The
Annuity

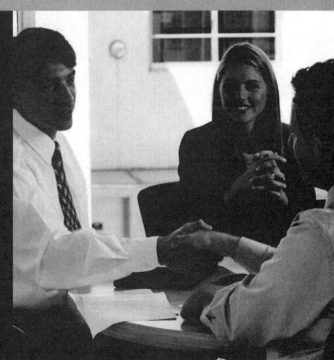

ohn L. Olsen,
CLU, ChFC, AEP

Michael E. Kitces,
MSFS, CFP®, CLU, ChFC

ADVISOR

ISBN: 0-87218-671-7

Library of Congress Control Number: 2005932230

1st Edition

Printed in U. S. A.

Dedications

John L. Olsen

To Katherine, who puts up with more than she should.

Michael E. Kitces

To my friends and family, for their understanding, patience, and support while I pursue my passion for financial planning.

Acknowledgements

The authors wish to express their special thanks to Debbie Miner and Joe Stenken at the National Underwriter Company for shepherding us through this project, and John Rudy for providing the initial connection that brought all of this about. We would never have finished it without you. We've also received help, encouragement, and wisdom from Terry Altmann, CLU, ChFC, CFP®, Jack Marrion, Rick Bueter, and Advanced Underwriting Consultants, Indianapolis, Indiana.

About the Authors

John L. Olsen

 John L. Olsen, CLU, ChFC, AEP is a financial and estate planner practicing in St. Louis County, MO. John has been involved in the financial services industry since 1973. He is a licensed life and health agent in several states, and is a Registered Representative with Securities America, Inc. (NASD/SIPC) and a Registered Advisory Associate with Securities America Advisors, Inc. (A Registered Investment Advisory firm). In addition to providing insurance, financial and estate planning services to his own clients, John works with other advisors on advanced cases and product selection and offers independent consulting on financial planning software.

John serves on the Board of Directors of the St. Louis chapter of the National Association of Insurance and Financial Advisors, is a former Board member of the St. Louis chapter of the Society of Financial Services Professionals, and is a member of the St. Louis Estate Planning Council. He is a highly sought-after speaker, having given presentations on financial, insurance, and estate planning, software selection, Monte Carlo simulation, and other topics to many industry groups. John can be reached at –

Olsen Financial Group
131 Hollywood Lane
Kirkwood, MO 63122
(314) 909-8818 (voice)
(314) 909-7912 (fax)
jolsen02@earthlink.net

Michael E. Kitces

 Michael E. Kitces, MSFS, CFP®, CLU, ChFC, RHU, REBC, CASL, is Director of Financial Planning for Pinnacle Advisory Group, a private wealth management firm located in Columbia, Maryland. In addition to the financial planning work he does on behalf of Pinnacle's clients, Michael is also a very active speaker, writer, and editor, works with other financial professionals on advanced financial planning topics, and is regularly interviewed by national consumer and trade publications on a broad variety of financial planning topics.

Michael serves on the Board of Directors for the Maryland chapter of the Financial Planning Association (FPA), as well as participating on numerous committees for FPA National. He is also a member of the Editorial Review Board for the Journal of Financial Planning, a Moderator for the bulletin boards at Financial-Planning.com, and a commentator on retirement distribution and retirement planning issues for Leimberg Information Services Inc. Michael is a co-founder of NexGen, a community of the next generation of financial planners that aims to ensure the transference of wisdom, tradition, and integrity, from the pioneers of financial planning to the next generation of the profession.

Michael welcomes your questions, comments, or inquiries at –

Pinnacle Advisory Group
Attn: Michael Kitces
6345 Woodside Court, Suite 100
Columbia, Maryland 21046
(410) 995-6630
michael@kitces.com

Foreword

This book is the child of frustration. The authors have both been dealing with annuities for many years, and we had each been despairing over the lack of understanding of these instruments and of the absurdly partisan way in which annuities are regarded by many who write about them. Most articles we read about annuities were either "for" or "against" them, as if an annuity could be inherently either "good" or 'bad". Articles appearing in insurance industry magazines routinely touted annuities as the greatest thing since sliced bread, while many financial journalists appeared to regard them as little better than satanic devices. Sadly, both conditions persist, with no sign of change, as we write this.

As co-moderators of the discussion forums on the website for *Financial Planning* magazine (www.financial-planning.com), we were painfully aware that even those involved in recommending or evaluating annuities–professional financial advisors–often demonstrate little understanding of how these tools work (and when they do not). Some forum messages about annuities, posted by insurance and financial planning professionals, were just plain wrong.

Something, we both felt, ought to be done. What was needed, we thought, was a source of information about annuities that would be both accurate and *balanced*. So, when we were approached by The National Underwriter Company for suggestions about potential book topics, the need for a book about annuities seemed clear, and we decided that we would take a stab at it.

The result is the book you are about to read. It was written, not for the consumer, but for the professional advisor–and that does not mean just those who sell annuities. Attorneys, accountants, financial planners, trust officers, and compliance officers–anyone who may be called upon to render professional advice regarding an annuity–will, we hope, find this book worth reading.

The authors have tried to present the facts and to be as objective as possible in our conclusions. We have included a large amount of material about the taxation of annuities (including content we have never seen elsewhere in print) and much about suitability and appropriateness. There is not a single sentence in here about how to sell annuities. (There are many books out there on that topic).

While we have tried very hard to document facts and substantiate our conclusions, fairness obliges us to admit that much of what you will read is opinion. You, the reader, will judge whether the opinions presented are sound.

We hope that you will find this book, not only instructive, but also genuinely useful.

– John L. Olsen, CLU, ChFC, AEP
– Michael J. Kitces, MSFS, CFP®, CLU, ChFC, RHU, REBC, CASL

Table of Contents

Chapter 1

Basics of Annuities

What is an Annuity?

The term "annuity" simply means a series of regular payments over time. In popular usage, however, "annuity" generally refers to a contract or policy, issued by an insurance company, providing for payment of a regular income by the annuity issuer to the *owner*, over a specified period or for the life of an *annuitant* (see "Parties to the Annuity Contract," below). These contracts, called "commercial annuities," are what we will be talking about throughout this book.

Types of Annuities

There are different types of annuities. Annuities are generally classified according to three different dichotomies:

1. how the annuity is purchased;

2. when annuity payments are to begin; and

3. how the cash value in the annuity is invested.

How the Annuity is Purchased

There are generally two different ways an annuity is purchased. A **Single Premium** annuity is a contract purchased with a single payment, or premium. No further premiums are required, or even allowable. A **Flexible Premium** annuity is purchased with an initial payment (to establish the contract) and typically contemplates a series of premiums that may be paid whenever, and in whatever amount, the purchaser wishes (subject to policy minimums and maximums).

There is very little difference, if any, in the important policy provisions, guarantees, and payout options of the two types, and their tax treatment is identical. The significance of this dichotomy is simply that in some instances, contracts offered as single premium cannot receive additional subsequent payments, and therefore do not allow additional contributions under the original contract's terms–instead, additional money must be deposited to a new annuity contract.

When Annuity Payments Are to Begin

An **immediate annuity** is one in which regular income–or annuity–payments begin to be made to the owner[1] within one year of purchase. Another label sometimes used to describe an immediate annuity is **payout annuity**.

A **deferred annuity** is one in which annuity payments are deferred until later than one year after purchase–perhaps much later. The life of a deferred annuity is divided into two phases:

- The **accumulation phase**. This is the period from purchase of the contract until **annuitization**. Annuitization is the exercise, by the owner, of a contractual option to begin receiving regular annuity payments, in accordance with an annuity payout option (see "Types of Annuity Payouts", below). Deferred annuity contracts typically require annuitization by some specified date or age by specifying a maximum annuity starting date or maturity date (e.g.; policy anniversary following annuitant's age 85 or annuitant's age 85). Newer contracts may permit further deferral of annuitization provided the request is received within a specified period of time prior to the maturity date.[2]

- The **distribution phase**. This is the period from annuitization until the annuity payments cease (which may be at the end of the annuitant's life or after a specified number of years (see "Types of Annuity Payouts", below)).

Note: It is essential that the advisor understand the difference between an annuity contract's required annuity starting date (i.e.; the date by which annuity payments must commence, absent an election to defer annuitization) and when annuitization is permitted under that contract. In January, 2005, a class-action lawsuit was filed alleging "unsuitability," asserting that the deferred annuity purchased by a senior citizen allegedly did not permit annuity payments to begin until the annuitant's age 115. However, it appears that age 115 was the contract maturity date, and annuity payments under the contract could start at any time the owner wished to annuitize. In fact, in some contracts a late maturity date is a benefit, allowing an owner to keep the contract in the accumulation phase as long as possible, if that is his/her wish.

There is no accumulation phase in the life of an immediate annuity, as annuity payments typically commence shortly after purchase, and must, by definition, commence within one year. Annuities that are in distribution phase (i.e.; deferred annuities that have been annuitized and all immediate annuities) are said to be in payout status.

How the Cash Value in the Annuity is Invested

A "fixed" annuity is an annuity in which the contract value is measured in dollars. A "variable" annuity is one in which the contract value is measured in terms of units–either accumulation units or annuity units, depending upon whether the contract is in the accumulation phase or the distribution phase. In both cases, the value of each unit can–and probably will–vary each business day, according to the investment performance of the separate accounts[3] chosen by the contract owner. We will look at how accumulation units and annuity units work shortly. First, however, let's understand the basic investment difference between fixed and variable annuities.

Fixed Annuities

In a fixed annuity the contract values are guaranteed by the issuing insurance company. These values (discussed below) are all measured, as we've noted, in dollars. There is a common misconception that "fixed," in the term "fixed annuity," refers to the rate of interest credited to the contract. This is not correct. While some fixed deferred annuities provide guarantees as to the period during which the current interest rate will be credited, and all deferred annuities provide a guaranteed minimum interest rate that will be credited during the entire accumulation period, the term "fixed," when used in reference to "fixed annuities," properly refers, not to the interest rate, but to the fact that the contract values are measured in fixed units–namely, dollars.

What are these contract values? In a fixed immediate annuity, or a fixed deferred annuity that has been annuitized, the contract value guaranteed by the issuing insurer is the dollar amount of the periodic annuity payment (which may be payable monthly, quarterly, semi-annually, or annually). In a fixed deferred annuity, there are several contract values:

1.   **Cash Value.** The cash value (or accumulation value) of a fixed deferred annuity is the value on which interest is computed and to which interest is credited. It is generally the sum of all premium payments received, plus all prior interest credited, less any withdrawals (and, in the case of certain "qualified" annuities, unpaid loan interest). The cash value of fixed deferred annuities is always guaranteed. The cash value of variable annuities is not, except for monies deposited into the "fixed account" option of such contracts.

2.   **Annuity Value.** The annuity value is the value to which an annuity payout factor will be applied if–and only if–the contract owner annuitizes the contract. In some deferred annuities, this value is identical to the cash value. In so-called "tiered annuities" (of the type where a higher interest rate is credited to the annuity value than is credited to the cash value) and in contracts providing for an "annuitization bonus," the annuity value is higher than the cash value.

3.   **Surrender Value.** The surrender value of a deferred annuity is the cash value, less any applicable surrender charge and market value adjustment (see Chapter Five: Basic Costs of Annuities), that will be paid to the contract owner upon surrender of the contract.

The basic investment difference between fixed and variable annuities is that in a fixed annuity (either immediate or deferred), the contract owner is offered no investment choices within the contract and assumes no investment risk. In a fixed deferred annuity, the cash value (which includes all premium payments and prior interest credited) is guaranteed against loss, as is a minimum interest rate. All fixed deferred annuities also offer a current–non-guaranteed–interest rate. Some (but not all) contracts guarantee the current declared rate for a certain period of time.

It is essential for the advisor to understand that the guarantees in fixed annuities are only as good as the ability of the issuing insurer to pay them.

Variable Annuities

Variable annuities work very differently from fixed annuities, in both the accumulation phase and in the distribution phase.

The Accumulation Phase

In the accumulation phase of a variable deferred annuity,[4] each premium payment purchases (after applicable contract charges are deducted) a number of accumulation units for each investment sub-account chosen by the contract holder.

> *Example:* Mr. Jones has chosen five investment sub-accounts from among those available in his variable deferred annuity. He has directed that each premium payment[5] be allocated to these accounts as follows:

Large Cap Growth Account A	20%
Midcap Value Account M	20%
Small Cap Value Account S	20%
International Stock Acct I	15%
Bond Account B	25%

The accumulation unit values of these accounts, on the day his premium is received, are as follows:

Large Cap Growth Account A	$21.435
Midcap Value Account M	$16.567
Small Cap Value Account S	$34.123
International Stock Acct I	$9.567
Bond Account B	$15.003

If he makes a premium payment of $1,000, and the contract charges applicable are $14, the net premium ($986) will purchase –

Large Cap Growth Account A	9.1999 units
Midcap Value Account M	11.9032 units
Small Cap Value Account S	5.7791 units
International Stock Acct I	15.4594 units
Bond Account B	16.4300 units[6]

Accumulation unit values can, and often will, change, each day, according to the investment performance of the sub-accounts, just as the net asset value of a mutual fund share does. However, there is a significant difference between the pricing of annuity accumulation units and that of mutual fund shares. When a mutual fund declares a dividend or capital gains distribution (through the realization of dividends or capital gains income by the fund) and the shareholder has elected to reinvest such distributions, additional shares are purchased for his account (and the price of all shares of the fund is reduced to reflect the distribution). If the shareholder has elected not to reinvest such distributions, he receives cash (and the share price is reduced). When a dividend or capital gain is realized by a variable annuity sub-account, the value of the accumulation unit is increased to reflect the dividend or gain received, but the number of units remains the same.

Investment Sub-Accounts

One of the main advantages to investing in a variable annuity is the access it provides to diversified investment types. The first variable annuities offered relatively few investment choices, and, often, the choices were limited to proprietary accounts (that is: accounts managed by the insurance company that issued the annuity, or a subsidiary). Many newer contracts offer sub-accounts representing a wide variety of asset classes,[7] managed by a variety of money management firms. Typically, the contract owner is permitted to choose several sub-accounts,[8] and to make exchanges among them (re-allocating existing contract values) and to re-allocate ongoing contributions without charge.[9] Moreover, exchanges among sub-accounts in a single contract are not taxable events for income tax purposes. These investment management features, together with features such as automatic portfolio rebalancing and dollar cost averaging from the annuity contract's "fixed account"[10] to the variable sub-accounts, make the modern variable annuity a robust and powerful investment management tool.

The Distribution Phase

In the distribution phase, fixed annuities–either immediate contracts or deferred contracts that have been annuitized–provide a regular income by application of a chosen annuity payout factor to the amount that is converted to an income stream. For example, if Mr. Smith purchases a fixed immediate annuity for $100,000 or annuitizes a fixed deferred annuity having an annuity value of that same amount, and if he elects a Life and 10 Year Certain payout arrangement, and if the annual annuity payout factor for that option, for his age and sex, is 5.67, his annuity payments will be $5,670 per year from that point until the later of his death or the expiration of ten years. Similarly, if he elects to annuitize a variable deferred annuity on a fixed annuity payout arrangement, and if the total value of the accumulation units in his contract, at the time of annuitization, is $100,000, he will receive that same income (assuming the same annuity payout factor).

If the annuity payout is to be on a variable basis, however, the amount annuitized (either a lump sum, in the case of an immediate variable annuity, or, in a deferred variable annuity, the current value of the accumulation units the owner wishes to annuitize[11]) is not converted to a fixed income stream by applying an annuity payout factor. Instead, the purchase payment or amount annuitized is used to buy a certain number of annuity units.[12] The process works as follows:

- First, the payment (or annuitization amount) is reduced by any contract fee applicable and by any State premium tax due, and allocated to the investment sub-accounts chosen by the contract owner.

- Next, the insurance company computes an initial income payment amount for that portion of the purchase payment or annuitization amount allocated to each sub-account, using (a) the age and sex[13] of the annuitant and (b) an assumed investment rate (AIR). Many variable annuity contracts allow the purchaser to choose among several AIRs (e.g.; 3%, 4%, 5%, and 6%). The higher the initial AIR chosen, the higher the initial variable income payment will be.

- Finally, the initial income payment is divided by the value of the annuity unit for each sub-account chosen. The result is the number of annuity units of that sub-account that will be purchased by that payment. Subsequent annuity payments will increase or decrease in proportion to the extent to which the net investment performance (after application of the separate account charges) of the chosen variable sub-accounts exceeds or lags the AIR.

Parties to the Annuity Contract

There are four parties to a commercial annuity contract.

- The **annuity company** is the party that issues the policy, and is obligated to keep all the promises made in it.

- The **annuitant** is the individual–and it must be an individual–a human being–who may or may not also be the owner of the policy. The age and sex of the annuitant determine–for life annuities–the amount of each annuity payment. The annuitant is merely the "measuring life" for purposes of annuity payment calculations. He or she has NO rights in the annuity contract as annuitant.

- The **beneficiary** is the party who will receive any death benefit payable under the annuity (whether as a lump sum or a continuation of annuity payments). However, not all annuities will have a beneficiary because if payments cease at the annuitant's death, there is nothing for a beneficiary to receive. In most cases the beneficiary has no other rights, except if the beneficiary is named irrevocably.

- The **owner** is the individual or entity (it need not be a human) that has all ownership rights in the contract, including the right to name the annuitant and beneficiary, to elect commencement of annuity payments, and to surrender the contract. Occasionally, advisors will suggest that a non-qualified annuity[14] be owned jointly (usually, when the owners are a married couple). As will be discussed in Chapter 3, this arrangement can produce unexpected problems, and should be avoided unless the client and advisors are aware of the implications of such ownership.

Types of Annuity Payouts

An immediate annuity, or a deferred annuity that has been annuitized (where the contract owner has elected to begin receiving annuity payments), produces an income stream. The nature of this income stream can vary, according to the type of payout arrangement chosen.

The first arrangement, and the simplest, is **Life Only, No Refund.** When the contract owner elects this option, he or she will, upon annuitization, receive an income guaranteed to last for the annuitant's entire lifetime–no matter how long that annuitant lives. At the annuitant's death, no further payments will be due–no matter when that occurs. Life Only, No Refund provides the highest payout of any of the annuity arrangements, because if the annuitant dies prematurely–even if after receiving only one payment–the insurance company's obligation ceases. The insurance company, in making a Life Only, No Refund annuity payment guarantee, incurs no cost for guaranteeing a survivor benefit (or, in the jargon of the insurance industry, a refund feature). It is the cost of these refund features which necessitates that annuity payments calculated using such a benefit be lower than the amount of a Life Only, No Refund annuity.

A second payout type is **Life Annuity, With Refund.** As with all "life" payout options, the main guarantee is that payments will continue for the annuitant's lifetime. But should the annuitant die during the "refund period," the insurance company must pay the refund amount to the designated beneficiary.

Refund arrangements come in various flavors. The **Period Certain** refund type says that if the annuitant dies before the end of a certain period of time, payments will continue to the beneficiary for the remainder of that period. For example, the most common payout arrangement is **Life and 10 Year Certain.** This arrangement provides for payments that are guaranteed to continue for the annuitant's life (no matter how long he or she lives), but also, if that annuitant should not live to receive 10 years' payments (if payments are monthly, that is 120 monthly payments), the remaining payments will continue to the beneficiary named in the policy until the 10 year term is complete.

The **Cash Refund** or **Installment Refund** payout option says that if the annuitant dies before receiving a specified amount (which may or may not be less than the amount originally annuitized), the balance will be paid to the beneficiary, either in a lump sum or in installments.

Not all annuities are payable for life. A third payout type–the so-called **Period Certain** option–pays an income for a certain period. A 20-year period certain payout option will pay for exactly 20 years and no more or fewer. If the annuitant dies during that period, payments continue to the beneficiary (or to a "contingent annuitant" if one is named). If the annuitant is still living at the end of 20 years, payments cease.

The terminology almost begs for misunderstanding. "Life and 10 Year Certain" sounds a lot like "10 Year Certain." But they are very different payout options. The first one will pay for the longer of 10 years or the annuitant's lifetime–however long that is. The second will pay, in any and all events, for exactly and only 10 years. No more, no less. Many prospective annuity buyers will miss this distinction. No matter how careful the advisor is in explaining how that arrangement works, some people hear just the "10 Years" part and focus on it. Many years ago, in talking with an elderly prospective client, one of the authors thought he had explained the "Life and 10 Year Certain" annuity he was recommending adequately. But, after he had finished, she expressed concern. "I like having that amount every month", she said, "and I especially like knowing that amount won't change, but I'm a bit worried. You see, I may live *longer* than ten years, and then what?"

One way of avoiding this confusion, when structuring life annuities, is to consider using either Cash Refund or Installment Refund arrangements to address the risk of the annuitant's dying prematurely. It is far more easily explained and understood, and does not let the duration of the "certain" element distract attention from the lifetime guarantee—which is, after all, the main purpose of the arrangement.

The fourth type of payout includes arrangements that cover more than one annuitant. The most common type is that of the various **Joint and Survivor** payout options and normally allows only two annuitants. These are life annuity payouts—they persist until both annuitants have died. The amount of the annuity payment may remain unchanged at the first death (this is called Joint and 100% Survivor) or may be reduced by some percentage or fraction (for example, Joint and ⅔ means that the surviving annuitant will receive, commencing at the death of the first annuitant, an income equal to ⅔ of the original annuity amount). Some contracts allow Joint and Survivor payouts with a refund feature. A much less common option than the Joint and Survivor arrangement is called **Joint Life**. It, too, covers two annuitants, but pays a benefit only until the first annuitant dies.

Now that we have the basics and terminology of annuities out of the way (and the authors thank you, dear reader, for your patience), let's get to what annuities are used for.

The Annuity as a Tool

Annuities are tools. They are acquired because the purchaser has a particular job to be done and is willing to exchange his money for a tool to do that job. In many ways, this exchange transaction is like the purchase of a hammer. The hammer has certain specifications (type and strength of the metal, length of the handle, size of the hammer head) and when purchased from a quality company, often comes with a guarantee that the product will perform as specified.

The important key to understand about this analogy is that we generally do not buy a hammer simply because it happens to be cheaper, or lighter, or shinier than any other hand tool in the hardware store. We purchase it because we have a need (for example, to pound a nail into a piece of wood), or anticipate having a need in the future that we want to be prepared for, and we believe that a hammer is the best tool to solve that need.

In addition, there are many different situations where we might need a hammer, and each of those situations may call for a different hammer – clearly, using a sledgehammer to drive a small nail into your drywall to hang a picture is the wrong tool for the job. Thus, the key in purchasing the right hammer is really about understanding the need, and the job you're hoping to accomplish with it. Only once you understand the right situation for any particular hammer can you determine whether a hammer is the right tool for the job, and which type of hammer you need.

To complete the analogy, the key to decision-making when it comes to annuities is to first understand the problems for which the annuity can represent a solution–only then can one actually determine whether an annuity is the right tool to solve the problem, and which sort of annuity will best accomplish it.

Overview – The Annuity as a Problem-Solving Tool

We are all familiar with the kinds of problems that hammers solve, such as driving a small nail, pounding a large nail, or forcing a wedge between two pieces of wood to separate them. The problems that the annuity-as-a-tool are meant to solve are quite varied, because of the broad number and types of annuity-tools that are available. That said, the problems that annuities solve–the needs that they meet–can be identified, and broken into several general categories:

1. **The need for a known income stream.** This is what annuities do best, because annuities, whether deferred or immediate, are really designed to generate income. The "known" part may be the amount of the income stream, the duration, or both. The amount might be fixed or determined by a formula. The duration might be for a specified period, for the lifetime of the annuitant, or the longer of the two. The amount of each annuity payment may be greater than one could obtain–with absolute certainty–from other savings or investment vehicles. However, it must be noted that annuity income (meaning regular annuity payments, not partial withdrawals) are part principal. An annuitant is not living "on her income," but on income and principal.

2. **The need for a guaranteed rate of return.** As we've noted, the current interest crediting rate in most deferred annuities may potentially be changed every quarter, year, or at the discretion of the insurance company. Recently, however, contracts have been devel-

oped which are sometimes termed "CD annuities." These are fixed annuities with multi-year current rate guarantees. Often, the rate guarantee extends to the end of the surrender charge period (which is usually six years or less). Depending upon contractual provisions (especially, the surrender charge schedule) and whether interest rates are rising or falling, longer rate guarantee periods may offer lower or higher rates than shorter periods. In any event, though, the rate of return is contractually guaranteed, which may be the exact need that an individual has.

3. **The need for a better non-guaranteed rate of return.** Although their current crediting rate is usually not guaranteed beyond an initial period, deferred annuities have, historically, paid somewhat higher current returns, as a class, than some other fixed-dollar investments, such as passbook savings and certificates of deposit.

4. **The need (or desire) for tax advantages.** One of the main appeals to a deferred annuity is tax-deferred growth. Although the gain will ultimately be taxed (tax-deferred does not mean tax-free), tax deferral maximizes the benefit of compounding. Moreover, annual growth not distributed is not recognized as income for any tax purpose, including the taxability of Social Security benefits. Immediate annuities, too, receive favorable income tax treatment. A portion of each annuity payment is considered return of principal and is not taxable.

5. **A guaranteed payment in the event of death.** Although annuities are not life insurance policies, and are not taxed as such, they can provide guaranteed death benefits. A fixed deferred annuity offers guarantee of principal (and previously credited interest), and most such contracts waive surrender charges upon death. Variable deferred annuities typically offer a guaranteed minimum death benefit. Immediate annuities, while designed to amortize both principal and earnings over the annuity payout period, may be structured with a refund feature to guarantee a minimum payout, whether to the living annuitant or her beneficiary (if the annuitant should die early). That said, annuities are designed primarily to provide living benefits. If a guaranteed death benefit is a client's main concern, life insurance is often a better tool (provided the client is insurable). Just as a hammer can be used to pry apart two-by-fours, a pry bar is probably a better choice (so long as the job does not involve driving nails).

Is an Annuity the Right Tool, and, if so, Which Kind Will Do the Best Job?

Now that we've defined some of the needs that annuities can solve, we will begin to focus on how to match particular kinds of annuities to manage the risks inherent in those needs, and understand the annuity as a **risk management** tool.

When the Client Needs a Known Income Stream

For the client who requires a certain income stream, commencing within one year, an immediate annuity is an almost intuitive choice. Providing income–certain as to amount, duration, or both–is what an immediate annuity does. But we need, first, to ask a key question: For how long will the income stream be required?

If the need is for an income for life, an immediate life annuity just makes good sense. It is the only financial instrument that can guarantee a specific amount of income for as long as the recipient lives. It allows the purchaser to manage the risk that the asset base that is used to create the payments may not earn an adequate rate of return, or may not be large enough to provide enough payments for life–i.e., the risk of outliving one's assets. Some immediate annuities can be structured so that annuity payments will increase, each year, by a specified percentage. (This is sometimes known as the COLA (cost-of-living-adjustment) option). Unfortunately, most insurance companies do not offer such an option in their immediate annuity portfolios.

Similarly, if the need is for an income for a specified period of years, an immediate period certain annuity may be an appropriate choice. It, too, manages the risk of an unknown future rate of return over the time period, and the risk that the asset base (the dollars used to create the income stream) may not be sufficient to produce the income required.

One risk often cited by critics of immediate annuities is that the buyer has "locked in" current interest rates. This criticism is generally voiced during periods when prevailing interest rates are unusually low. How valid is this criticism? In the authors' opinion, it has merit, from a purely investment perspective. The interest rate used in the calculation of the annuity payout factor (the number of dollars, per thousand dollars of purchase payment that the annuitant will receive each period) is, indeed, locked in. Should prevailing interest rates rise over the period of time during which annuity payments are made, those annuity payments will not reflect that rise. However, the authors feel that, from a risk management perspective, this criticism is misdirected. If the goal is to ensure an income level, the relevant risk is whether the dollars invested to produce that income can do so. A rise in prevailing rates would not present that risk, but a decline would. To transfer that risk from the annuity buyer to the insurance company, the buyer must incur a cost. Locking in the annuity interest rate is part of that cost.

It should be noted, though, that the changes in interest rates used in immediate annuity calculations over the past two decades have been far less dramatic than the changes in interest rate for short-term instruments such as savings accounts and certificates of deposit. While it is true that the purchaser of an immediate annuity in January, 2005 is locking in an interest rate lower than would have been used for someone the same age and sex in, say, January, 1982, the difference is not nearly as great as one might think. By the same token, if interest rates should trend sharply upward in the next 10 years, the locked in rates ten years hence will probably not be substantially greater than the current ones.

When the Client Needs a Guaranteed Rate of Return

When a specific minimum return on investment and preservation of principal is required to accomplish a particular goal, an immediate annuity makes no sense, because it does not preserve principal. The income payments from an immediate annuity, while they may be larger than might be achievable from alternatives, are not a return on investment, but a combination of return on and return of investment. However, a deferred annuity offering a multi-year interest rate guarantee may well provide a solution. The risk of getting an inadequate rate of return is managed by transferring it to the insurance company issuing the annuity that provides a total or minimum rate of return that is guaranteed to equal or exceed the return required. However, it is important to note that there is the lack of liquidity cost associated with these annuities. This is because the insurance company makes its guarantees assuming that it will have use of the money used to purchase the annuity. Typically, a deferred annuity contract does not become profitable for an insurer until after it has been in force for several years, due to commissions, other issuing charges and administrative costs, deferred acquisition costs, taxes, and reserve requirements. If the annuity owner elects to surrender or take withdrawals from the annuity in the early contract years, he will usually be required to pay a surrender charge (the amount and terms of which vary considerably from contract to contract).

Recently, many variable deferred annuities have been marketed with guaranteed living benefits. The structure and provisions of these policies vary greatly, but it should be noted that the guarantees provided are typically not equivalent to the guaranteed minimum rate of return of fixed annuities, and usually require annuitization, minimum holding periods, or other conditions for the guarantees to be effective. (For an extensive discussion of the various living benefits available with variable annuities, see Chapter 6.)

When the Client Needs a Better Non-Guaranteed Rate of Return

With the exception of fixed annuities with multi-year current rate guarantees (so-called "CD annuities"), no deferred annuity guarantees the current rate of return for more than a year at most (although all fixed annuities offer a guaranteed minimum rate of return). Variable deferred annuities generally do not offer any guarantees of return or of principal, except where the fixed investment account is used or as provided by optional riders. That said, we should bear in mind that most other long-term investments do not offer such guarantees either. For clients who require a guarantee of principal and are willing to accept a current rate that may change, deferred fixed annuities may offer better returns than certificates of deposit or individual bonds. The interest rate history of many fixed annuities has exceeded that of CDs, although there can be no assurance that this will hold true in the future.

When comparing the interest crediting rate of a deferred annuity with that of an alternative, the diligent advisor will point out not only any applicable surrender charges, but also the early distribution penalty that applies to withdrawals taken prior to age 59½ (unless an exception is available) (See Chapter 2 for an in-depth discussion of the income taxation of annuities). Those are essential elements in any sound risk management decision. So, too, is the fact that earnings in deferred annuities are not taxed until distributed.

When the Client Wants and Needs Income Tax Deferral

Tax deferral is perhaps the most advertised and promoted advantage of deferred annuities. Earnings are not taxed until distributed (either to living contract owners or beneficiaries). The advantages of such deferral are well-recognized. However, the *cost* of such tax deferral, granted by Section 72 of the Internal Revenue Code, is a requirement in that same section that all distributions from annuities be taxed at ordinary income rates. No capital gains treatment is ever available under current law. Whether this trade-off is favorable, or appropriate, is a matter of considerable controversy. In the authors' view, it is always a matter of individual facts and circumstances, for reasons that will be discussed in later chapters.

When the Client Needs a Guaranteed Payment in the Event of Death

An often overlooked feature of annuities is the right of the beneficiary to receive a guaranteed payment (or a payment determined by a guaranteed formula) in the event of death. This payment may not occur until the distant future, but upon purchase of the contract the owner knows exactly what the payment will be or how it will be determined, guaranteed, at that point in the future.

When is this important? When the client requires that a certain amount be available upon death, regardless of investment performance in the meantime. This guarantee allows an annuity owner to manage the risk that inadequate investment performance will cause a smaller amount to pass to her beneficiaries than desired, regardless of actual investment performance over the time period until death. The authors strongly believe, however, that, when the need for such guaranteed death benefit is a primary concern, life insurance generally represents a far more efficient solution, if available.

Summary: The Annuity as a Tool

The guarantees that the annuity-tool provides allow clients and their advisors to solve certain problems and to meet certain needs. Specifically, it allows us to meet those needs despite risks that might cause us to fail. Thus, at its most fundamental level, annuities serve as tools that allow us to manage risks–specifically, the risks that:

- **Distributions** from an investment will be inadequate to meet specified goals;

- **Earnings** on an investment will be inadequate to meet specified goals; and

- The **amount available to heirs,** from the investment, will be inadequate to meet specified goals

Our discussion of annuities, and potential applications for them, throughout the remainder of this book will proceed with the understanding that annuities are nothing more than risk management tools that allow us to accomplish certain needs and goals with certainty (or at least increased likelihood) because of the underlying guarantees that they hold.

Determining When a Risk Management Tool (Annuity) is Appropriate

In all cases, the annuity tool solution will have a cost associated with it–the cost of the annuity and the guarantees that it provides–and, because of these costs, the solution provided often will not be the solution with the highest expected value or projected return on investment. However, the decision to accept a lower expected value (net of costs) in exchange for a higher (or entirely guaranteed) probability of success is a risk-return tradeoff that can and should be examined and made on a case-by-case basis. In many instances, when presented with both options, the client will choose the option most likely to succeed, not the one with the highest expected return.

It is also important to remember that, in the search to maximize the probability of success, it is entirely possible that the client will not actually need to utilize the guarantees provided by an annuity. Annuities manage risks of loss; there is no guarantee that such losses will occur in the first place. Annuities offer purchasers options to utilize certain guarantees; they do not require the exercise of those options. Thus, it may be that a guarantee within a client's annuity is never actually put to use. Nonetheless, owning the annuity may very well have still been the right choice. That the guarantees may never be put to use does not mean the cost of those guarantees was a waste. Your house may never burn down, but it is still prudent to maintain your homeowner's insurance and pay premiums for years. Doing so buys you a guarantee that you will not lose the entire value of your house, may produce ancillary benefits (such as allowing you to obtain a mortgage), and in any event, can provide you with invaluable peace of mind, and the ability to better enjoy your life knowing that a particular risk had been transferred—insured—away.

Chapter Endnotes

1. Some insurance companies will issue annuity checks to a non-owner annuitant if requested to do so by the owner.

2. Such deferral may require the insurance company's approval.

3. These are also referred to as investment sub-accounts.

4. As we have noted, there is no accumulation phase in a variable *immediate* annuity.

5. After deduction for contract charges.

6. We have illustrated four decimal places precision for units purchased and three decimal places for unit values in this example. Some insurers use greater precision and some use less.

7. Asset classes are investment types having distinct risk/return characteristics, such as US Large Cap Growth Stocks, Foreign Stocks, US Real Estate, US Long Term Gov't Bonds, etc.

8. Some contracts require a minimum initial and/or ongoing contribution per sub-account.

9. Most contracts impose a maximum on the number of exchanges permitted per month and may levy a charge for additional "excess" exchanges. These restrictions are generally in place to prevent "active" trading using the investment sub-accounts, but are not intended to restrict "normal" occasional trading and re-balancing.

10. The "fixed account" in a deferred variable annuity typically guarantees a minimum interest rate and may offer a guaranteed duration for the current declared interest rate. In addition, the principal (including all prior credited interest) is typically guaranteed against loss.

11. Some variable deferred annuities permit partial annuitization. Others require that the entire value of the contractholder's accumulation units be annuitized.

12. Some variable annuity literature describes this process as a conversion of the existing accumulation units to annuity units.

13. If the annuity uses unisex annuity factors, the sex of the annuitant is not considered. Most commercial annuities use sex-distinct factors; unisex factors are most often seen in contracts used to fund qualified retirement plans, where sex-distinct factors in such an employment context are considered to impose potentially unlawful discrimination.

14. An annuity purchased with after-tax dollars that will not fund an IRA or tax-qualified plan.

Chapter 2

Taxation of Annuity Benefits During Owner's Lifetime

The rules regarding taxation of annuities are complicated, and, in many instances, not entirely clear. It is, unfortunately, very easy for an advisor to make mistakes in advising clients as to ownership, beneficiary designations, or distribution requirements, as well as a myriad of rules applicable to withdrawals from deferred annuities while alive. Mistakes in these areas can have serious consequences both for the client and advisor. For these reasons, we will devote considerable attention in this chapter not only to the rules themselves (including some that may be unfamiliar to the reader), but also to the practical, "every day" applications and implications of those rules.

The rules governing taxation of annuities are contained in Internal Revenue Code section 72 ("the Code") and the applicable Treasury Regulations. However, it is extremely important for the reader to understand that most of Section 72 deals only with so-called "non-qualified" annuities (annuities purchased with after-tax dollars and not to fund individual retirement accounts (IRAs) or tax-qualified retirement plans). The tax rules regarding the deferral of tax on annual earnings within annuities and methods for determining how much of each annuity payment is taxable refer only to non-qualified annuity contracts. "Qualified" annuities[1] are governed by parts of the Code dealing with the specific type of plan the annuity is funding (e.g.: Section 408 for traditional IRAs, Section 408A for Roth IRAs, and Section 401 for pension plans). The rules that would govern an annuity that is not purchased to fund an IRA or qualified plan (the rules for non-qualified annuities) are totally inapplicable to an annuity which is purchased to fund such a plan (a qualified annuity). This is often not understood, and one of the most common mistakes made by advisors in the area of retirement planning is an attempt to apply "regular annuity rules" to a "qualified" annuity. The rules discussed in this chapter apply only to "non-qualified" annuities, except where indicated.

While Code section 72 also deals with policy dividends and forms of premium returns, we will focus, in our discussion, on two types of payments:

1.   "Amounts received as an annuity" (i.e., annuity payments); and

2.   "Amounts not received as an annuity" (i.e., withdrawals, surrenders, and other non-annuity payouts).

All distributions from an annuity, whether made to a living owner or beneficiary, or as a death benefit, are one or the other of these two types.

Before we examine these two types of distributions, however, one very important point bears repeating: Distributions made from an annuity while the owner of the annuity contract is living are taxable to that owner–even if made to an annuitant who is a different individual. If A owns an annuity of which B is the annuitant, payments are generally made to A. Some annuity issuers will issue checks directly to a non-owner annuitant if the owner directs, but, even so, the tax liability is that of the owner.

Amounts Received as an Annuity

"The term *annuity* includes all periodic payments resulting from the systematic liquidation of a principal sum."[2] It "refers not only payments made for the life or lives, but also to installment payments that do not involve a life contingency; for example, payments under a 'fixed period' or 'fixed amount' settlement option."[3] Amounts "received as an annuity" are taxed under Code section 72 (discussed below), which considers each payment to be part principal and part gain. The part representing principal is excluded from tax (as a return of principal); the part representing gain is taxable as ordinary income.[4] The formula for allocating the amount of principal and gain of each payment for fixed annuities is different from that used with variable annuities.

In the case of a fixed annuity, this calculation is done by applying an "exclusion ratio," which is the total investment in the contract (adjusted for the value of any refund feature elected) divided by the expected return (which, for life annuities, takes into account life expectancies). In the case of a variable annuity, the expected return is unknown and is considered (for purposes of the exclusion calculation) to be equal to the investment in the contract. The ratio used to determine the portion of each variable annuity payment includible in income is the investment in the contract, adjusted for the value of any refund feature elected, divided by the number of years over which it is anticipated that the annuity will be paid.[5] (For a detailed description of each method, see Appendix B). Once all principal has been received tax-free, the entire annuity payment is taxable as ordinary income.[6] It is important to note that, where the annuity starting date was prior to January 1, 1987, the exclusion ratio continues to apply, even after all the principal has been recovered–consequently, when addressing the taxation of an existing annuity payment stream, it is absolutely critical to know when payments began.

"Annuity" payments (or amounts "received as an annuity") include payments from an immediate annuity, or from a deferred annuity that has been "annuitized" (where the owner of a deferred annuity has elected to commence regular annuity payments under an annuity option offered by that contract).

Amounts Not Received as an Annuity

The tax treatment of annuity distributions other than regular annuity payments, including partial withdrawals, surrenders, and other non-annuitized payouts, depends upon when the annuity contract was issued.

Contracts Entered Into After August 13, 1982

For contracts entered into after August 13, 1982, non-annuity distributions are taxed according to the "interest first" rule, sometimes referred to as "LIFO" (Last In, First Out). All distributions that are "amounts not received as an annuity" are considered income until all "gain" in the contract has been received.

Amounts "not received as an annuity" are any amounts received from an annuity that do not qualify as amounts "received as an annuity." This distinction may appear obvious, but it is not quite that straightforward because of how Section 72 treats the word "received." "Amounts not received as an annuity" include not only outright distributions such as partial withdrawals and death benefits not taken under an annuity option, but also policy dividends (unless retained by the insurer as premiums or other consideration[7]), amounts received as loans, "the value of any part of an annuity contract pledged or assigned,"[8] and amounts received on partial surrender. Such amounts "are taxable as income to the extent that the cash value of the contract immediately before the payment exceeds the investment in the contract."[9]

The preceding two sentences merit closer attention, because many advisors are unaware of these provisions. First, amounts taken from annuity contracts as loans are taxable,[10] although non-qualified annuity contracts generally do not contain loan provisions. Second, merely pledging an annuity as collateral for a loan causes recognition of income to the extent of the lesser of any "gain" or the portion of the annuity thus pledged.

Multiple Deferred Annuities – The "Anti-Abuse Rule"

One method of reducing the impact of the "LIFO" treatment of deferred annuities, for purchasers who contemplate using partial withdrawals, is to use multiple contracts.

> *Example:* If A purchases a single deferred annuity for $100,000. Five years later, it is worth $120,000. If A then withdraws $15,000, the entire $15,000 is taxable as ordinary income. Moreover, if A is under age 59½, he must pay the 10% penalty tax for "premature distributions" (unless an exception to the penalty applies). If, however, A purchases ten annuities for $10,000 each, and each is worth $12,000 five years later, a surrender of one contract (for $12,000) and a withdrawal from a second, for $3,000, would produce a taxable amount of only $4,000 (the "gain" in the two annuities) for the same $15,000 withdrawal. Moreover, the penalty tax would be $400, instead of $1,500, as the penalty applies only to the tax-able portion of early distributions.

Congress recognized this technique as abusive and enacted a provision treats all annuities issued during a single calendar year and issued by the same insurance company as one annuity, for purposes of taxing withdrawals.[11] This provision does not apply to partial withdrawals or surrenders of deferred annuity contracts issued in the same calendar year by different insurance companies.

Contracts Entered Into Before August 14, 1982

Amounts "not received as an annuity" from contracts entered into before August 14, 1982 and allocated to investments made before August 14, 1982 are taxed under the "cost recovery" rule, a treatment sometimes referred to as "FIFO" (First In, First Out). Under this rule, "the taxpayer may receive all such amounts tax-free until he has received tax-free amounts equal to his [total] pre-August 14, 1982 investment in the contract; [subsequent withdrawal] amounts are taxable only after such basis has been fully recovered."[12] It should be noted that this does not mean that all amounts "not received as an annuity" from an annuity contract entered into before August 14, 1982 are treated thus. Only amounts allocable to investments made before August 14, 1982 receive this treatment.

> *Example:* If taxpayer had an annuity that was purchased in 1981 (thus, before August 14, 1982) for $25,000, and it is currently worth $125,000, the first $25,000 of withdrawals are received tax-free, and subsequent withdrawals are taxable as gain. If the taxpayer had made a total of $50,000 of deposits by adding another $25,000 in 1984, the taxpayer would still only be able to receive the first $25,000 tax-free, because the second deposit, although attributable to a pre-August 14, 1982 annuity, would not be allocable to a pre-August 14, 1982 investment in the contract. Note that if the taxpayer's two deposits had occurred in 1983 and 1984 (thus, after August 14, 1982), the post-August 14, 1982 rules would apply and the contract with a $50,000 investment and a $125,000 current value would be taxed as gains first (to the extend of the $75,000 of gain inherent in the contract), and only then would withdrawals be a tax-free recovery of basis. Alternatively, if the $125,000 contract were annuitized, a portion of each payment would be a tax-free recovery of basis. This illustrates the three different ways that basis may be allocated to withdrawals from a contract–all basis first and then gains for pre-August 14, 1982 contracts, all gains first and then basis for post-August 14, 1982 contracts, and pro-rata basis and gains on each payment for annuitized contracts.

Deferral of Tax on Undistributed Gain

One of the most often-cited advantages of deferred annuities is that the annual increase in the cash value of these contracts is not subject to tax until the gain is withdrawn. Indeed, this "tax-deferred growth" is often touted as the most important benefit offered by deferred annuities.[13] The authors believe that this is both an oversimplification and a mischaracterization. A deferred annuity is not merely a tax-management instrument. It is also a platform for various investment strategies, and a mechanism for ensuring a known or determinable stream of income for a definite period or for the whole of one or two lifetimes. But above all, in the authors' judgment, a deferred annuity (or an immediate annuity, for that matter) is a potent risk management tool.

Advisors sometimes ask what specific section in the Internal Revenue Code states that growth in the cash value of a deferred annuity is not taxable until distributed. As we have noted, the tax treatment of non-qualified annuities is governed by IRC section 72, but there is no specific line or paragraph in that section granting such tax deferral. Rather, the various subsections of Section 72(e) define what distributions (including "imputed" distributions, such as policy gain in an annuity pledged as collateral for a loan) will be taxed as "amounts not received as an annuity." Growth in the cash value (or "annuity value" or "surrender value") is not among the items defined as such. It is therefore not taxable, currently, by implication.

When Does a Deferred Annuity NOT Enjoy Tax-Deferred Treatment?

Not all deferred annuities enjoy the benefit of tax-deferred growth. Contributions made after February 28, 1986 to annuity contracts held by a corporation or other entity that is not a "natural person" will not be treated as an "annuity contract" for tax purposes[14] and will not enjoy tax deferral. "Income on the contract"[15] will be treated, each year, "as ordinary income received or accrued by the owner during such taxable year."[16]

There are five exceptions to this rule.[17] It does not apply to a contract that:

(A) is acquired by the estate of a decedent by reason of the death of the decedent;

(B) is held under a qualified pension, profit sharing, or stock bonus plan, as an IRC Section 403(b) tax sheltered annuity, or under an individual retirement plan;

(C) is a qualified funding asset[18] (as defined in IRC Section 130(d) but without regard to whether there is a qualified assignment);

(D) is purchased by an employer upon the termination of a qualified pension, profit sharing, or stock bonus plan or tax sheltered annuity program and held by the employer until all amounts under the contract are distributed to the employee for whom the contract was purchased or to his beneficiary; or

(E) is an immediate annuity (i.e., an annuity that is purchased with a single premium or annuity consideration, the annuity starting date of that is no later than one year from the date of purchase, and which provides for a series of substantially equal periodic payments to be made no less frequently than annually during the annuity period).

Another very important exception to this general rule is granted by a sentence at the end of Section 72(u)(1), which states that "for purposes of this paragraph, holding by a trust or other entity as an *agent for a natural person* (emphasis supplied) shall not be taken into account." In other words, if the nominal owner of the annuity is not a "natural person" but the beneficial owner is, the annuity will be treated as held by a "natural person" and treated as an annuity for tax purposes.

In what circumstances does this "exception to an exception" apply? It generally occurs when a trust owns the annuity for the benefit of another person. However, we would like to draw attention to one specific observation from that discussion, worthy of the reader's attention:

It is clear that if all contributions to the contract are made after February 28, 1986 the requirements apply to the contract. It seems clear enough that if no contributions are made after February 28, 1986 to an annuity contract, a contract held by a nonnatural person is treated for tax purposes as an annuity contract and is taxed under the annuity rules. . . . However, if contributions have been made both before March 1, 1986 and after February 28, 1986 to contracts held by nonnatural persons, it is not clear whether the income on the contract is allocated to different portions of the contract and whether the portion of the contract allocable to contributions before March 1, 1986 may continue to be treated as an annuity contract for income tax purposes. The Code makes no specific provision for separate treatment of contributions to the same contract made before March 1, 1986 and those made after February 28, 1986.[19]

What about a deferred annuity owned by a Family Limited Partnership? Here, the applicability of the "agent of a natural person" exception is particularly unclear. The authors have not been able to locate any private letter rulings in which the Service has held that such a partnership would qualify as such an agent, but Letter Ruling 199944020 is worthy of note. In this ruling, the Service provides notice of a taxpayer withdrawal of a letter ruling request -

> "Two rulings were requested on the transaction described below. The first was whether the transfer of annuity contracts to a partnership in exchange for limited partnership interests qualified for nonrecognition under §721 (nonrecognition of gain or loss on contribution). The second is whether the annuity contracts after the transfer to the partnership will be considered as held by a natural person under §72(u)."[20]

Although the taxpayer requesting the Ruling withdrew the request, Letter Ruling 199944020 states that -

> "We reached a tentatively adverse conclusion only with regard to the second requested ruling dealing with §72(u) (treatment of annuity contracts not held by natural persons)...

> Under the present facts, Partnership is not a mere agent holding the deferred annuities for natural persons, rather it is proposed that Partnership actually receive and possess the deferred annuities as property of Partnership, thus, subjecting this property to any possible claims of creditors against Partnership. By way of contrast, the example set forth in the drafting history of §72(u) clearly demonstrates that the agency exception was limited to a situation where a pure agency was created as the nonnatural person holding the property had no interest other than as agent. S. Rept. No. 99-313, 99th Cong., 2d Sess. 567 (Group annuity held by a corporation as agent for natural persons who are the beneficial owners, the contract is treated as an annuity). See also Joint Committee on Taxation Staff, General Explanation of the Tax Reform Act of 1986, 99th Cong., 2d Sess. 658 (1987) (If an employer holds a group policy to satisfy State group policy requirements, but has no right to any amounts contributed to the contract and all amounts are employee contributions, the employer is merely the nominal holder of the contract and the contract is not treated as held by a nonnatural person)."[21]

What is the significance of this Letter Ruling? First, it is only a Private Letter Ruling. Moreover, its "tentatively adverse conclusion" was reached based on specific facts and circumstances. However, the authors believe that the conclusion reached was both logical and valid, and that the mere agency required for an entity to qualify as the "agent of a natural person" under Section 72(u)(1) is fundamentally incompatible with the nature of a valid business partnership in general, and, in specific, with the business purpose requirement the Service has applied to Family Limited Partnerships in an estate planning context. At the very least, a Private Letter Ruling approving the claiming of the Section 72(u)(1) exception should be obtained before recommending that an annuity be owned by a Family Limited Partnership.

Penalty for Early Distributions from a Deferred Annuity

In granting the benefit of tax-deferral to deferred annuities, Congress intended that they should be retirement plans. To discourage the use of annuities as short-term financial instruments by young people, it enacted IRC section 72(q), which imposes a 10% penalty tax on certain "premature" payments (distributions) from annuity contracts. The penalty applies only to payments to the extent that they are includible in taxable income, and there are certain distributions to which the penalty does not apply,[22] including those –

(A) made on or after the date on which the taxpayer attains age 59½;[23]

(B) made on or after the death of the holder (or, where the holder is not an individual, the death of the primary annuitant);

(C) attributable to the taxpayer becoming disabled;[24]

(D) which are a part of a series of substantially equal periodic payments (not less frequently than annually) made for the life (or life expectancy) of the taxpayer or the joint lives (or joint life expectancies) of the taxpayer and his designated beneficiary;[25]

(E) from a qualified pension, profit sharing, or stock bonus plan, §403(b) annuity plan, or IRA;

(F) allocable to investment in the contract before August 14, 1982;[26]

(G) under a qualified funding asset;

(H) subject to the 10% penalty for withdrawals from a qualified retirement plan;[27]

(I) under an immediate annuity contract;

(J) which are purchased by an employer upon the termination of a qualified plan and which is held by the employer until such time as the employee separates from service.

It is important to note that, under the exemption for an immediate annuity, Revenue Ruling 92-95 states that "where a deferred annuity contract was *exchanged* (emphasis added) for an immediate annuity contract, the purchase date of the new contract for purposes of the 10% penalty tax was considered to be the date upon which the deferred annuity was purchased. Thus, payments from the replacement contract did not fall within the immediate annuity exception to the penalty tax."[28] This illustrates a significant common pitfall: where an immediate annuity is purchased directly, its payments will always be penalty-free; however, where an immediate annuity is acquired as part of an exchange from a deferred annuity contract, annuitization is not penalty free unless the payments happen to meet another exception.

> *Example.* Assume individual A (under age 59½) purchases an immediate annuity for a 5-year period certain payout, and individual B (also under age 59½) acquired an immediate annuity via an exchange from an existing deferred annuity for a 5-year period certain payout. Individual A's payments will be penalty-free. Individual B's payments, however, will not, because a contract that was initially a deferred annuity and is converted to an immediate annuity later does not meet the immediate annuity requirements.[29] On the other hand, let's assume that both individuals A and B selected lifetime annuitization options. In this case, individual A's payments will again be penalty free; individual B's payments will also be tax-free in this case, but not because the exchanged-for contract was an immediate annuity – instead, individual B's payments should be tax-free because they will *also* satisfy the requirements of subparagraph D (substantially equal periodic payments).

Tax Deduction for Annuity Losses

An income tax deduction for a loss may be taken by a taxpayer only when the loss is incurred in connection with the taxpayer's trade or business or in a transaction entered into for profit.[30]

"Generally, the purchase of a personal *annuity* contract is considered a transaction entered into for profit. Consequently, if a taxpayer sustains a loss upon surrender of a refund annuity contract, he may claim a deduction for the loss, regardless of whether he purchased the contract in connection with his trade or business or as a personal investment. The amount of the loss is determined by subtracting the cash surrender value from the taxpayer's "basis" for the contract. His "basis" is gross premium cost less all amounts previously received tax free under the contract (e.g., any excludable dividends and the excludable portion of any prior annuity payments). The loss is ordinary loss, not capital loss. Rev. Rul. 61- 201, 1961-2 CB 46; *Cohan v. Comm.*, 39 F.2d 540 (2nd Cir. 1930), aff'g 11 BTA 743. But if the taxpayer purchased the contract for purely personal reasons, and not for profit, no loss deduction will be allowed. For example, in one case, the taxpayer purchased annuities on the lives of relatives, giving the relatives ownership of the contracts. Later he acquired the contracts by gift and surrendered them at a loss. The court disallowed a loss deduction on the ground that the contracts were not bought for profit but to provide financial security for the relatives. *Early v. Atkinson*, 175 F.2d 118 (4th Cir. 1949)."[31]

How is this loss claimed on taxpayer's income tax return? There is some dispute as to the correct method for claiming the loss. "Some say that the loss should be treated as a miscellaneous itemized deduction that is not subject to the 2% floor on miscellaneous itemized deductions. Others, including some at the Service in unofficial comments, say it is a miscellaneous itemized deduction subject to the 2% floor. And finally, others take a more aggressive approach and say that the loss can be taken on the front of the Form 1040 on the line labeled 'Other gains or (losses).'"[32]

The authors believe that the proper place to take this deduction is as a miscellaneous itemized deduction subject to the 2% floor, in light of IRC section 67(b) which states that all deductions are miscellaneous itemized deductions unless specifically listed in Section 67(b)(1) through 67(b)(12)–and deferred annuities surrendered at a loss are not so enumerated.

Exchanges of and for Annuities

Under IRC section 1035, "no gain or loss shall be recognized on the exchange of" a life insurance policy for an annuity[33] or an annuity contract for another annuity contract,[34] under the so-called "like-kind exchange" rules. Instead, the acquired annuity receives a carryover basis from the surrendered insurance or annuity policy.[35] It is notable that an exchange of an annuity policy for a life insurance policy is not eligible for 1035 exchange treatment,[36] although the reverse transaction is.

Where a policy is exchanged not solely in kind, and is instead exchange for another policy of lesser value and the owner also receives cash or other property "to boot," this boot causes recognition of taxable gain for the lesser of the amount of boot received or unrecognized gain.[37] However, if the owner has exchanged an annuity at a loss, the receipt of boot does not cause the loss to be recognized;[38] if an annuity meets the provisions of Section 1035, then no loss will be recognized, and the receipt of boot cannot change this. In addition, it is notable that application of Section 1035 is mandatory when its provisions are met–it is not an election, but is instead an automatic provision that applies when its stipulations are met.

When a life insurance policy with a loan is exchanged for an annuity, the extinguishing of the loan with the proceeds of the insurance policy is considered to be the receipt of boot to the extent of the loan. Consequently, gain recognition will occur for the lesser of boot received (loan extinguished) or gain in the contract. Unfortunately, while transfer of the loan to an acquired life insurance contract will allow the insurance policy owner to avoid boot treatment,[39] this option is not available for an annuity, because a loan against an annuity is considered a withdrawal.[40]

Over the years, the IRS has clarified its views on what does and does not constitute a 1035 exchange through a series of Revenue Rulings, and to some extent through Private Letter Rulings. Thus, the IRS has declared that a surrender and immediately subsequent purchase of an annuity does not qualify as a 1035 exchange if the taxpayer ever has control of the proceeds of the initial annuity.[41] However, a taxpayer can exchange an annuity into an existing annuity,[42] can combine multiple policies into a single annuity,[43] or can exchange a policy plus cash to a receiving annuity[44] (although the receipt of cash in an exchange can be taxable boot, the addition of cash to the exchange is not boot).

For many years, there was question about whether a taxpayer could complete a *partial* 1035 exchange, where a partial surrender from an annuity is exchanged for a new annuity contract. The Service fought transactions of this nature, for fear that taxpayers would use it as a tax avoidance scheme where a partial exchange is completed and the new annuity is subsequently surrendered for a smaller recognized taxable gain than would have occurred if the original annuity contract had been partially surrendered. However, after losing a partial 1035 exchange case in court,[45] the Service finally acquiesced to allow partial 1035 exchanges.[46] Under current rules, partial 1035 exchanges are allowed, as long as the taxpayer does not intend to surrender the newly-acquired contract within two years of purchase.[47] When a partial 1035 exchange is completed, basis is divided pro-rata between the old contract and the new one based on the relative value of the contracts when the split occurred.

Annuity contributions generally retain their original character after a 1035 exchange. Consequently, a contract with pre-August 13, 1982 contributions will retain treatment of those contributions even if the contract is subsequently exchanged via Section 1035[48] (see prior discussion of contracts entered into before August 13, 1982). (Note, however, a contract with pre-October 21, 1979 contributions will *not* retain their step-up in basis treatment at the death of the owner.[49]) However, this 'tracing' of the original contract contributions has its drawbacks – when a deferred annuity is exchanged for an immediate annuity, the original contribution date holds as the purchase date for the immediate annuity, and if not within one year of original purchase, the immediate annuity will not qualify for Section 72(q)(2)(I) provisions for the avoidance of the early withdrawal penalty.

A planning technique sometimes recommended by aggressive planners involves the "harvesting" of an otherwise non-deductible loss in a life insurance policy by using a tax-free exchange of that policy, under IRC section1035, for a deferred annuity having no surrender charges, and subsequent surrender of that annuity (which will have acquired the substituted cost basis of the exchanged life policy) for an allegedly deductible loss. In the authors' opinion, the success of this strategy is questionable if the annuity is surrendered shortly after the exchange. The IRS may well regard this as a "step transaction" and disallow the loss deduction, holding that the substance of the transaction (the surrender of the original life insurance policy) holds over the form of the transaction (the apparent surrender of an annuity policy).

Gift or Sale of an Annuity

If the owner of an annuity transfers that annuity, by sale, to another taxpayer, there may be both gift tax and income tax consequences. Annuities may also be transferred by gift. Although gifts are not subject to income tax, they may be subject to federal and/or state gift tax.

Gift of a Deferred Annuity

An individual who transfers an annuity contract issued after April 22, 1987, for less then full and adequate consideration, is treated as having received as "an amount not received as annuity" an amount equal to the excess of the cash surrender value of the contract at the time of transfer over the investment in the contract at that time.[50] Thus, the *transferor* realizes, in the year of the transfer, any gain on the contract allocable to investment in the contract after August 13, 1982. The transferee's cost basis will be the donor's adjusted cost plus the donee's cost (if any), adjusted for (increased by) any gift tax actually paid.

Note, however, that "upon maturity or surrender by the donee of an annuity or endowment contract issued before April 23, 1987, that portion of the gain on the contract which had accrued up to the date of the gift will be taxed *to the donor* not the donee (emphasis supplied). Thus, the *donor* will have taxable gain from the contract in the year the contract values are received by the donee to the extent that the cash surrender value at the time of the gift exceeded the donor's premium cost (less any excludable dividends he has received). It is ordinary income, not capital gain."[51] It is notable, though, that when the donee makes only *partial* surrenders of the gifted annuity contract, the timing of tax recognition that traces back to the donor will depend on whether contributions under the contract are allocable to investment in the contract before August 13, 1982 ("FIFO" basis-first treatment) or after ("LIFO" gains-first treatment). If there is gain attributable to both the donee (post-transfer) and the donor (pre-transfer), it is unclear which party will be required to recognize gain first where there is a partial surrender and not all gain is recognized in a single year. In any event, when the entire contract is surrendered, all gain accrued up to the date of the gift will be taxed to the donor.

Not all such gratuitous transfers[52] result in this recognition of gain by transferor. This rule does not apply to transfers between spouses (or between former spouses incident to a divorce and pursuant to an instrument executed or modified after July 18, 1984).[53] In addition, "the IRS has ruled privately that the distribution of an annuity contract by a trust to a trust beneficiary will not be treated as an assignment for less than full and adequate consideration (i.e., a gift) since, for purposes of this rule, the trust is not considered to be an individual."[54]

A question often asked by advisors is whether a taxpayer who owns a deferred annuity containing as-yet-untaxed "gain" may avoid tax on that gain by making a gift of the annuity to a charity. The simple answer is no. However, it is important to note that, as discussed above, annuities issued since April 22, 1987 will be taxed to the donor on transfer, while the gift of an annuity issued prior to this date will not be taxed until it is surrendered by the donee. Congress has considered legislation allowing the donation of deferred annuities to charities to avoid recognition of gain on a transfer, but no such legislation has been passed.

Of course, the taxpayer who makes a gift of a deferred annuity to a qualifying charity will be allowed an income tax deduction for the charitable gift. However, since annuities are ordinary income property, the deduction amount of the cost will be limited to the cost basis, and not the current value.[55] In addition, when property is donated with a fair market value that is less than the cost basis (i.e., property at a loss) the amount of the gift is restricted to the fair market value of the property.[56]

Consequently, it will virtually always be best to surrender an annuity first, and then donate the proceeds, allowing the donor to recognize the annuity loss, or recognize the gain but ensure that the charitable deduction will be for the fair market value of the contract (i.e., the full cash proceeds of the annuity are received and then donated as cash, and thus are not restricted to the cost basis limitation of an in-kind annuity donation).

Sale of a Deferred Annuity

The naming of a new owner of an annuity in exchange for full and adequate consideration is a sale of the annuity. The seller must recognize any gain as ordinary income.[57] However, there is no clear case law, statute, or regulations regarding the tax treatment of an annuity sale where the sale price exceeds the surrender value of the contract.[58]

"However, where an annuity contract is sold after maturity,[59] the cost basis of the contract (for purpose of computing the seller's gain) must be reduced by the aggregate excludable portions of the annuity payments that have been received. But the adjusted cost basis cannot be reduced below zero (for example, where the annuitant has outlived his life expectancy and was able to exclude amounts in excess of his net premium cost on a contract that was annuitized prior to January 1st, 1987).[60] The taxable gain can never be greater than the sale price.

Where an annuity contract is sold for less than its cost basis, apparently the seller realizes an ordinary loss."[61]

Transfers of Annuities to Trusts

Generally speaking, the transfer of ownership of an annuity is a taxable event for both income tax and gift tax purposes, as discussed above. When ownership of an annuity is transferred to a trust, though, the tax consequences depend upon the nature of the trust.

1. The transfer of an annuity from an owner to the owner's revocable trust is not a taxable event for income tax purposes, under the "grantor trust"[62] rules because the grantor is still considered the owner of the trust for income tax purposes, so no taxable transfer has taken place. In addition, it is not a gift–since the trust is fully revocable and the annuity could be re-titled back to the grantor at any time, the grantor has not "completed" the gift.[63]

2. The transfer of an annuity from an owner to the owner's irrevocable grantor trust is not a taxable event for income tax purposes (under the same grantor trust rules noted above), but the transfer may be a taxable gift (since the gift is irrevocably completed).

3. The transfer of an annuity from an owner to the owner's irrevocable non-grantor trust will trigger recognition of policy gain, because the owner of the trust for income tax purposes is someone other than the grantor (by virtue of the trust not being a grantor trust).[64] In addition, if the transferee trust does not qualify as the "agent of a natural person," the contract will no longer qualify as "an annuity" for income tax purposes,[65] and any income on the contract will be treated as taxable ordinary income to the owner.[66] Moreover, the full value of the annuity will be considered a taxable gift for gift tax purposes, less the annual exclusion amount[67] (if applicable).

Chapter Endnotes

1. Technically, "qualified annuity" refers only to an annuity purchased to fund a "qualified retirement plan" offered by a participant's employer, such as a pension or profit sharing plan, 403(b) plan, SEPP, etc. An IRA (either "traditional" or Roth) is not a "qualified plan," in the strict sense of that term. However, many (but not all) of the rules governing IRAs are similar to (and in some cases, identical to) those governing qualified plans (such as the Required Minimum Distributions of IRC Sec. 401(a)(9)) and very different from the rules governing ordinary savings plans, so that the terms "qualified annuity" and "qualified money" (to describe money held in a "qualified" plan) are commonly used in reference to an annuity purchased to fund a "qualified plan" *or* an IRA.

2. *Tax Facts on Insurance & Employee Benefits*, The National Underwriter Co. (2005), Q. 1.

3. *Ibid.*

4. IRC Sec. 72(b); Treas. Reg. §1.72-3.

5. Treas. Reg. §1.72-2(b)(3).

6. IRC Sec. 72(b)(2).

7. IRC Sec. 72(e)(1)(B); *Tax Facts on Insurance & Employee Benefits*, The National Underwriter Co. (2005), Q. 3.

8. *Tax Facts on Insurance & Employee Benefits*, The National Underwriter Co. (2005), Q. 3.

9. *Tax Facts on Insurance & Employee Benefits*, The National Underwriter Co. (2005), Q. 3; IRC Sec. 72(e)(3).

10. IRC Sec. 72(e)(4)(A).

11. IRC Sec. 72(e)(11).

12. *Tax Facts on Insurance & Employee Benefits*, The National Underwriter Co. (2005), Q. 3; IRC Sec. 72(e)(5).

13. It is worth stating, again, that the word "deferred," in the term "deferred annuity" does not refer to the tax treatment just described, but to the fact that annuity income will not commence immediately upon purchase of the contract, but will instead be deferred until some point in the future. Some deferred annuities impose a limit upon deferral by mandating that annuity payments commence no later than at annuitant's attainment of a certain age.

14. IRC Sec. 72(u)(1)(A).

15. " 'Income on the contract' is the excess of (1) the sum of the net surrender value of the contract at the end of the taxable year and any amounts distributed under the contract during the taxable year and any prior taxable year over (2) the sum of the net premiums (amount of premiums paid under the contract reduced by any policyholder dividends) under the contract for the taxable year and prior taxable years and any amounts includable in gross income for prior taxable years under this requirement. IRC Sec. 72(u)(2)." *Tax Facts on Insurance & Employee Benefits*, The National Underwriter Co. (2005), Q. 2.

16. IRC Sec. 72(u)(1)(B).

17. IRC Sec. 72(u)(3).

18. A qualified funding asset is any annuity contract issued by a licensed insurance company that is purchased and held to fund periodic payments for damages, by suit or agreement, on account of personal physical injury or sickness. IRC Sec. 130(d).

19. *Tax Facts on Insurance & Employee Benefits*, The National Underwriter Co. (2005), Q. 2.

20. Let. Rul. 199944020.

21. *Ibid.*

22. The authors' descriptions of the IRC Sec. 72(q)(2) exceptions have been abbreviated for clarity. For more detailed descriptions, see *Tax Facts on Insurance & Employee Benefits*, The National Underwriter Co. (2005), Q. 4.

23. In the authors' opinion, "Taxpayer," here, refers to the taxpayer responsible for paying the tax on a distribution. If A, age 81, owns an annuity of which B, age 55, is annuitant, and requests a withdrawal, that withdrawal is not subject to the 10% penalty because A, as owner of the contract, is liable for tax on the distribution, even if the distribution is made directly to B, at A's direction.

24. "Disabled" is defined in IRC Sec. 72(m)(7), which states: "[F]or purposes of this section, an individual shall be considered to be disabled if he is unable to engage in any substantial gainful activity by reason of any medically determinable physical or mental impairment which can be expected to result in death or to be of long-continued and indefinite duration. An individual shall not be considered to be disabled unless he furnishes proof of the existence thereof in such form and manner as the Secretary may require."

25. Under IRS Notice 2004-15, 2004-9 IRB 526, taxpayers seeking substantially equal periodic payments from annuities under IRC Sec. 72(q)(2)(D), may rely on the guidance of IRS Notice 89-25 1989-1 CB 662 (as modified by Revenue Ruling 2002-62, 2002-2 CB 710), which provides explanation and rules regarding substantially equal periodic payments from retirement accounts under IRC Sec. 72(t).

26. This provision is actually somewhat redundant. IRC Sec. 72(q)(1) already indicates that the penalty will apply only to amounts includable in gross income, and IRC Sec. 72(e)(5) already indicates that withdrawals allocable to investment in the contract before August 14th, 1982 will not be included in income (and thus could not be subject to penalty).

27. This prevents the imposition of an IRC Sec. 72(q)(1) early withdrawal penalty on a 'qualified' annuity that is already subject to the early withdrawal penalty rules under IRC Sec. 72(t).

28. Rev. Rul. 92-95, 1992-2 C.B. 43.

29. IRC Sec. 72(u)(4)(B) requires the annuity starting date to be no later than 1 year *from the date of purchase* to qualify as an "immediate annuity" – when the purchase date of the *original* contract must be applied under Revenue Ruling 92-95, it will almost always be beyond the 1-year period.

30. IRC Sec. 165.

31. *Tax Facts on Insurance & Employee Benefits*, The National Underwriter Co. (2005), Q. 26.

32. *Ibid.*

33. IRC Sec. 1035(a)(1).

34. IRC Sec. 1035(a)(3).

35. IRC Sec. 1035(d)(2); IRC Sec. 1031(d).

36. Treas. Reg. §1.1035-1(c).

37. IRC Secs. 1035(d)(1), 1031(b).

38. IRC Secs. 1035(d)(1), 1031(c).

39. Let. Ruls. 8604033, 9044022.

40. IRC Sec. 72(e)(4)(A).

41. Let. Ruls. 8515063, 8810010.

42. Rev. Rul. 2002-75, 2002-2 CB 812.

43. Let. Rul. 9708016.

44. Let. Rul. 9820018.

45. *Conway v. Comm.*, 111 TC 330 (1998).

46. See Rev. Rul. 2003-76, 2003-2 CB 355.

47. See Notice 2003-51, 2003-33 IRB 361. However, in Let. Rul. 200342003, the Service agreed to non-recognition treatment for a taxpayer that only stipulated a one-year promise not to surrender.

48. Rev. Rul. 85-159, 1985-2 CB 29.

49. See Rev. Rul. 79-335, 1979-2 CB 292, Let. Rul. 9245035, and TAM 9346002.

50. IRC Sec. 72(e)(4)(C).

51. *Advanced Sales Reference Service*, The National Underwriter Co., Sect. 52, ¶330.10; Rev. Rul. 69-102, 1969-1 CB 32.

52. Gratuitous transfers, or gifts, are those not made for full and adequate consideration. When an annuity is transferred in exchange for a fair price, the transfer would be considered a sale.

53. IRC Sec. 72(e)(4)(c)(ii).

54. *Advanced Sales Reference Service*, The National Underwriter Co., Sect. 52, ¶330.10. See Let. Ruls. 9204010, 9204014.

55. IRC Sec. 170(e).

56. Treas. Reg. §1.170A-1(c)(1).

57. *First Nat'l Bank of Kansas City v. Comm.*, 309 F.2d 587 (8th Cir. 1962) aff'g *Katz v. Comm.*, TC Memo 1961-270; *Roff v. Comm.*, 304 F.2d 450 (3rd Cir. 1962) aff'g 36 TC 818; *Arnfeld v. U.S.*, 163 F. Supp. 865 (Ct. Cl. 1958), *cert. denied* 359 U.S. 943.

58. For example, assume an annuity with a $50,000 cost basis and a $75,000 surrender value were sold for $85,000 (perhaps because it provides a contractual interest rate guarantee that is more appealing than current market rates). Clearly the $25,000 gain from cost basis to surrender value must be taxed as ordinary income; however, it is not clear whether the additional $10,000 of gain would be taxed as though it were an "amount not received as an annuity" (i.e., ordinary income treatment), or the sale of the entire annuity contract as though it were a capital assets (i.e., capital gain treatment).

59. "After maturity" means "after annuity starting date" – i.e. a contract that has been annuitized.

60. Treas. Reg. §1.1021-1.

61. *Tax Facts on Insurance & Employee Benefits*, The National Underwriter Co. (2005), Q. 28.

62. IRC Secs. 671-677.

63. Treas. Reg. §25.2511-2(c).

64. The same recognition-of-gain rules that would apply on any transfer of the annuity to a new individual or other party. This rule is actually the "norm", and the grantor trust rules described above represent the exception to that rule.

65. IRC Sec. 72(u)(1).

66. IRC Sec. 72(u)(1)(B).

67. IRC Sec. 2503(b).

Chapter 3

Taxation of Annuity Death Benefits

The taxation of death benefits of non-qualified annuities is a particularly difficult subject for many advisors. Most of the difficulty lies not in whether or how such proceeds are taxable, but in when and how they must be paid out to beneficiaries. The rules governing required payouts upon death are complicated and sometimes unclear. In at least one important area (when and how a non-spousal beneficiary of a deferred annuity must take death proceeds), the rules in the Internal Revenue Code appear to be contradictory (see "What About Section 72(h)," below). Fortunately, not all of the rules are this difficult. We will begin our examination with the "easier stuff" – the relatively straightforward rules of how death proceeds of non-qualified annuities are treated for Estate Tax purposes.

Estate Taxation

If the value of an annuity contract does not terminate entirely upon the death of the contract owner (leaving nothing to pass to owner's estate or beneficiaries), any remaining value is taxable in owner's estate for estate tax purposes.[1] Whether any value remains depends upon whether the contract is, at the time of owner's death, in "payout status" or not, and, if so, the terms of the payout arrangement. An annuity is said to be in "payout status" on or after its "annuity starting date."[2] The "annuity starting date" is "the first day of the first period for which an amount is received as an annuity."[3] "In the case of a single premium immediate annuity contract, the annuity starting date is usually the date of purchase. For example, if an individual purchases an immediate annuity on July 1, 1987 which provides for monthly payments beginning August 1, 1987, the annuity starting date is July 1, 1987 (the first monthly payment is for the period beginning July

1st). Payments under settlement options, however, usually commence at the beginning, rather than at the end of the month or other payment period; hence the annuity starting date is the date of the first payment."[4]

Estate Taxation of Annuities in "Payout Status"

What is the Estate Tax value of an annuity "in payout status?" This depends upon the payout arrangement. Let's examine each of the five possibilities:

1. If the decedent was receiving a "life only" annuity,[5] payments ceased with her death; thus, no property interest remains to be included in her gross estate.[6]

2. If the decedent was receiving a life annuity with a "refund feature" that was still operative, the value of that refund feature is includible in decedent's gross estate.

    Example A: Decedent elected to take a life annuity, payable monthly, with a 10 year certain refund feature,[7] commencing on June 1, 1995. She died in May, 2004, after receiving 108 monthly payments. Twelve additional payments were due under the refund feature. The value of these payments, to be included in the decedent's estate, is what the insurance company issuing the annuity would charge for a contract paying a comparable annuity (12 monthly payments).[8] Value at date of death is used, even where the executor elects alternate valuation.[9]

    Example B: Decedent elected a life annuity with a cash refund feature. If annuity payments received by her, during her lifetime, were less than the value of the cash refund,[10] "the value includible [in decedent's estate] is presumably the amount received by the beneficiary."[11]

3. If the decedent was receiving a life annuity with a refund feature that had expired, payments ceased with her death; thus, no property interest remains to be included in her gross estate.

    Example: Decedent elected to take a life annuity, payable monthly, with a 10 year certain refund feature,[12] commencing on June 1, 1995. She died in August, 2005, after receiving 123 monthly payments. As the number of payments guaranteed in the refund feature had been received by the decedent during her lifetime, the refund feature had been satisfied. No payments were due to any beneficiary, and no value remained to be includible in decedent's estate.

4. If the decedent was receiving, and was the owner of, a Joint and Survivor annuity, the value of the survivor's annuity is "the amount the same insurance company would charge the survivor for a single life annuity as of the date of the first annuitant's death."[13] The amount includible in decedent's estate depends on who paid for the annuity and whether the joint annuitants were husband and wife. If the deceased owner/annuitant (in a non-married situation) contributed the entire purchase price, the full value of the survivor's annuity is includible in the deceased's estate. If not, the annuity is includible in decedent owner's estate only to the extent of his or her contribution.[14] If the annuity was paid for entirely by the surviving annuitant, its value is not includible in deceased annuitant's estate.[15]

5. If the decedent was receiving a Period Certain annuity, the value of the remaining payments includible in decedent's estate is what the same insurance company would charge for a Period Certain annuity for the number of payments remaining.[16]

It is worth noting that in some situations, interest rates or even mortality tables may have changed from original annuity issuance to the date of decedent's death–consequently, the valuation of the survivor's portion of the annuity could be substantially more or less expensive that the pricing may have been at the original purchase date.

Estate Taxation of Annuities not "In Payout Status"

A deferred annuity where the owner has not yet elected an annuity settlement option ("annuitization") – that is, where the owner dies before the annuity starting date - is not "in payout status."[17] The death benefit (including any "death benefit enhancements") of the annuity as of owner's death is fully includible in owner's estate, either under Code section 2039 (which relates to the estate taxation of annuities) or under Code section 2033 (which relates to property which the decedent had an interest in), for estate tax purposes.

What if the owner is not the annuitant? The annuitant of a deferred annuity not in payout status generally has no property rights under the contract. The annuity is property and both the income tax and estate tax liabilities are those of the owner. However, because the tax code, and many annuity contracts, may make reference to both the annuitant and the owner at various points, the tax rules can get very complicated (as we will see later on) where owner and annuitant are not the same individual.

Income Taxation of Death Benefits

Annuities in "Payout Status" (Immediate Annuities and Deferred Annuities, Where Holder Dies After Annuity Starting Date)

Death proceeds of an immediate annuity or a deferred annuity that has been "annuitized" are governed by Code section 72(s)(1)(A), which states that

> "if any holder of such contract dies on or after the annuity starting date and before the entire interest in such contract has been distributed, the remaining portion of such interest will be distributed at least as rapidly as under the method of distributions being used as of the date of his death."

If the death proceeds ("the remaining portion of such interest") are taken by the beneficiary either as a lump sum or in installments other than payments calculated by application of a new annuity option,[18] proceeds will be excludible from income until the total amount beneficiary receives, when added to the amounts annuitant received tax-free, equal annuitant's "investment in the contract," unadjusted for the value of the refund feature.[19] Amounts received by the beneficiary in excess of the "investment in the contract" are taxed as ordinary income. Note that this "FIFO" (first-in, first-out) basis-first treatment of beneficiary payments is different than the standard, income/gains-first treatment of annuity withdrawals and different from the pro-rata exclusion-ratio treatment of annuitized payments. If the total payments thus made to the beneficiary are less than annuitant's investment in the contract and the annuitant's annuity starting date was after July 1, 1986, the beneficiary may take an income tax deduction for any such unrecovered investment.[20]

Important Note: "Whose Tax is it, Anyway?" – Annuitant, Owner (Holder), Taxpayer?

Unfortunately, for those trying to make sense of annuity taxation, the relevant rules in the Code and the Treasury Regulations, as well as many reference sources that cite the law, often refer to "annuitant" when applying tax rules. The implication is that the owner and the annuitant are the same individual. This is generally a holdover from a time when all annuities were "annuitant-driven" (that is, an annuity paid a death benefit upon the death of the annuitant) and when tax law focused upon the annuitant, rather than the owner (which the Code and Regulations consistently refer to as the "holder"). Where the annuitant and owner (or holder) are the same individual, there is no distinction to be made or inferred, but where the two are not, the rules–and the explanations of those rules in even the best reference sources–can be confusing. It is vital that we remember that the tax liability for payments made from annuities (whether "amounts received as an annuity" or "amounts not received as an annuity") are generally the tax responsibility of the contract owner if that owner is living, even if the payments are actually made to another individual (such as a non-owner annuitant). However, if the payments are made to a beneficiary, by reason of the death of either the annuitant or owner, the tax liability is that of the beneficiary/payee.

Consider, for example, the following explanation from *Tax Facts on Insurance & Employee Benefits (2005 edition)*, Q. 18:

> "The beneficiary will have no taxable income unless the total amount the beneficiary receives when added to amounts that were received tax free by the annuitant (the excludable portion of the annuity payments) exceeds the investment in the contract."

Strictly speaking, that ought to read "…that were received tax-free by the annuitant, or contract owner, if the owner was not the annuitant". Similarly, the statement above that "proceeds will be excludible from income until the total amount beneficiary receives, when added to the amounts annuitant received tax-free, equal annuitant's 'investment in the contract', unadjusted for the value of the refund feature" would be more accurate if stated as "proceeds will be excludible from income until the total amount beneficiary receives, when added to the amounts **annuitant received without tax to the owner,** equal **owner's** *'investment in the contract'*".

However, such "precision" would very likely be a "cure worse than the disease"– increasing, rather than reducing, reader confusion. The authors merely wish to make clear that references such as "annuitant's investment in the contract" should be understood to mean "owner's investment" in the case where owner and annuitant are two different individuals.

Annuities Not in Payout Status (Deferred Annuities, Where Holder Dies Before Annuity Starting Date)

The income tax rules regarding death benefits of deferred annuities not in "payment status" constitute one of the most difficult and confusing areas of annuity planning. Most of this confusion lies not in how taxable amounts are determined (though that is certainly complicated), but in how and when death proceeds must be received by the beneficiary under tax law. To understand this (how and when death proceeds must be taken) we must first understand when death proceeds are payable–that is, whose death triggers the payment of the proceeds.

An annuity is said to be "annuitant-driven" when payment of the death benefit to the beneficiary will be made upon the death of the annuitant. When the death benefit is payable to the beneficiary upon death of the owner, the annuity is said to be "owner-driven."

One might think that any annuity contract is either one or the other, but it is not quite that simple. All deferred annuity contracts issued since January 18, 1985, are owner-driven, because no annuity contract issued since that date will be treated as an "annuity contract" for tax purposes unless it contains language requiring the "force out" provisions of Code section 72(s).[21] That Code provision mandates distributions from annuity contracts upon the death of "the holder."[22]

Code section 72(s) is entitled "Required Distributions Where Holder Dies Before Entire Interest Is Distributed." It is a very important section that should be well understood by anyone selling or offering advice on the subject of annuities. **Failure to understand the rules set out in this section can be hazardous to your career!** If the owner, annuitant, and beneficiary designations of an annuity are made without a clear understanding of the rules discussed below, the result could be a required distribution of that annuity at a time and in a manner never intended or desired by the client.

Before getting into a detailed examination of Section 72(s), the authors want to make three observations about it. First, it is not nearly as simple or straightforward as it may appear. Second, it applies only when the holder of an annuity contract dies. Third, holder is an exceedingly slippery term. Generally speaking, it means owner–the individual named as owner of the annuity contract. However, for certain purposes, when an annuity is owned by a "non-natural" entity (such as a Trust or Corporation), the Code will deem an individual to be the holder, even if that individual is not the owner named in the contract.

With those observations in mind, let's look at what Section 72(s)(1) says:

In General.—A contract shall not be treated as an annuity contract for purposes of this title [i.e. for income tax purposes] unless it provides that–

(A) if any holder of such contract dies on or after the annuity starting date and before the entire interest in such contract has been distributed, the remaining portion of such interest will be distributed at least as rapidly as under the method of distributions being used as of the date of his death, and

(B) if any holder of such contract dies before the annuity starting date, the entire interest in such contract will be distributed within 5 years after the death of such holder.

We have seen the first rule (Section 72(s)(1)(A)) before, in our discussion of the income tax treatment of annuities in "payout status." This refers to immediate annuities and deferred annuities that have been annuitized.

The second rule (Section 72(s)(1)(B)) is the default rule for annuities not in payout status (i.e., deferred annuities that have not been annuitized). It says that, upon the death of the holder, the proceeds of the annuity must be paid out within five years of holder's death. This rule applies unless an exception is available. The subsections that follow (Sections 72(s)(2) and 72(s)(3)) provide the two allowable exceptions. Neither exception is available unless the annuity is payable to a "designated beneficiary," which is defined by Section 72(s)(4) as "any individual designated a beneficiary by the holder of the contract."

The key word here is "individual." An "individual" must be a natural person–a human being. A trust, for example, cannot be a designated individual. It is important to note that, unlike recent new regulations regarding distributions from IRAs payable to trusts, there are no "look-through" provisions for trust beneficiaries of annuities–since the trust itself is not a natural person, it cannot be a designated beneficiary! And any beneficiary that is not a "designated beneficiary" (a natural person) is not entitled to either of the two exceptions we are about to discuss.

The first exception to the default "five year rule" allows the designated beneficiary to take the proceeds over a period longer than five years. Section 72(s)(2) permits proceeds to be distributed "over the life of such designated beneficiary (or over a period not extending beyond the life expectancy of such beneficiary)". Note that it does not require that the beneficiary take proceeds over his or her remaining lifetime, but merely states that the distribution period cannot be longer than that. A "period certain" annuity payout (e.g., 20 Year Certain) is acceptable, provided that beneficiary's life expectancy is at least 20 years.

If an annuity option (e.g. a life annuity [with or without a "refund feature"] or a period certain annuity) is elected by the beneficiary, the payments will be taxed according to the "regular annuity rules" of Section 72(b)(1). "The exclusion ratio for the payments would be based on the deceased annuitant's [remaining] 'investment in the contract' and the beneficiary's 'expected return.' If life contingency is involved in the settlement arrangement, the beneficiary's life expectancy as of his or her annuity starting date would be used in computing expected return."[23]

If the insurance company that issued the annuity permits, the beneficiary may also elect to take death proceeds in an arrangement often referred to as a "stretch annuity." This arrangement, first permitted in Private Letter Ruling 200151038, allows the beneficiary to take proceeds by using a "fractional" method, whereby the amount of each payment would be determined by applying divisors from the "Unified Table" used for Required Minimum Distributions from IRAs and qualified plans. For younger beneficiaries, the required minimum payments thus calculated are substantially smaller in the earlier years than those that would be required under any life annuity or period certain option, allowing these beneficiaries to defer receiving a greater amount of proceeds to later years. As the "gain" in proceeds not yet received (or constructively received) is not yet taxable, this represents an opportunity for greater tax deferral. But how should each income payment to the beneficiary be taxed? PLR 200151038 is silent on this point, stating "Specifically, no opinion is expressed on whether payments made to the designated beneficiary under the procedures described in Requested Rulings 1, 2, and 3, above (the optional distribution procedures), are "amounts received as an annuity," taxable under §72(a) and (b), or "amounts not received as annuity" taxable under §72(e)."

However, a subsequent Letter Ruling, PLR 200313016, held that such payments, made in accordance with the "life expectancy fraction method," will, to the extent that they do not exceed the amounts required by such calculation, qualify as "amounts received as an annuity." Under such treatment, a portion of each annuity payment is excluded from tax, as a "return of principal" (see Chapter 2).

A caveat should be noted, with regard to this conclusion. The options available to beneficiaries of the annuity issued by the insurance company that requested the ruling were allowed two additional options, after having elected one of three payout arrangements (of which one was the "fractional method"). "Option 1" permitted the beneficiary to take, at any time, the entire remaining balance in a lump sum. "Option 2" permitted additional partial withdrawals (over and above those distributions required by the payout method). The ruling specifically stated that the result stated above–that payments made in accordance with any of the three payout methods specified in the ruling request (including the "fractional method")–applies only to beneficiaries who elect Option 1. No opinion is expressed regarding those who elect Option 2.

What can we say about what these rulings allow a beneficiary of a non-qualified annuity? First, we are obliged to note that they are only private letter rulings. They may not be relied upon by anyone other than the taxpayer to whom they were issued. Second, whether the IRS will consider "fractional method" annuity payments made to beneficiaries as "amounts received as an annuity" is moot if the issuer of the annuity will not permit such a payout arrangement. Some do not. It is essential that the advisor discussing this option be aware of whether the issuer of the annuity in question will permit it in the first place.

When it is permitted, it can be extremely attractive. Many beneficiaries also select this option because it allows payments to occur across the lifetime of the beneficiary without actually requiring annuitization of the proceeds, which provides additional liquidity for beneficiaries that do not require the guarantees of annuitization. Furthermore, some annuity companies will allow the annuity owner, while still alive, to select a particular beneficiary payout period to be established as part of the contractual annuity agreement, thereby potentially preventing the beneficiary from having fully liquid access to the proceeds at the owner's death without necessitating the use of a trust.

The second exception to the "five year rule" of Section 72(s)(1) is available only to a beneficiary who is the surviving spouse of the holder. This exception, allowed under Section 72(s)(3), permits that surviving spouse/beneficiary to treat the decedent's annuity as her own as if she were owner of the contract from inception. It is extremely important that the advisor understand that spousal continuation applies only in the situation just stated. It is not available, for exam-

ple, to a surviving spouse who is trustee of a trust named as beneficiary of decedent spouse's annuity.[24] It is also not available to a beneficiary who owned an
annuitant-driven annuity of which his spouse was annuitant–for example, where
H is the owner and W is the annuitant of an annuitant-driven contract, and W
dies, H receives the death proceeds of the annuity he owns and must recognize
the income without the opportunity to elect spousal continuation.

The Section 72(s)(2) annuitization exception (to the five year rule) requires
that "such distributions begin not later than 1 year after the date of the holder's
death or such later date as the Secretary may by regulations prescribe." Many
advisors interpret this to mean that the beneficiary has one year from the date of
holder's death to elect this option. Indeed, some insurance companies may, by
current practice, allow the beneficiary up to one year to make such an election.
This interpretation could pose a serious problem for clients – and advisors – rely-
ing upon it. Why? Because of a Code section often ignored–Section 72(h).

What About Section 72(h)?

Section 72(h) is entitled "Option To Receive An Annuity In Lieu Of A Lump
Sum". It states that –

If —

(1) a contract provides for payment of a lump sum in full discharge of an
obligation under the contract, subject to an option to receive an annuity in
lieu of such lump sum;

(2) the option is exercised within 60 days after the day on which such lump
sum first became payable; and

(3) part or all of such lump sum would (but for this subsection) be includible in gross income by reason of subsection (e)(1),

then, for purposes of this subtitle, no part of such lump sum shall be considered as includible in gross income at the time such lump sum first
became payable.

What does this mean, in normal English? It means that if an annuity provides
the beneficiary the option to take death proceeds as an annuity, in lieu of taking
a lump sum settlement and, if the beneficiary exercises, within sixty days of

owner's death,[25] the option to take an annuity, and if part or all of the proceeds would be includible in beneficiary's estate if taken in a lump sum (e.g.: the contract was an annuity, not qualifying for the tax-free treatment of death benefit that life insurance contracts enjoy under Code section 101(a)), then the entire taxable portion of this death benefit will not be taxable to beneficiary in the year of the owner's death. The beneficiary, by electing to take proceeds as an annuity, will, instead, be taxed on those proceeds as received, under the "regular annuity rules"–provided that he or she exercises such an "annuitization" option within sixty days of the owner's death.

This sixty-day requirement of Section 72(h)(2) appears to conflict with the one-year requirement of Section 72(s)(2)(C), even though they are not speaking of the same thing. The latter requirement concerns only when the first annuity payment must be made if "regular annuity rule" taxation is to be available; the former says when the exercise of the annuity option must be made to achieve that result. Conceivably, one might elect to take death proceeds as an annuity within sixty days of the death of the annuitant or owner, with the first payment to commence within one year of that result, thus satisfying both rules – because the election of the annuity option is the exercise thereof. However, insurance companies typically offer beneficiaries annuity payment options only on an immediate annuity basis – where the first payment will commence one month or so from the date of election. Practically speaking, this means that the first annuity payment must probably be made much sooner than one year from death, but, in any event, the exercise of the option to receive payments must be made within sixty days.

Some commentators believe that Section 72(s) trumps Section 72(h), arguing that the former section is some twenty years newer than the latter. Moreover, it is argued, the legislative history of Section 72 shows a Congressional intent to bring "parity" to the rules governing required distributions from non-qualified annuities and those governing required distributions from IRAs and qualified plans. The "default" five year rule, an exception for annuitization not extending life expectancy commencing within one year, and the "spousal continuation" provisions of Section 72(s) certainly resemble corresponding provisions in Section 401(a)(9). However, Section 72(h) was neither modified nor repealed by Congress, either when it enacted Section 72(s) or when it later amended it. Moreover, Section 72(s) says nothing about when or how distributions from an annuity must be recognized by the beneficiary as income for tax purposes; it merely mandates what distributions must occur from the contract for it to qualify as "an annuity contract" in the first place.

By contrast, Section 72(h) specifically speaks directly to the taxability of death benefits, declaring (basically) that if a beneficiary of a contract which allows a lump sum payout as an alternative to an annuity does not exercise the option to take proceeds as an annuity within 60 days, that beneficiary will be in "constructive receipt" of the entire contract gain in the year of owner's or annuitant's death. In other words, if the beneficiary has the option to take a lump sum, and does not elect an annuity payout within 60 days of the date of death, the beneficiary must recognize all of the gain, and must do so regardless of whether he actually withdrawals all or any of the death benefit proceeds that year.

In the authors' opinion, a beneficiary's election to take the death proceeds of an annuity, as an annuity, must be made within sixty days of the date on which those proceeds first became available. This applies both to deferred annuity and immediate annuity contracts. An insurance company may, by its current practice, permit a beneficiary to make such election as late as one year after holder's death, and may issue tax reporting forms reflecting the availability of "regular annuity rule" tax treatment. But the IRS may not accept such a position, because Section 72(h) is still on the books. It may be that a "late" election by a beneficiary to take proceeds as an annuity will escape IRS notice, particularly if the insurance company issues Forms 1099 reflecting "regular annuity rule" taxation, but, to be sure of that treatment, the beneficiary should make this election within sixty days.

It should be noted, at this point, that the apparent conflict between Sections 72(h) and 72(s) does not come into play when the annuity death benefit is paid by reason of the death of a non-owner annuitant (where the annuity contract was annuitant-driven and the non-owner annuitant died). Section 72(h) applies when the death benefit of any annuity contract is payable, as long as it provides for both lump sum and annuity payouts to the beneficiary. Section 72(s) applies only when the holder (owner) of an annuity dies. But some annuities pay a death benefit upon the death of either the owner or the annuitant. What are the income tax rules in that situation?

When Section 72(s) Does Not Apply – Income Tax Treatment of Death Proceeds of an Annuity "Not in Payment Status" When Non-Owner Annuitant Dies

Annuities that are not annuitant-driven (i.e., are owner-driven) pay a death benefit only upon death of the owner, and the income tax rules governing those death benefits are those we have just reviewed. However, annuities that are annuitant-driven pay a death benefit upon the death of the annuitant or the owner (the annuitant under contractual annuitant-driven provisions, and the owner under required provisions as dictated by Section 72(s)(1)), and in the case of an annuitant-driven annuity where the annuitant and owner are different individuals and the annuitant has died but the owner has not, the rules are somewhat different.

In the situation just described, Section 72(h) applies. If the beneficiary does not elect, within 60 days of annuitant's death, to take proceeds as an annuity (if the contract even offers this option), the proceeds will be considered "amounts not received as an annuity."[26] The proceeds in excess of the "investment in the contract" (i.e. the "gain") will be taxable to the beneficiary in the year of annuitant's death.[27] In this case, because there has been no death of a holder to which Section 72(s) might apply, there are no grounds to make an election under any time period except during the 60-day "window" of Section 72(h).

If the beneficiary is the surviving spouse of either the owner or annuitant, the "spousal continuation" option of Section 72(s)(3) is not available in this situation, because that option applies only when the beneficiary is the surviving spouse of a deceased holder (owner). If the beneficiary is under age 59½, the exemptions from the 10% penalty tax (under IRC Section 72(q)) that would apply had the owner died are similarly unavailable.

Due to all of these complications, including the time requirements of Section 72(h), loss of spousal continuation options of Section 72(s), and the potential premature distribution penalties of Section 72(q), the authors strongly caution against ever establishing an annuitant-driven contract where the owner and annuitant are different individuals.

Jointly Held Annuities

Non-qualified annuities sold to married individuals are often placed in joint ownership. Often, there are good reasons for this, but the advisor should be aware of potential problems with this arrangement. Ownership of assets held jointly, with rights of survivorship (JTWROS) ordinarily vests immediately, upon the death of one tenant, in the surviving tenant(s). This does not apply, however, to annuities owned in this manner. As we have seen, IRC section 72(s)(1)(B) requires that when any owner of an annuity dies before the annuity starting date, the proceeds of that annuity must be distributed within five years, unless the exceptions of Sections 72(s)(2) or 72(s)(3) apply.

Section 72(s)(3) provides what is often termed the "spousal continuation" option, whereby the surviving spouse of the deceased owner may elect to treat the annuity as his or her own. In the authors' opinion, this applies only when the surviving spouse is the designated beneficiary of the deceased owner. If the annuity is owned jointly by a husband and wife, but the beneficiary is their daughter, and either of the couple dies, the distribution must be made to the daughter under the terms of Section 72(s). This view is not shared by some insurance companies. Both of the authors have been informed, in conversations with insurance company representatives, that the contracts of a particular insurance company provide that under the fact situation given above, the surviving spouse/owner would be able to exercise the "spousal continuation" option of Section 72(s)(3). In one conversation, the insurance company representative stated that this would be so if the contract were not annuitant-driven, but that if it were, payment to the daughter as beneficiary would be required to be made, in accordance with the Section 72 rules.[28]

The authors know of no authority supporting this position, or, for that matter, the position that a surviving owner can ever elect "spousal continuation" if he or she is not the designated beneficiary of the deceased owner. On what basis might one assert the contrary? At least one insurance company's annuity provides that if the contract is owned jointly, the surviving owner will be deemed to be primary beneficiary, regardless of any prior beneficiary designation. That is certainly an interesting approach, but it relies, not on any putative right of the surviving owner, but on the fact that he or she would be the primary beneficiary. The authors have heard of (but have not been able to verify) an annuity that defines the death benefit as payable, when the contract is owned jointly, only upon the death of the second joint owner, but would have serious concerns that this might contravene the "death of any holder" language of Section 72(s)(1)?

The authors offer a strong suggestion to the reader to be very careful in dealing with joint ownership of annuities. If you believe that joint ownership is appropriate, and especially if a third party will be named as beneficiary, you should be certain of the insurer's policies with regard to payment of death benefits.

When the Beneficiary is a Trust

Probably the most confusing area of annuity taxation is that of which distribution rules apply when (a) the annuity is not "in payout status" and (b) the owner and/or beneficiary is a trust and (c) either the annuitant or owner of the annuity dies. This is such a complicated area that the authors have devoted a separate chapter of this book to it (see Chapter 8, Annuities and Trusts).

Annuities and Step-up in Basis at Death

Variable annuity contracts issued before October 21, 1979 are potentially eligible for a "step-up in basis" at the death of the owner under IRC section 1014.[29] This step-up in basis applies to contributions made to these contracts (including any contributions applied to an annuity contract pursuant to a binding commitment entered into before that date)[30] and their attributable earnings.

> The basis of the contract in the hands of the beneficiary will be the value of the contract at the date of the decedent's death (or the alternate valuation date). If that basis equals the amount received by the beneficiary there will be no income taxable gain and the appreciation in the value of the contract while owned by the decedent will escape income tax entirely. Rev. Rul. 79-335, 1979-2 CB 292. But where a variable annuity contract purchased before October 21, 1979 had been exchanged for another variable annuity contract under IRC Section 1035 after October 20, 1979 and the annuity owner died prior to the annuity starting date, the beneficiary was not entitled to a step-up in basis. TAM 9346002; Let. Rul. 9245035.[31]

It is important to note that these rulings apparently apply only to variable annuities. Fixed deferred annuities, whether acquired prior to 1979 or after, are apparently not eligible for step-up in basis treatment under Section 1014.

Beneficiary's Income Tax Deduction for Federal Estate Tax Attributable to Annuity Gain – IRC Section 691(c)

As was noted earlier, the value of an annuity is includible in the estate of the owner, for estate tax purposes, and the as-yet-untaxed gain is taxable to the beneficiary for income tax purposes. This "double taxation" is reduced (but not avoided entirely) by an income tax deduction available to the beneficiary under IRC section 691(c), under the so-called "Income in Respect of a Decedent" rules:

> Income in respect of a decedent is subjected to the federal estate tax in the decedent's estate and to federal income tax in the hands of the person who receives it. Also, such income may be subject to the generation-skipping transfer tax. . . Section 691(c) alleviates the hardship of the "double" taxation somewhat by allowing the recipient an income tax deduction for that

portion of these taxes attributable to the inclusion of the net value of the income right. Where the income would have been ordinary income in the hands of the decedent, the deduction is an itemized deduction. Rev. Rul. 78-203, 1978-1 CB 199.

The amount of the deduction is determined by computing the federal estate tax (or generation-skipping transfer tax) with the net income in respect of a decedent included and then recomputing the federal estate tax (or generation-skipping transfer tax) with the net income in respect of a decedent excluded. The difference in the two results is the amount of the income tax deduction. Thus, the amount deductible equals (a) the federal estate tax on the taxable estate, *minus* (b) the federal estate tax on the taxable estate less net IRD.

If two or more persons will receive income in respect of the same decedent, each recipient is entitled to that share of the total deduction which is in the same proportion that his share of income in respect of a decedent bears to the total gross income in respect of a decedent that was included in the gross estate. For example, a recipient who is entitled to 1/4 of the income is also entitled to 1/4 of the deduction. This is so, even though none of the federal estate tax is attributable to the income received by that particular recipient — for example where his income was offset by an equivalent amount of deductions. IRC Sec. 691(c).

The deduction is taken only as the income is received, and in the same proportion. For example, say that the income in respect of a decedent will be received by only one person, and will be received in equal amounts over a 10-year period. The recipient may take 1/10 of the total deduction in each of the 10 taxable years.[32]

It should be emphasized that the deduction is only for the gain in the contract, and only to the extent of the Federal estate tax. Any state estate or inheritance tax would not be considered for purposes of this deduction.

Chapter Endnotes

1. IRC Secs. 2039, 2033.

2. Also referred to as "Annuity Commencement Date."

3. IRC Sec. 72(c)(4); Treas. Reg. §1.72-4(b) further defines "annuity starting date" as "The first day of the first period for which an amount is received as an annuity shall be whichever of the following is the later:

(i) The date upon which the obligations under the contract became fixed, or

(ii) The first day of the period (year, half-year, quarter, month, or otherwise, depending on whether payments are to be made annually, semiannually, quarterly, monthly, or otherwise) which ends on the date of the first annuity payment."

4. *Advanced Sales Reference Service*, The National Underwriter Co., Sect. 52, ¶310.1.

5. Also called "straight life annuity" or "life annuity with no refund."

6. *Tax Facts on Insurance & Employee Benefits 2005*, The National Underwriter Co., Q. 500.

7. This arrangement is variously called "Life with 10-Year Certain", "Life-10 Yr. Continuous & Certain" or the like. If annuity payments are to be made monthly, it may be called "Life and 120 Months Certain."

8. Treas. Reg. §20.2031-8(a).

9. IRC Sec. 2032(a)(3).

10. The value of the cash refund guaranteed is typically less than the amount annuitized under this option.

11. *Advanced Sales Reference Service*, The National Underwriter Co., Sect. 54, ¶24.3.

12. This arrangement is variously called "Life with 10-Year Certain," "Life-10 Yr. Continuous & Certain" or the like. If annuity payments are to be made monthly, it may be called "Life and 120 Months Certain."

13. *Tax Facts on Insurance & Employee Benefits 2005*, The National Underwriter Co., Q. 503.

14. Treas. Reg. §20.2039-1(c), ex. 1.

15. Treas. Reg. §20.2039-1(c).

16. Treas. Reg. §20.2031-8(a).

17. An immediate annuity is "in payout status" by definition.

18. If the beneficiary elects to change the amount or duration of annuity payments, this constitutes electing a new annuity option. This election would cause the payments to be taxed under the "regular annuity rules." However, such a change will not be permitted if the payments would not distribute proceeds "at least as rapidly" as the annuitant had been receiving them. IRC Sec. 72(s)(1)(A).

19. Treas. Reg. §1.72-11(c).

20. IRC Sec. 72(b)(3)(A).

21. It is important to note, with regard to this "owner-driven" vs. "annuitant-driven" distinction, that certain riders and enhanced death benefits of deferred annuities may be 'annuitant-driven' and take effect only at the death of an annuitant, despite the fact that the annuity itself must be paid out to the beneficiary on the death of the owner, per IRC Sec. 72(s)(1). For this reason, the advisor should be very cautious about annuitant-driven contracts where the owner and annuitant are different individuals.

22. IRC Sec. 72(s)(1) was amended by the Tax Reform Act of 1986, changing "the holder" to read "any holder." This change had serious implications for jointly held contracts (as discussed later in the text), and applies to contracts issued since April 22, 1987. Also added were Sections 72(s)(6) and 72(s)(7), which deal with annuities held by other than "natural persons."

23. Treas. Reg. §1.72-11(e).

24. Let. Rul. 200323012, issued to the surviving spouse who was trustee of a joint revocable trust named as beneficiary of annuity contracts owned by that trust, of which decedent husband was annuitant, held that the surviving spouse/beneficiary could elect the IRC Sec. 72(s)(3) "spousal continuation" option, but the facts of that case were unusual – the spouse had such liberal powers and access to the trust that it was as though she were the directly named beneficiary. Most commentators believe that the trustee of a trust named as beneficiary of an annuity will not be able to elect such treatment or the "annuitization" option of IRC Sec. 72(s)(2) in all normal cases. Moreover, most insurance companies, in the authors' experience, will, at this time, not consent to such a result without, at the very least, a ruling from the IRS.

25. Presumably, the date of owner's death would be the date on which "such lump sum first became payable."

26. In this instance, the "60 day vs. one year" conflict discussed above is irrelevant. IRC Sec. 72(s) does not apply, because the death benefit is paid by reason of the death of the annuitant, not the owner.

27. IRC Sec. 72(e)(2)(B).

28. In addition, it is important to note that in this situation, the surviving spouse would be the owner of an annuity that must be paid to the beneficiary (the daughter), and consequently could be deemed to make a gift to the daughter of the annuity death benefit upon the death of any holder. This is not unlike the similar consequences when a husband owns an insurance policy on his wife, with his daughter as the beneficiary, and the wife dies, causing the death benefit owned by the husband to be paid to the daughter.

29. In theory this step-up in basis for pre-1979 contracts may no longer apply if Section 1014 ceases to apply in the face of a repeal of estate taxes.

30. Rev. Rul. 79-335, 1979-2 C.B. 292.

31. *Tax Facts on Insurance & Employee Benefits 2005*, The National Underwriter Co., Q. 36. See also Rev. Rul. 70-143, 1970-1 C.B. 167.

32. *Advanced Sales Reference Service*, The National Underwriter Co., Sect. 53, ¶20.15(d).

Chapter 4

Basic Costs of Annuities

Thus far in this book, we've examined the basic *structures* of annuities and how distributions are taxed. Later, we will consider the *benefits* annuities can provide. In this chapter, we will focus on one of the most controversial–and often misunderstood–aspects of annuities: their *costs*. The controversy (and misunderstanding) is chiefly due to two conditions:

1. The cost factors are almost always very complicated–sometimes, bewilderingly so.

2. These cost factors are often poorly communicated–both by the advisor to the purchaser to whom the annuity is being recommended, and to that advisor by the insurance company issuing the annuity contract.

The responsibility for this poor communication is a matter of considerable debate. Some "consumerists" hold the advisor chiefly, if not solely, responsible for a purchaser's lack of understanding. Class-action lawsuits have asserted that the onus lies, ultimately, with the insurance companies, citing confusing (even allegedly misleading) training and marketing materials. The authors believe that, where an annuity purchaser can legitimately state that he or she did not understand the costs of the annuity, there is plenty of blame to go around. The same holds true with respect to the benefits of that annuity.

That being said, the fact remains that the costs of nearly all annuity contracts offered today are often hard to understand and appreciate fully, especially when the benefits derived from those costs are also complicated. Complex cost and benefit structures, however fully disclosed, run the risk of being misunderstood, and even the best explanations can be recalled imperfectly. The annuity advisor must have a very clear understanding of the costs and benefits of those contracts he or she deals with and be willing to spend whatever time is required in perfecting a clear explanation of both.

Cost Factors in Immediate Annuities

The least complex cost structure is that of the fixed single premium immediate annuity (fixed SPIA). These contracts generally assess no front-end sales charge or annual contract charges. A few fixed SPIAs permit commutation[1] or partial withdrawals, and may assess a charge for these distributions. Most, however, do not permit these changes to the original payout structure, but instead require that, once annuity payments have commenced, no withdrawals or lump sum surrender will be permitted. The only cost component in these contracts is reflected in the payout factors (both those guaranteed in the contract and those offered on a currently available basis).

Annuity Payout Factors

An annuity payout factor (or annuity factor) is a number, usually expressed with two decimal precision. It represents the dollar amount of each annuity payment, per thousand dollars of proceeds placed under the annuity option.

> *Example:* The sample table below shows that the annual payment for a "life only" annuity,[2] for a male age 65 or a female age 59,[3] will be $6.38, for each thousand dollars of annuity purchase payment. Thus, a single premium of $125,500 will purchase an annual annuity payment of $800.69 (125.5 x 6.38). The same sum would purchase an annual annuity of $672.68 (125.5 x 5.36) if payments are to persist for the greater of the life of the annuitant or twenty years ("Life & 20 Years Certain").

Male Age	Female Age	Life Only	L&10YC	L&20YC	L&Cash Ref
65	59	6.38	6.09	5.36	5.61
66	60	6.57	6.24	5.42	5.72

The amount of each payment is guaranteed never to change, unless the annuity provides for a cost of living adjustment (COLA). At the time of this writing, most annuities–both immediate and deferred–do not provide for any COLA adjustments. Some offer a single fixed COLA choice (e.g., payments to increase at 3% per year). Very few offer a choice of different COLA percentages (e.g., 3% or 5%), or any kind of COLA that adjusts to a specified inflation factor (e.g., the Consumer Price Index (CPI)). Fortunately for consumers, there is a trend in newer annuity contracts toward offering COLA choices. In the authors' opinion, this is both necessary and long overdue.

Annuity payout factors reflect an insurance company's estimate of life expectancy (mortality), expenses, and interest rates. These estimates change over time. The annuity payout factors offered to current purchasers of immediate annuities and to owners of deferred annuities choosing to annuitize their contracts can change as frequently as weekly. Of course, once one purchases an immediate annuity or elects an annuitization option in one's deferred annuity, the payout factor used to calculate the initial payment is all that matters. All future payments will be based upon that same and sole factor, which never changes once payments begin.

For purchasers of deferred annuities, there are two sets of annuity factors which may come into play. Every deferred annuity contract contains guaranteed minimum annuity payout factors. These are based on very conservative assumptions, and are generally considerably lower (that is, providing for lower annual payments per thousand dollars annuitized) than the current factors offered by the same insurer, for use with the same annuity. In fact, in the authors' experience, there has never been a time when the current factors were not significantly higher than the guaranteed ones.

Does this mean that the cost of these guaranteed annuity payout factors is "wasted money?" In the authors' view, the answer is "no"–even though these guaranteed factors have never yet been as attractive as the "current" ones. Americans are living longer with each passing decade. A breakthrough in gerontological medicine producing greatly increased average life expectancies, especially if accompanied by a prolonged period of low interest rates (or particularly a period of deflation) could produce future current annuity payout factors less attractive than those guaranteed in existing deferred annuity contracts. Is this likely? Perhaps not. But, as we have noted before, an annuity is primarily a risk management instrument. The presence of these guarantees allows the purchaser to manage the risk that future annuity payout rates (based on longer life expectancies or lower interest rates) will not produce sufficient income.

The other type of immediate annuity is the variable single premium immediate annuity (variable SPIA). Like its fixed cousin, the variable SPIA provides for an income commencing within one year of purchase; unlike the fixed variety, however, the amount of each annuity payment is not fixed,[4] because the annuity cash value is invested in "variable sub-accounts." A variable annuity, whether immediate or deferred, assesses expense charges at both the sub-account and contract (wrapper) levels. These charges, the form of which is generally the same for immediate annuities as for deferred ones, will be covered in the discussion on costs in variable deferred annuities.

Cost Factors in Deferred Annuities

The "overhead costs" of deferred annuities are considerably more complex than those of immediate contracts. Historically, fixed deferred annuities have contained fewer, and simpler, charges than variable deferred contracts, but, in recent years, the complexity of both types has increased substantially.

> Note on Nomenclature: While immediate annuities are always purchased with a single premium, a deferred annuity, of either the fixed or variable type, may be purchased either with a single premium (single premium deferred annuity, or SPDA) or may permit (but not necessarily require) ongoing periodic premiums (flexible premium deferred annuity, or FPDA). As if this were not complicated enough, the labels SPDA and FPDA are typically used in connection only with fixed contracts, just as the term SPIA (for single premium immediate annuity) is, in common practice, applied only to fixed contracts, even though it is properly applicable to variable contracts as well. To avoid adding to the confusion, the authors suggest using complete terminology (e.g., "fixed SPIA," "variable SPIA," "flexible premium deferred variable annuity," etc.)

Fixed Deferred Annuities

Charges assessed in fixed annuities may include any or all of the following:

Front-End Sales Charge

Until fairly recently, an initial sales charge, or "load" (generally, a percentage of the initial premium) was a common contract expense. Very few fixed deferred annuities offered today assess such a charge, as it was notably unpopular with consumers.

Surrender Charges

A surrender charge, as its name implies, is assessed upon the surrender of an annuity contract, or upon withdrawal of more than the policy's "free withdrawal" amount. Typically, fixed annuities allow the contract owner to withdraw up to 10% of the account balance, per year, without penalty. There are numerous variations of this provision (such as permitting this penalty-free amount to be cumulative or allowing a penalty-free withdrawal of all previously credited interest), but 10% per year without penalty is fairly standard.

Surrenders, or withdrawals in excess of this penalty-free amount, are generally subject to a surrender charge. While the mechanics of this charge vary widely from contract to contract, the usual format is a declining surrender charge schedule–such as 6% in the first contract year, 5% in the second, 4% in the third, and so on, until the surrender charge reaches zero. In flexible premium contracts, the surrender charge schedule may be fixed, terminating at the end of N years from issue, or "rolling," applying the schedule separately to each deposit. This is a moot point with single premium annuities, which, as we have noted, do not allow subsequent deposits.

Many deferred annuities, both fixed and variable, include provisions that waive the imposition of surrender charges in certain circumstances. Most contracts waive the charges upon the death of the owner (or annuitant, if the contract is annuitant-driven). Many also provide a waiver if the owner (or annuitant) is confined to a nursing home, is disabled, or suffers one of several listed "dread diseases."

Considering how much criticism is leveled at surrender charges by many financial journalists and those who simply don't like annuities on principle, a comment or two may be in order, at this point, on why surrender charges exist in the first place.

A schedule of surrender charges is an alternative to a front-end sales charge. Both exist to allow the issuing company to recover acquisition costs–the costs of putting the annuity policy in force. Even in today's high-tech world, this cannot be done for free. The most controversial–even notorious–acquisition cost is the selling commission, paid to the agent who sells the annuity. Most annuities are sold by commissioned advisors, who are compensated in this fashion. Practically all fixed annuities are of this sort. However, not all variable annuities are commissionable. An increasing number of variable annuities are of the type usually called "low load." They pay no sales commissions. Not coincidentally, they generally assess no surrender charges.

If, at this point, you are thinking that the purpose of surrender charges is to pay the sales commission, you are basically right. The insurance company pays that commission when it issues the annuity and it needs to recover that cost. But the surrender charge almost always declines over time–after a few years, to zero. Why is that?

It is because the insurance company knows that, if the annuity owner keeps the policy in force for long enough, it will recover its acquisition costs from other "moving parts" in the annuity contract. In the case of a fixed annuity, the "interest rate spread"–the difference between what the company earns on invested annuity premiums, and what it credits to those annuities–will, in time, not only make up the commission cost, but make the annuity contract profitable to its issuer. In the case of a variable annuity, there's no "interest rate spread," and it is the insurance costs (see below) that bring about this same result.

A front-end sales charge would do the job, too. But front-end sales charges are unattractive to buyers, which is why most annuities no longer impose them.

So, if the sales commission is an acquisition cost, surrender charges (in lieu of an initial sales charge) pay that cost, right? Basically, yes. (It's not quite that simple, but that's the gist of it). So, if the annuity pays no sales commission, there's no need for surrender charges.

Seems simple enough. But sales commissions are not the only acquisition costs. Even when an insurance company markets a particular annuity contract through fee-only advisors as a "commission-free" product, it cannot produce that product for free. Not only are there development costs which any prudent company will expect to recover, but also costs of issue and administration. And then, there is the matter of profit. The insurance company expects to make money selling the annuity, and prices it with that expectation. In the case of a fixed annuity, profit–and cost recovery–comes from the interest rate spread. In a variable annuity, which has no such spread, they come mainly from insurance charges. Thus, insurance companies attempt to make up for the fact that there are not any surrender charges on such "low load" or "commission-free" products by other costs, or by the attempt to generate additional sales with the marketability of a "low load" or "commission-free" label.

Market Value Adjustment

There may be a market value adjustment (MVA) upon surrender of the contract, or upon a partial withdrawal. If so, then the surrender value or withdrawn amount is usually decreased if a benchmark interest rate (a specified, well-recognized external index) is higher, when the contract is surrendered, than it was at the time of issue. The surrender value will be increased if the reverse is true. The purpose of this adjustment is to compensate the insurance company for the risk that contact owners will withdraw money when the market value of the investments backing the annuity (in the case of fixed annuities, this generally means bonds) is low. Since bond prices are inversely related to interest rates, the market value of the investments backing the annuity will generally be lowest when interest rates have risen, which, generally, is the exact time that investors may want to withdraw their money (to re-invest in a new contract with higher then-current rates)–thus the need for the insurance company to protect itself from this risk. However, MVAs are a risk-sharing feature, because, if the external index is lower at time of withdrawal or surrender than it was at issue, and the value of the underlying bonds is correspondingly higher (again, because bond prices are inversely related to interest rates), the contract owner benefits from the adjustment. Generally, an MVA is assessed only on withdrawals in excess of the penalty-free withdrawal amount, and usually does not apply after the expiration of the surrender charge period.

Interest Rate Spread

In a fixed deferred annuity, the issuing company's profit derives chiefly from the interest rate spread–the difference between what the company can earn on invested annuity premiums and what it will credit to the cash value of those contracts. In a sense, this spread is a cost of the contract, if one assumes that the annuity investor would otherwise be able to earn the same rate as the insurance company. However, this assumption may not be reasonable.

In nearly all fixed deferred annuities, this spread is not guaranteed, or even revealed directly to the contract holder. It may be calculated, of course, provided one knows both the rate credited to an annuity during a certain period and the rate the insurance company earned during that same period. However, not all insurers credit interest in the same manner, or even credit interest in the same manner to all fixed annuities they have issued. To understand how interest rate spread works, as a contract cost, we must understand how interest is credited to fixed deferred annuities.

Guaranteed Interest Rate

All fixed deferred annuities guarantee a minimum interest crediting rate. Regardless of future conditions, interest will be credited, each period, to the annuity at a rate at least equal to this guaranteed rate. In addition, every deferred annuity of which the authors are aware also provides for the crediting of current, non-guaranteed interest at a rate, which may be higher, but cannot be lower, than the guaranteed rate.

Current Interest Rate Crediting Methods

There are four basic methods of crediting current interest to fixed annuities.

1. Portfolio Method. For an annuity that uses this method, all contracts will be credited, each period, with the same current, non-guaranteed interest rate, regardless of when annuity contributions (premiums) were received, except for contracts that are still within an interest rate guarantee period.

2. New Money (or Pocket of Money) Method. For an annuity using this method, the rate of interest credited to all contracts will depend upon when the premiums were received. For flexible premium annuities, this can mean that a particular annuity contract might receive, on any given interest crediting date, several different rates, each applied to the "pocket of money" received during the time period specified forth that "pocket."

    Example: Mr. Jones' flexible premium annuity was issued June 30, 1999. Interest is credited each year, at a rate determined annually. On June 30, 2002, the contract is credited with the following:

    a. 4.00% for all premiums received in the period 1/1/1999 – 12/31/1999

      b.   3.89% for all premiums received in the period 1/1/2000 – 12/31/2000

      c.   3.80% for all premiums received in the period 1/1/2001 – 12/31/2001

      d.   3.56% for all premiums received in the period 1/1/2002 – 12/31/2002

3.   Tiered Interest Rate Method–Type One

In this method, the interest rate credited to a contract depends upon the cash value of the annuity.

Example: Ms. Smith's annuity credits interest according to the following current schedule:

      a.   4.00% for the first $50,000 of cash value

      b.   4.25% for the next $50,000 of cash value

      c.   4.5% for cash value in excess of $100,000

4.   Tiered Interest Rate Method–Type Two

In this method, interest is credited at one rate if the owner annuitizes the contract and at a lower rate if the contract is surrendered. In these contracts, the value is generally reported as two separate items: (a) the annuity value and (b) the cash value (or "contract value"). The cash value will be reduced, on surrender of the contract, by any surrender charge applicable. The amount payable at the owner's (or annuitant's) death may be either the cash value or annuity value, depending upon contract terms, and a surrender charge may or may not apply.

Interest Rate Guarantee Period

Sometimes the current interest rate of a newly issued fixed deferred annuity may be guaranteed for a specific period. If so, then at the expiration of this period, renewal interest is credited according to the crediting method used for that particular contract–subject, of course, to the guaranteed minimum rate.

Interest Rate Renewal History

One item that every advisor who is considering recommending a fixed deferred annuity must consider is the history of the issuing insurance company with regard to renewal interest rates. Renewal rates, except for contracts in the interest rate guarantee period, are entirely at the discretion of the issuing insurer (subject, of course, to the minimum rate guaranteed in the contract). Some insurers have a distinguished history of declaring renewal interest at competitive levels. Others, unfortunately, do not. In the 1980s and 90s, a few insurers offered fixed deferred annuities at initial rates well above the level offered by most competitors and, as soon as the interest rate guarantee period elapsed, renewed these contracts at, or barely above, the guaranteed rate. Most insurance companies did not play this game, fortunately for consumers. But the risk of this sort of "bait and switching" is one the prudent advisor must take into consideration. The authors strongly advise a close look at the published history of renewal crediting rate of any insurance company whose products you are considering.[5]

A final observation on this subject of interest rate crediting is in order. It may appear, to the advisor inexperienced in fixed deferred annuities, that renewal interest rates, while they may drop from the initial level to as low as the guaranteed rate, may also rise at that point–even beyond that initial level–if interest rates are increasing at that time. That may appear logical, but it is not likely to happen. In the authors' experience, insurance companies simply do not declare renewal interest rates at a level higher than the initial rate. This may, of course, be due to the fact that, for the past thirty years and more, interest rates have, in general, been trending downward. Nevertheless, there have been short periods, during those decades, during which rates increased. In those periods, the initial rate offered by insurance companies, on their fixed deferred annuities, did increase–but the renewal rates for existing contracts did not.

"Bail-Out" Interest Rate

Some fixed deferred annuities provide that, if renewal interest is ever credited below a certain specified rate (the "bail-out" rate), surrender charges will be waived for a certain time period, allowing the contract owner to "bail out" of the contract without charges. Of course, the premature withdrawal penalty of Code section 72(q) will apply if the owner is under age 59½ and no other exception to the penalty is available. "Bail-out rate" annuities were very popular in the volatile interest environment of the 1980s and 90s, but are much less common today.

"Bonus" Interest Rates

A policy feature that has become very popular in both fixed and variable deferred annuities is the crediting of so-called "bonus" interest. Typically, bonus interest is interest, over and above the current rate, that is applied to deposits in the first year or first few years,[6] and is immediately vested (that is, the contract owner is not required to keep the contract for a set period, or to annuitize, to earn it). However, it is important to note that generally the surrender charges may be slightly higher on such contracts, the interest guarantees may be lower, or the current crediting rate may be lower–in other words, the general paradigm that "there's no such thing as a free lunch" still holds true, and the insurance company likely will still find some way to make up the cost of the bonus payment.

A variation on this theme is the "annuitization" bonus, which provides that a certain interest rate (e.g., 5%) will be credited to the contract, in addition to the regular interest, upon annuitization.

"CD-Annuities"

A relatively recent development in fixed deferred annuities is the so-called "CD-annuity." This type of contract typically guarantees the initial interest crediting rate for the duration of the surrender charge period (which is typically six years or less). As its name suggests, this product was developed as an alternative to certificates of deposit. While the assurance of receiving a known interest rate for several years, with freedom from surrender charges at the end of that period, is certainly attractive, especially when the tax liability for all the interest is deferred, the existence of the Section 72(q) penalty makes this type of contract a questionable short-term savings vehicle for those who will be under age 59½ at its "maturity."

Contract Charges

Some fixed deferred annuities assess an annual contract charge, though most do not. Some contracts that do assess an annual contract charge will waive that charge when the account balance exceeds a certain amount (e.g., no contract charges for annuities with a balance in excess of $50,000).

Let's look now at the costs of variable deferred annuities. As was noted, the number and complexity of charges in variable annuities is greater than those in fixed contracts, and it is the former that are usually being referred to in critics' attacks on annuity costs.

Variable Deferred Annuities

Front-End Sales Charges

Front-end sales charges are generally equally as unpopular with variable annuities as they are with fixed annuities. Interestingly, though, some issuers of variable deferred annuities are offering new contracts with a front-end sales load in lieu of surrender charges. These contracts, sometimes called "A-share"-type annuities, may owe their existence to the heightened regulatory scrutiny and frequent "bad press" aimed at "B-share"-type mutual funds and traditional variable annuity costs. In addition to imposing no surrender charges, they may offer smaller annual costs (including mortality and expense charges).

Surrender Charges

Surrender charges in variable annuities work just as they do in fixed annuities.

Insurance Charges

The "insurance charges" in variable annuities are just plain confusing to almost everyone. Part of this confusion stems from the practice of some commentators on annuities to refer to the total insurance costs of these policies as "mortality and expense" charges. However, mortality and expense–or M&E, as it is usually called–is only one of the components of insurance expenses. In this discussion, we will use the classification employed by Morningstar, Inc., which works like this:

The category of Total Insurance Expense consists of three elements:

1. Mortality and expense charges (M&E)

2. Administrative charges

3. Distribution charges

The mortality and expense charge is defined by Morningstar as "the percentage of the subaccount's assets that the insurance company deducts to cover costs associated with mortality and expense risk. Specifically, it can serve as a source of profit for the insurance company [if mortality is more favorable than expected] in addition to compensating the company for offering features such as the variable-annuity death benefit and for compensation."[7]

Administrative charges are defined by the same source as "the percentage of the subaccount's daily net assets deducted by the insurance company to cover the costs involved in offering and administering the variable annuity, such as the cost of distribution and printing of correspondence."[8]

Of distribution charges, Morningstar says, "When applicable, these fees compensate the agent, broker, or financial planner who sold the policy."[9]

What does all that mean in English? It means that these insurance charges are imposed -

- First, to compensate the issuing company for risks it incurs related to mortality (basically, the risk that they have under-estimated longevity) and expenses (under-estimation of various operating expenses, including government-imposed premium taxes), and

- Second, to pay selling and distribution expenses, including printing costs and agents' commissions.

As we have noted, these separate charges are not imposed by fixed annuities. But fixed annuities have the "interest rate spread," from which the cost of these risks can be, and is, recovered.

We also need to note that M&E is but one component of total insurance expense. Some commentators, when they use the term M&E mean just that component, but others–probably most–use it to mean the total figure. It is important, when comparing different variable annuities, to be sure to compare "apples with apples." One low load annuity, for example, is reported as having an M&E charge of ten basis points, but a total insurance expense of 30 basis points. Advisors must not mix the two terms.

As if that were not confusing enough, we need, also, to be aware that the benefits paid for by the total insurance expense of one variable annuity contract may not be the same as those paid for by the total insurance expense of another contract. The minimum death benefit, for example, could be significantly different. Or there may be other optional benefits, the charges for which are included in total insurance expense.

We will look, in Chapter 5, at some of the optional benefits commonly offered in variable annuity contracts, as well as some of the enhancement features used. But, first, it is essential that we understand that, for variable annuities, the total annual overhead cost to the contract owner is not just the sum of the annual contract charge plus the total insurance expense. There is also the annual expense charge imposed at the separate account level. This charge, called "fund expense," is analogous to the expense ratio of a mutual fund, and is defined in Morningstar's *Principia®* as "the percentage of assets deducted each year for underlying fund operating expenses, management fees, and all other asset-based costs incurred by the fund, excluding brokerage fees."[10]

Fund expenses vary considerably, both from contact to contract, and–especially–according to the type of account. Money market and index accounts typically have the lowest fund expense, with bond accounts somewhat higher, general equity accounts higher, and specialty accounts (e.g., natural resources, real estate) with the highest fund expense.

The sum of (a) fund expense and (b) total insurance expense equals the total annual overhead cost to the annuity contract owner. Well, almost. There may also be an annual contract charge, but that is usually about $30 per year (and is often waived for contracts with balances exceeding specified levels), not a percentage of the annuity balance.

What do these various charges and expenses amount to, in percentage terms? Morningstar's *Principia®* service (January, 2005 edition) reports that, of all the variable annuities in its database, the average M&E charge is 1.22% (of account balance). The average total insurance expenses (M&E, administrative, and distribution) are 1.37%. The average fund expense is 0.97%, and the average total expense (total insurance expenses plus fund expenses) is 2.35%. This does not count the contract charge, which is measured in dollars, or the surrender charge, as the surrender charge is payable only on surrenders or withdrawals in excess of the penalty-free amount.

Chapter Endnotes

1. "Commutation" is the right of an annuity contract holder to surrender a policy in "payout status" for a lump sum, in lieu of the remaining annuity payments. This is generally determined as the present value of remaining payments, with some minor adjustments to compensate the insurance company for the change.

2. A life only annuity pays for the life of the annuitant. Payments cease at the annuitant's death, regardless of when death occurs.

3. Most annuity contracts are issued on a "sex-distinct" basis, recognizing that females live longer, on average, than males. A few contracts use "unisex" rates (where the payout factor for a male is always the same as for a female of the same age); these are usually employed in group retirement plans where "sex-distinct" annuity factors have been judged to be discriminatory.

4. Variable SPIAs typically offer a "fixed account" option, which does provide for fixed amounts; the present discussion refers, however, to amounts placed under the "variable" payout option.

5. This applies, not just to annuities, but also to other products–notably, universal life policies. Many insurance companies publish their interest rate crediting history. In addition, an excellent, and unbiased, source for such information is A.M. Best (www.ambest.com).

6. Some contracts provide for the payment of bonus interest at certain policy anniversaries (e.g., at the end of the 5th and 10th year).

7. Morningstar® *Principia®* software, Variable Annuity/Life module. Quoted from the "online help" section.

8. *Ibid.*

9. *Ibid.*

10. *Ibid.*

Chapter 5

Optional Costs in Variable Annuities

The total insurance expenses described in Chapter 4 are the standard costs for the standard features of a typical variable deferred annuity. The principal benefits typically purchased by these expenses are:

1. The Guaranteed Death Benefit provided by the contract (without election of optional, extra-cost "riders");

2. The Guaranteed Annuity Payout Factors, providing a minimum annuity payment if the contract is annuitized under one of the annuity payment options, regardless of future changes in longevity or interest rates.

Most deferred variable annuities marketed today offer additional, optional benefits (at additional cost). New policy enhancements are introduced by one company or another nearly every month, and the variety–and complexity–of options available is downright staggering. Some relate to the guaranteed value at the death of the annuitant or owner, and are generally termed death benefit enhancements (discussed at the end of this chapter). Others–indeed, most of the recently-introduced options–fall into the category of living benefits.

Living Benefits

The living benefits offered in deferred variable annuity contracts refer to benefits that a contract holder that can exercise while still alive (that is, they are not triggered by the death of either the annuitant or owner). Strictly speaking, the term should include benefits such as the guaranteed annuity payout factors, the availability of the various investment sub-accounts and cost-free transfers among those sub-accounts, dollar cost averaging, and automatic rebalancing. However, in practice, living benefits–especially when the reference is to enhanced living benefits–generally means any of these three enhancement features:

1.   Guaranteed minimum income benefit (GMIB)

2.   Guaranteed minimum accumulation benefit (GMAB)

3.   Guaranteed minimum withdrawal benefit (GMWB)

Availability of "Enhanced Living Benefits"

Some annuity contracts permit these enhanced living benefit options to be elected only at the time of contract issue. Others permit them to be added later. Some contracts permit election of only one of these benefits. After electing one of these benefits, the contract owner may or may not be permitted to discontinue it (and to cease paying its cost).

Guaranteed Minimum Income Benefit

The guaranteed minimum income benefit (GMIB) guarantees a minimum income to the annuitant, regardless of adverse investment performance of the variable annuity contract. The amount of the guaranteed income is typically calculated by applying a guaranteed interest rate (usually 5-7%) to the initial payment to produce a benefit base[1] from which the GMIB payments are calculated. It is extremely important that the advisor understand that this rate does not guarantee a future account balance that may be withdrawn as a lump sum. The only thing guaranteed by a GMIB benefit is the amount of income the annuitant will receive (utilizing the benefit base and certain payout factors), and that guarantee comes only with certain conditions.

Annuitization Generally Required

Variable annuity contracts offering a GMIB benefit generally require that the contract be annuitized for the GMIB to be applicable. Usually, the annuitization must be for the life of the annuitant, and, in some cases, must be elected within a 30 or 60-day window each year (typically, immediately following a contract anniversary), following the expiration of a waiting period, which is usually 7-10 years. Annuitization that uses the GMIB benefit base is not available during the waiting period. Often, the GMIB provision will also require an annuitization age setback (typically, from 3 to 7 years), where the actual age of the annuitant will be reduced (by the number of years specified in the setback requirement), and the special GMIB annuity factor for that adjusted age is used to determine the annuity amount. It is important to note that the downward adjustment of the annuitization age will spread payments over a longer period of time, resulting in a lower payment amount–this represents an indirect cost of utilizing the GMIB rider.

Calculation of the GMIB

The GMIB is calculated by using special annuity payout factors which are generally significantly lower[2] (that is: they produce lower annuity payments, per dollar of principal applied) than the factors the insurer offers to owners of deferred annuity contracts wishing to annuitize on a "regular" basis, using the cash value or annuity value of their contracts.[3] The special GMIB payout factor for the payout option chosen (e.g: Life & 10 Year Certain) and the annuitant's age–or adjusted age, if applicable–is applied to the benefit base, rather than the cash value or annuity value of the contract, to determine the Guaranteed Minimum Death Benefit.

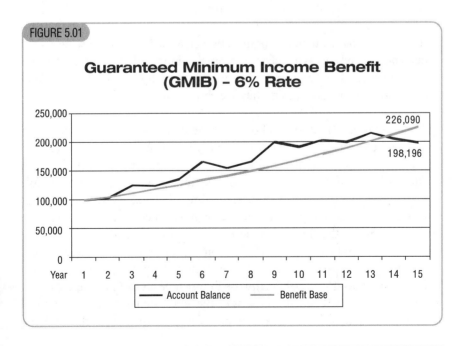

FIGURE 5.01

Guaranteed Minimum Income Benefit (GMIB) – 6% Rate

(Chart showing Account Balance and Benefit Base over Years 1–15. Benefit Base reaches 226,090; Account Balance reaches 198,196.)

Obviously, electing the GMIB payout (with its reduced annuity factors) would not be advisable if the contract value exceeds the benefit base (that is, the investment performance produced a greater sum than the initial premium, compounded at the GMIB guarantee rate). However, if the benefit base exceeds the actual account balance (the cash value or annuity value), that greater amount is used to produce the GMIB annuity amount. (In the above graph, the account balance, at the end of 15 years, is $198,196, and the benefit base is $226,090). This represents the primary potential benefit of the GMIB rider–the ability to elect to annuitize a lifetime stream of payments based on a higher benefit base if market performance turns out to be unfavorable, thereby guaranteeing a certain income stream in the future regardless of market performance while still providing the investor the opportunity to participate in the investment potential of the variable sub-accounts selected.

What is not so obvious is that the election to annuitize using the GMIB may not be advantageous for the contract owner even if the benefit base is higher than the account balance. This is because the lower payout factors used in the GMIB, and the age setback, if applicable, may produce a lower annuity amount than the higher "regular" payout factors applied, using the annuitant's actual age, to the account balance. Advisors should be aware of this potential, especially when discussing the feasibility of electing a GMIB payout.

The GMIB typically requires annuitization on a fixed basis. That is, the special annuity factor used creates an income stream that is not only guaranteed, but also fixed in amount. Some annuity contracts may offer this benefit in connection with variable annuitization, using variable annuity units.

Because of the complexity in how the benefit base is determined, and even greater complexity in how the GMIB annuity payments are calculated (due to the application of different annuity factors and potentially an age setback), it is often advisable to focus on the actual guaranteed annuity payment, in dollars, at a particular point in the future. By comparing actual guaranteed dollar payments at a particular point in the future, it becomes easier to compare the GMIB benefit to other income options in the contract or to GMIB riders of other variable annuity contracts. Some companies may offer a lower interest rate applied to the benefit base but higher annuity factors, or apply an unusually high interest rate to the benefit base but include a substantial age setback. By viewing the GMIB benefit in terms of the actual dollar payments that will be received, evaluation may be easier, and clearer, despite all of the "moving parts." But be certain to properly evaluate the time value of money inherent in receiving guaranteed payments in the future based on a lump sum deposited today.

Withdrawals and the GMIB

GMIB options often permit the contact owner to make withdrawals before, or even after, exercise of the GMIB option. Such withdrawals reduce the benefit base, from which the guaranteed minimum income is calculated. Two methods of reduction are used:

1. "Dollar For Dollar" reductions adjust the benefit base downward by one dollar for each dollar withdrawn. Usually, this dollar for dollar treatment (if offered) is available only for withdrawals up to a specified percentage of the prior year's account balance or benefit base.[4] Withdrawals in excess of this percentage then reduce the benefit base proportionally.

2. "Proportional" reductions (also called pro-rata reductions) adjust the benefit base downwards by the proportion that the withdrawal represents of the current account value.

Where the benefit base exceeds the account value, the proportional method will produce a greater reduction in the benefit base (less favorable for the annuity holder) than a dollar-for-dollar method. Conversely, where the benefit base is less than the account value, the proportional method will produce a smaller reduction in the benefit base than the dollar-for-dollar method.

These same two methods are used in the guaranteed minimum death benefit discussed below. See that discussion for an example.

"Step-Up" and the GMIB

Often, the GMIB rider includes a "Step-Up" option. This allows the contract owner to "step up," or increase, the benefit base if the account balance has increased beyond the level of the benefit base. Typically the comparison between the account balance and the benefit base is applied on the contract anniversary. In the chart below, the GMIB benefit base is stepped up to the (greater) account balance in year 6. This option is typically subject to restrictions as to the number and timing of step-ups.

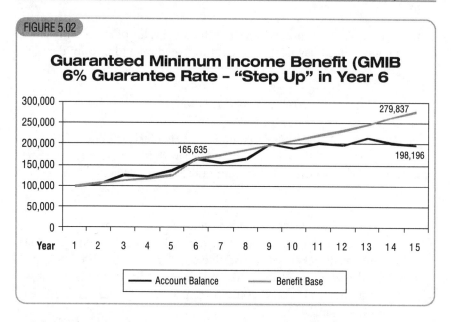

FIGURE 5.02

Guaranteed Minimum Income Benefit (GMIB 6% Guarantee Rate – "Step Up" in Year 6

It is worth noting that some (but not all) contracts that include both an annual growth rate on the benefit base and a potential step-up feature on the benefit base will continue to apply the growth rate to the original contribution(s), while other contracts offering both those features will apply the growth rate to the current benefit base, thereby accruing this growth on top of step-up adjustments. This difference can be significant, and reminds us that it is critical to read the details of the provisions regarding death benefit options as they appear in the prospectus. Reading the brochure designed for the client or even the "Agent's Guide" is not enough.

Cost of the GMIB

The cost of a GMIB varies, from contract to contract, but is generally in the range of 35-50 basis points per year.[5] In some contracts, this cost is assessed against the account value; in others, it is assessed against the benefit base.

Guaranteed Minimum Accumulation Benefit

The guaranteed minimum accumulation benefit (GMAB) is the second of the three optional living benefits offered in variable deferred annuity contracts. As with the other two enhanced living benefits, the GMAB consists of several "moving parts."

Guarantee Period

Unlike the GMIB, which promises a future minimum income value, the GMAB guarantees a future account value. It does not do this by guaranteeing a minimum growth per year, but by promising that the account balance will equal, at a minimum, to the GMAB guarantee amount at the end of the guarantee period,[6] which is typically 7-10 years. Thus, if the account value is less than the GMAB guarantee amount at the end of the guarantee period, the account value itself will be adjusted upwards to equal the GMAB guarantee amount.

The guarantee amount is generally the initial investment (in the case of single premium contracts) or all contributions made during the guarantee period (in flexible premium contracts). This guarantee of principal is sometimes referred to as the "base guarantee" of the GMAB provision.

"Step-Up" Provision

The "step-up" provision in a GMAB rider operates to provide additional "downside" guarantees in the event that the cash value of the annuity rises above the initial amount. (Note that this is different from how step-up provisions work with GMIB riders.) The opportunity to step-up the GMAB guarantee amount to the current cash value may be available every certain number of years, every year, or at any policy anniversary where the current value exceeds the prior anniversary's value by a certain percentage. When a step-up option is exercised, a new guarantee period begins, and the new, stepped-up value guarantee is not applied to the contract to adjust the account value until the end of this new period (see chart below). However, the original benefit amount (the contract owner's contributions) is, in many contracts, guaranteed indefinitely, from the end of the original guarantee period.

The chart below illustrates a GMAB where the policy owner elected to step up the GMAB benefit base to the cash value at the end of the 5th year. The GMAB had a 7-year guarantee period, meaning that the greater of the original contribution or this "stepped up" amount was available at the end of the 12th policy year. Typically, GMAB riders do not require annuitization.

Asset Allocation May Be Required

Most insurers manage the risk to themselves inherent in the GMAB by imposing restrictions upon the asset allocation permitted to contract holders who purchase the GMAB rider. Often, funds with high volatility are not avail-

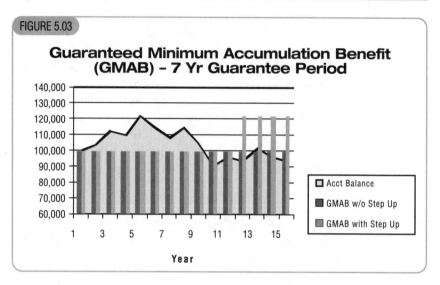

FIGURE 5.03

Guaranteed Minimum Accumulation Benefit
(GMAB) – 7 Yr Guarantee Period

Year

□ Acct Balance
■ GMAB w/o Step Up
■ GMAB with Step Up

able, and many contracts require that the contract owner choose one of several defined model portfolios. Alternatively, the insurer may reserve the right to move funds from the variable sub-accounts chosen to fixed accounts.

Withdrawals

Withdrawals may be (but are not always) permitted from contracts in which the GMAB rider has been purchased. If so, they may reduce the guarantee amount on a dollar-for-dollar basis, a proportional basis, or a combination of the two (e.g., dollar-for-dollar, for withdrawals not exceeding 5% of the guarantee amount, and proportional, for any excess).

Annuitization Generally Not Required

Unlike the GMIB, the GMAB generally does not require annuitization. The guaranteed amount is available as a lump sum, if desired (although surrender charges may apply). It is worth noting that if the GMAB rider is applied at the end of the guarantee period, the account value itself is typically adjusted upwards as appropriate immediately, providing additional amounts for future investment in the contract from that point forward.

Cost of the GMAB

The cost of the GMAB, like the cost of the other enhanced living benefits discussed, varies from contract to contract, but the usual range is around 20-25 basis points per year, although earlier GMAB riders on existing contracts may cost as little as 10 basis points per year. That cost is typically assessed against the annuity account value.

Guaranteed Minimum Withdrawal Benefit

The newest of the three basic enhanced living benefits is the guaranteed minimum withdrawal benefit.[7] The GMWB guarantees a return of principal, or of a "protected withdrawal value," over time, through systematic withdrawals. The amount guaranteed to be available via withdrawals may be the owner's total contributions to the annuity (the principal) or a greater "protected withdrawal value," such as the annuity cash value at the time of the first withdrawal.

The GMWB provision specifies a maximum percentage (typically, 5, 6, or 7%) of the protected withdrawal amount that may be withdrawn without "resetting" that protected withdrawal amount. The benefit of the GMWB to the contract owner–and the risk to the issuing insurance company–is that the insurer must permit withdrawals, not exceeding the specified percentage, of the remaining principal or the protected withdrawal amount, even if the annuity cash value has fallen to zero due to adverse investment performance. This means that the annuity holder may be able to deposit an amount to the annuity contract, and withdraw that entire principal amount at a specified percentage annually until all principal has been recovered, regardless of investment performance, as can be seen in the graph below.

FIGURE 5.04

GMWB Benefit
7% of Purchase Payment Withdrawn Annually

It is vitally important that the advisor know the impact upon the GWMB guarantee if the contract owner makes withdrawals exceeding the specified percentage. Some contracts will, in this circumstance, "reset" the "protected withdrawal amount" to the then-current cash value, which in a declining market (while withdrawals are also occurring) could be substantially lower. In some contracts, this reset can occur if any excess withdrawals occur, even if that excess is only a dollar.

When does the presence of a GMWB add value? As the following graph shows, the GMWB rider provides value only if the account balance falls to zero before the expiration of the GMWB period. In the example, the rider guarantees the contact owner the right to take withdrawals up to 7% per year until the guarantee amount is exhausted. In this case, that is approximately 14.3 years (100/7).

GMWB May Require No Waiting Period

Typically, GMWB provisions do not require a waiting period (although some contracts impose such a requirement). Some contracts offer a "bonus" (an increase in the protected withdrawal amount) if no withdrawals are made during a specified period of years following election of the option.

Asset Allocation May Be Required

Some GMWB provisions (like most GMAB provisions) impose restrictions on the investment choices available to the contract owner. Certain variable

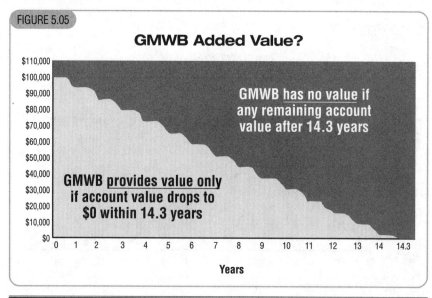

FIGURE 5.05

GMWB Added Value?

GMWB has no value if any remaining account value after 14.3 years

GMWB provides value only if account value drops to $0 within 14.3 years

Years

sub-accounts (typically, those having high price volatility) may be unavailable, or election of a diversified "model portfolio" may be required.

"Reset" Option

Some GMWB provisions allow the contract owner an option, similar to the step-up option often permitted by GMIB provisions, to reset the protected withdrawal amount to the annuity cash value if that value has risen due to investment gains. The owner may, thus, lock in these gains. In so doing, the contract owner who has elected the GMWB option ensures a greater guaranteed withdrawal amount (because the GMWB withdrawal percentage will apply to this greater protected withdrawal amount). Reset may be permitted only at certain option dates (such as every five years) or on each contract anniversary, or at any anniversary where the annuity cash value has increased by at least a certain percentage over the previous year's value.

Cost of GMWB

The cost for the GMWB option is typically in the range of 35-50 basis points per year. Some contracts waive this cost if no GMWB withdrawals are made within a specified period (e.g., 7 years) following election of the option, but will continue the GMWB provision in force.

It is vitally important that the advisor understand that all of the living benefit guarantees described above (GMIB, GMAB, and GMWB) operate only in the accumulation phase of the annuity; that is, prior to annuitization. When the contract owner elects an annuity payout option–whether fixed or variable, all of these guarantees expire. Of course, in the case of the GMAB and the GMIB, it may be more appropriate to say that the benefits mature. If the GMAB value exceeds the cash value of the contract and the waiting period has passed, the annuitization value of the contract will be the GMAB value–because the cash value will have been stepped-up to the GMAB value at the end of this waiting period. If the GMIB value exceeds the cash value, the higher (former) value may be used as the annuitization value–but this will require use of the special GMIB payout factors. As noted above, these factors are usually significantly less than the regular payout factors available to contract holders wishing to annuitize the cash value. This could result in a lower annuity payment than would be payable by annuitizing the (lower) cash value, using the "regular" payout factors.

Combination "Living Benefit" Riders

At the time of this writing (March, 2005), at several insurance companies have introduced new riders combining the features of the GMAB, GMIB, and GMWB. While the provisions of these "combination riders" vary considerably, they generally provide more flexibility and all of the combined features to work in concert, something often not permitted by the individual GMAB, GMIB, and GMWB provisions. The cost of these riders is, at the time of this writing, roughly 60 basis points per year.

Death Benefit Enhancements

The industry standard death benefit in variable annuities was, for many years, the greater of (a) the amount originally invested (less any withdrawals) or (b) the account balance at death. Often, surrender charges were waived upon death, and most contracts offered today contain this waiver.

Most variable deferred annuity contracts available today offer much more liberal death benefit guarantees, though these enhanced death benefits are generally available only at extra cost (either by additional cost for the rider, or by incorporating the guarantee into the base contract for a higher M&E cost). Some contracts offer a choice of several death benefit provisions.

The typical enhanced death benefit of a modern variable deferred annuity is a guarantee to pay the highest value of –

1) Total contributions made (less withdrawals)

2) The cash value at the time of death, usually without regard for any surrender charges

3) The highest cash value as of certain prior dates, such as "as of any prior policy anniversary" or "as of the 5th, 10th, 15th, or 20th policy anniversaries." This is often referred to as a "ratcheted" death benefit, and is typically restricted to policy anniversaries prior to a certain maximum age (e.g., age 85).

4) Total contributions made (less withdrawals), accumulated at a specified rate of interest (e.g., 5%). This option typically provides that accrual ceases at a certain maximum age (e.g., age 85).

The cost of such an enhanced death benefit is typically 35 basis points or less per year. As with some living benefits, the cost may be calculated based on the annuity account value, or the guaranteed death benefit amount.

Impact of Withdrawals on Death Benefit

An extremely important provision in any variable deferred annuity contract is the one specifying what adjustments will be made to the death benefit as a result of any partial withdrawals. Some contracts reduce the death benefit by withdrawals made, on a dollar for dollar basis. Others reduce it proportionally, by the percentage that the withdrawal represents of the cash value.

If the death benefit equals the current cash value, these two formulas will produce the same result. However, if the death benefit does not exceed the current cash value, the proportional method produces a higher remaining death benefit after withdrawal. The death benefit may be less than the current cash value if:

1. The death benefit is a basic return-of-premium death benefit and the contract has appreciated since inception;

2. The death benefit is a guaranteed return on contributions structure where the sub-accounts have outperformed the guaranteed interest rate; or

3. The death benefit is an annual step-up option, and the contract value has increased since the last anniversary step-up occurred, but the increase will not be credited until the next anniversary.

Example - Where Death Benefit Does Not Exceed Current Cash Value

Total Contributions To Annuity	$100,000
Current Cash Value	$150,000
Death Benefit Guarantee	$125,000
Withdrawal	$ 10,000

"Dollar For Dollar" Reduction in Death Benefit

$125,000 - $10,000   = $115,000 (Death Benefit following withdrawal)

"Proportional" Reduction In Death Benefit

$10,000 / $150,000   =   6.6666+%
$125,000 x 6.6666+%   = $8,333
$125,000 – $8,333   = $116,667 (Death Benefit following withdrawal)

Example – Where Death Benefit Exceeds Current Cash Value

However, when the death benefit *exceeds* the current cash value, the "dollar for dollar" method results in a *higher* after-withdrawal death benefit than the "proportional" method. (In the following example, the annuity owner invested $100,000. At one point, a later policy anniversary, the cash value had grown to $150,000. Subsequently, the cash value dropped to $75,000 due to poor investment results. The annuity offers an "annual ratchet" death benefit guarantee, whereby that earlier "high water mark" of $150,000 was "locked in" as the guaranteed death benefit).

Total Contributions to Annuity	$100,000
Current Cash Value	$ 75,000
Death Benefit Guarantee	$150,000
Withdrawal	$ 10,000

"Dollar For Dollar" Reduction in Death Benefit
$150,000 - $10,000   = $140,000 (Death Benefit following withdrawal)

"Proportional" Reduction In Death Benefit
$10,000 / $75,000   = 13.3333+%
$150,000 x 13.3333+% = $20,000
$150,000 – $20,000   = $130,000 (Death Benefit following withdrawal)

This distinction can be very important if the client is concerned with the amount to be left to heirs. It is particularly significant when a client is considering making a partial tax-free exchange of an existing annuity to a new annuity under Code section 1035. If the existing contract uses a "dollar for dollar" method for reducing the death benefit, and the account value is less than the death benefit, then a partial withdrawal of all but the minimum amount necessary to maintain the existing contract can leave much of that contract's death benefit intact while allowing the client to invest most of its former cash value in a new, and better, annuity. (It is presumed that the client, and his advisor, would not consider making the exchange unless the new annuity is significantly better, for the client's purposes, than the existing one).

Whose Death Triggers
the Death Benefit Guarantee?

As was discussed in Chapter Three, all annuities issued since January 18, 1985 must provide that the contract value will be paid to the beneficiary upon the death of the contract owner ("holder"), in accordance with rules specified in Code section 72(s). This rule of tax law mandates only that the contract value be paid upon the death of the contract owner. It does not mean that the guaranteed minimum death benefit of the contract will be payable. Whether that is the case is not a matter of tax law, but, rather, depends upon the terms of the annuity contract. Some (but not all) contracts are "annuitant-driven;" that is, they state that the contractual death benefit (including any optional, or enhanced death benefit guarantees) will be payable only upon the death of the annuitant. If the annuitant and the owner are different individuals, the owner's death will trigger payout of the contract value, under Code section 72(s), but will not trigger payment of the guaranteed minimum death benefit. Of course, where annuitant and owner are the same individual, this point is moot. But where they are not, it is extremely important that the advisor and the client know whose death will trigger the death benefit minimum guarantee.

Death Benefit Guarantee is Not Applicable After Annuitization

A point that may be overlooked in many sales presentations is the fact that the guaranteed minimum death benefit–a point often emphasized in these presentations–is operative only when the annuity contract is in the accumulation phase (that is, before the owner has exercised an option to annuitize the contract). Upon annuitization, the death benefit guarantees described above cease to exist. If the advisor is emphasizing the advantages to the client, and the client's family, of the death benefit guarantees in a deferred annuity, it is essential that he or she make clear when those guarantees are no longer operative.

Chapter Endnotes

1. This value is also known as the "Income Base" or "Protected Value."

2. The interest rate used in calculating these special payout factors is less than the rate used to calculate the "regular" payout factors. Often, this "special" interest rate is 2 or 2.5%, although it may be as high as 3.5% in some older GMIB riders.

3. See "Annuity Payout Factors" in Chapter 4.

4. However, in the older first generation of GMIB riders, unlimited dollar-for-dollar treatment was more common.

5. A *basis point* is 1/100th of a percent. Therefore, 30 bps = 0.30%. Basis points are useful terms for describing the magnitude of difference between two values, each of which is expressed in percentage terms. For example, if A = 6% and B = 4%, B is 200 basis points less than A. To say that "B is 2% less than A" would be incorrect, literally speaking. (100% - 2% = 98%, and 98% of 6% is 5.88%).

6. Also called the "waiting period" or "vesting period."

7. Also known as the Guaranteed Partial Withdrawal Benefit.

Chapter 6

The Variable Annuity as an Investment

In earlier chapters, the authors have made the point that an annuity is primarily a risk management tool and only secondarily an investment. Arguably, there are exceptions. A short-term "CD" annuity and, perhaps, an index annuity might be properly viewed as primarily a savings instrument. On the whole, however, many–if not most–deferred annuities are purchased and sold as investments, and this is particularly true of variable deferred annuities.

Because the variable deferred annuity is typically sold as an investment, we will, in this chapter, examine it as an investment. We will use as our framework a model that one of the authors uses to describe the process of financial and estate planning. We will relate various characteristics of the variable annuity to three key aspects of the overall planning process, focusing on the extent to which these characteristics provide solutions to the needs that cause consumers to purchase financial instruments–investments–in the first place.

The Model

The process of financial and estate planning may be described as a "3-legged stool." The "legs" are:

- Accumulation

- Conservation

- Distribution

From the standpoint of the planning process, each leg, or aspect, represents a need (or combination of needs) that must be satisfied if the plan is to be successful. From the standpoint of a deferred variable annuity, each aspect is reflected in one or more characteristics of the annuity, designed to satisfy the need in question. We will examine each leg, first as a component of the planning process, and then, as a need for which certain features of the variable annuity were designed to provide a solution.

Accumulation

The accumulation goal, as many investors perceive it, is to amass as much capital as possible, by achieving the highest investment returns possible, consistent with acceptable risk. The authors believe that, while this may a valid investment objective, it is not a good planning objective. Rather, we think, one should aim for maximizing the probability of achieving one's goals. Often, goals are expressed in the form of income. To satisfy these income goals, a tool designed specifically to create income may be more efficient than one designed to create a future lump sum that can then be tapped to create income. There is good evidence that a combination of (a) instruments designed for pure wealth accumulations and (b) purely income instruments can produce higher probabilities of overall plan success than pure accumulation instruments by themselves.[1] In so doing, a combination is actually addressing both the client's accumulation goal and his or her conservation goal.

That said, let's stay focused on the accumulation goal, and ask: How can a variable annuity help the investor to achieve this goal?

The Variable Deferred Annuity as Accumulation Instrument

The efficient accumulation of wealth is the object of all investment methodologies, including the widely used and popular Modern Portfolio Theory (MPT). This theory holds that, to achieve the highest returns possible, with the least amount of investment risk (or, viewed another way, to minimize the investment risk necessary to achieve a given portfolio rate of return), one should construct a diversified portfolio, composed of asset classes, that:

1)   Offers the opportunity, through a broadly diversified portfolio, to achieve the return necessary to achieve planning goals with the least amount of risk (where risk is traditionally defined as volatility–usually measured by standard deviation).

2)   Reduces risk by constructing the portfolio "efficiently" from compo-
     nents that represent asset classes that are, to the extent possible, as
     weakly correlated–or even negatively correlated–as possible. This
     requires that the investment vehicle provide a sufficient variety of asset
     classes to allow construction of such a portfolio.

3)   Can be adjusted periodically. Many theorists believe that periodic
     rebalancing of the portfolio is essential, by selling those components
     that have outperformed expectations and buying those that have
     underperformed, so as to bring the proportions of the components
     back to the original "optimum" mix. How often such rebalancing
     should occur is a matter of considerable debate.

4)   Can be adjusted with as little expense (e.g., transaction costs, taxes,
     etc.) as possible.

How Does a Variable Annuity Allow
the Investor to Build Such A Portfolio?

1.   A Broadly Diversified Portfolio.

     Early variable annuities offered only limited investment choices,
often managed by the issuing insurance company. Today's contracts typically provide the policy owner access to a wide variety of investment
sub-accounts,[2] managed by several different independent money management firms, in addition to a fixed sub-account (which acts much like
a fixed annuity, and for which separate management charges are not
assessed). Some variable annuities offer thirty or more variable sub-
accounts from dozens of money managers. Generally, these sub-accounts
are actively managed, and are sometimes said to be "clones" of mutual
funds offered outside the annuity by the money manager. It is very
important that the advisor understand that the term "clone," in this connection, is misleading. For example, an annuity may contain a sub-
account called "Atropos Growth Opportunities," managed by, say,
"Olympia Capital Investments." And Olympia may offer, outside the
annuity, a mutual fund with the exact same name. But this does not mean
either that they are managed by the same individuals or that they have
precisely the same investment objectives or investment policies. Nor does
it mean that the fees and expenses are the same. Even when the same
individual manages both, and when the investment policies of both are

essentially the same, that manager may employ different strategies in the annuity than for the mutual fund. Tax considerations alone might suggest different strategies. (Realized gains in a mutual fund must, by law, be distributed to shareholders of a mutual fund, and are currently taxable even if reinvested.)

Advisors should avoid referring to these sub-accounts as clones, and, most certainly, should never use the performance history of one when discussing the other. Moreover (as was noted in Chapter 1), the pricing of a variable annuity sub-account is different from the pricing of a mutual fund. Reinvested gains in a mutual fund purchase additional shares, having (at the time of distribution) the same value as the original shares. By contrast, gains in a variable annuity sub-account do not purchase additional shares. Instead, the value of the shares is adjusted to reflect those reinvested gains.

Most variable sub-accounts are actively managed, as are most mutual funds. Recently, more and more variable annuities have added passively managed sub-accounts designed to match the performance of an external index such as the S&P 500.

2.   An "Efficient" Portfolio.

The availability of a wide variety of investment sub-accounts, representing many asset classes, may allow the owner of today's variable annuity to construct a portfolio that is not only diversified but theoretically efficient–that is, it is comprised of asset class components that are weakly, or even negatively, correlated, such that they do not perform in lock step with one another. We say "may allow" because few, if any, variable annuity issuers provide the annuity owner (or his or her advisor, for that matter) with a tool to construct such an "efficient" portfolio. This construction is usually done by means of a technique known as "Mean-Variance Optimization," and the software tool used to employ it is usually known as an "optimizer." As of this writing, the authors know of no variable annuity issuer that provides either the client or the client's advisor with an optimizer, either on a website or in illustration software.

Of course, the client's advisor may have access to such an optimizer, either incorporated in a financial planning software package or a "stand alone" software package. However, even access to this tool will not suffice unless the advisor also knows some vitally important data about the sub-accounts to be used to create the "optimum" portfolio. The required data includes:

- The expected mean return of the asset class.[3]

- The expected volatility of the asset class, as measured by its Standard Deviation (SD).

- The coefficient of correlation of the performance of every sub-account to be considered, to the performance of every other sub-account to be considered.

- The historical time period to which these data refer.

Few, if any, variable annuity issuers provide all of this information. All provide historical return data, however, and an advisor who has access to an analysis tool such as Microsoft Excel, expertise in using its statistical functions, and historical return data for all sub-accounts to be considered for a common time period of significant duration (we suggest at least ten years) can derive the remaining data, which can then be plugged into an optimizer.[4]

Few advisors will do this. First, because it requires statistical expertise which many advisors do not possess, and, second, because there is a much easier way to do the optimization. Or, at least, there appears to be.

Some advisors will choose specific investment sub-accounts within the annuity to represent asset classes (e.g., "Olympia Giant Growth" to represent large cap growth stocks) and create an optimized portfolio from those accounts, using optimizer software and the statistical data (Mean, SD, and coefficient of correlation) supplied with the software, representing the asset classes themselves. The sub-accounts will, in this procedure, be acting as "proxies" for the asset classes.

Use of an optimizer program in this way is fairly common among advisors seeking to build optimized portfolios from actively managed mutual funds. Applying it to actively managed variable annuity sub-accounts is not much different, and the results should be no less credible.

The problem is, the results will not be credible, whether it is mutual funds or variable annuity sub-accounts that are being optimized–not if they are actively managed.

The manager of an actively managed fund or variable annuity sub-account seeks to distinguish the performance of the account from its peers (hopefully, by outperforming them). That is what sells the fund and that is what produces the manager's bonus. If the benchmark for a fund is a particular index, the fund manager will seek to outperform that index. But the whole idea of using a proxy for something is to obtain results as close as possible to the values that would be produced if that something were the thing used. The very idea of a proxy–a substitute–deliberately managed to produce results different from the object for which it is substituted is self-contradictory.

In the authors' opinions, use of Mean-Variance Optimization (MVO) has its uses, but it is not nearly the ideal tool that many advisors suppose when it's used as just described. By definition, any fund or sub-account with a low "R-Squared" value,[5] in relation to the asset class for which it is standing proxy, will not perform in accordance with the expectations for that asset class. The lower the R-Squared value, the greater the dissonance. The authors believe that MVO is a much more reliable and credible tool when the correlation between the asset classes chosen–to which the return, SD, and coefficients of correlation apply directly–and the proxies chosen to represent those asset classes is as close as possible. There is a fairly simple way to accomplish this objective: The proxies should be designed to mirror the asset classes they represent. If the asset class is, say, "US Small Cap Growth"–as measured by the Russell 2000 Growth Index–then an excellent proxy would be an index fund or sub-account deliberately constructed to perform like that index.

At the time of this writing, most variable annuities include few, if any, such sub-accounts, but the industry trend appears to be toward offering more of them. Some variable annuities now offer Exchange Traded Fund (ETF) accounts, constructed to mirror the performance of various indices, and many offer at least a few index sub-accounts similar to index mutual funds. Typically, the expense ratio of these accounts is significantly lower than for their actively managed cousins. All other things being equal, lower cost is good.

But are all other things equal? The debate between "actively managed" and "passively managed" still rages. Many commentators and a few scholars argue that active management can provide additional value, over and above the value expected from the asset class to which a fund is most closely related. For those who agree with this argument, a variable annuity offers a significant benefit that is often under-appreciated.

As noted earlier, many variable annuities offer dozens of separate sub-accounts managed by perhaps a dozen or more money management firms. Often, these managers are chosen by the insurance company because they represent a specific style expertise. "Olympia Capital Investments," for example, may be a highly respected growth manager that is particularly adept and successful at managing client money using that style. By contrast, "Asgard Asset Management" may be well known and respected as a value manager. Another management firm may be highly successful at bond investing. By including all three firms in its stable of managers, an annuity offers the policyholder the opportunity to choose, not only those asset classes which comprise the most appropriate portfolio for his or her goals, but to select managers for each class that are unusually good at managing that particular kind of investment.

3.   Periodic Adjustment.

Nearly all variable annuities allow the switching of money among the various sub-accounts without cost.[6] Moreover, such a transfer is not a taxable event for income tax purposes. This allows the annuity owner to adjust her portfolio to reflect changed objectives or time horizons, because a manager has consistently underperformed, or to rebalance the portfolio (to return the investment mix to original, or revised, percentage allocations). Most variable annuities offer the policy owner the opportunity to elect such re-balancing automatically, at various intervals (typically: annually, semi-annually, quarterly, or monthly) or when the existing percentage allocation of a holding varies from its target by at least a certain amount or percentage. Typically, there is no charge for this feature.

A related benefit allowed by many variable annuities is sometimes referred to as "dollar cost averaging." This feature allows the contract owner investing with a lump sum, who may be concerned about the risk of investing in the market at the wrong time, to deposit the lump sum into the fixed account of the annuity in an arrangement where a portion of this lump sum will be automatically transferred, each month, to variable sub-accounts that she has selected, so that the entire sum will be transferred evenly across a certain time period (typically, six months or one year).

4.   Low Annual Cost.

The owner of a modern variable annuity can construct a portfolio of many individual sub-accounts, representing a wide variety of investment types and managed by a diverse "stable" of professional money managers with different styles and expertise. She can adjust this portfolio periodically (in some contracts, as often as desired) at no cost and with no tax consequence, and may elect to have adjustments made automatically, at no cost. These are powerful and attractive portfolio management benefits, rarely available to regular taxable accounts, which are all too often ignored when the variable annuity is considered as a wealth accumulation tool.

Conservation

The second leg of our 3-legged stool model is wealth conservation. Here, the investor's goal is to keep his accumulated assets as safe as possible from loss, including loss due to:

- Poor investment performance;

- Taxes;

- Bankruptcy or other failure by the institution holding the investment; or

- Attacks by creditors.

How can a variable annuity help the investor achieve this goal?

1.   Loss from Poor Investment Performance.

Loss due to poor investment performance can adversely affect both the annuity owner during his or her life and the owner's beneficiary, if the owner dies before the contract is surrendered or annuitized. Today's variable annuities contain several risk management features that can help the annuity owner manage the risk of such losses.

Living Benefits

As described in Chapter 5, the living benefits in modern variable annuity contracts provide the contract owner with three basic assurances:

1. A guarantee of a minimum future accumulation value, through the guaranteed minimum accumulation benefit.

2. A guarantee of a minimum income, through the guaranteed minimum income benefit.

3. A guarantee of no loss of principal, through the guaranteed minimum withdrawal benefit.

Newer combination riders, incorporating elements of all three benefits, provide these same assurances while offering greater flexibility.

Death Benefits

As discussed in Chapter 5, the Guaranteed Death Benefit in today's variable annuity contracts assures the owner that her beneficiary will receive at least the amount originally invested, plus (depending upon policy terms) a minimum rate of return on that investment or all or part of previously credited gains.

Both the living and death benefits are, of course, insurance features. They are, however, arguably relevant to a proper evaluation of the variable annuity-as-investment, for anyone whose overall financial planning goals include a desire for conserving his invested wealth.

2. Loss Due to Taxes.

One of the most-cited benefits of any deferred annuity (including a deferred variable annuity) is that undistributed gain is not subject to current income taxes. Indeed, tax deferral is often said to be the main attraction of deferred annuities. This, in the authors' opinion, is unfortunate–for two reasons.

First, this narrow focus ignores the many benefits offered by deferred annuities that have nothing to do with taxation. The investment aspects of a variable annuity just described may be sufficiently attractive to an investor to justify the annuity costs, irrespective of tax deferral. Moreover, an annuity is the only financial instrument that can guarantee its owner an income that he or she cannot outlive.

Second, the argument that tax deferral is the main benefit to be gained from owning a deferred annuity necessarily implies that anyone purchasing a deferred annuity inside an IRA or qualified plan foregoes that main benefit. It is certainly true that the holder of an IRA annuity does not get tax deferral, by reason of owning the annuity, because the IRA itself provides such deferral. However, there are other reasons why one might wish to fund an IRA (or qualified plan) with a deferred annuity. We will consider several of these reasons in Chapter 11.

All that said, the tax deferral enjoyed by annuities is clearly a benefit. Dollars that would otherwise be lost to annual income tax are, in a deferred annuity, able to earn further gain. The "miracle" of compound interest (in which gain on an investment can, itself, earn yet more gain) is enhanced by another layer–to produce what is sometimes called "triple compounding" (1. principal earns gain; 2. after-tax gain earns gain; and 3. gain that would otherwise be surrendered to pay tax can also earn further gain). Of course, tax deferred does not mean tax free! The untaxed gain will eventually be taxed, either to the living annuity holder or to the beneficiary. And it will be taxed as ordinary income. Whether the trade-off of tax deferral (a benefit) for ordinary income treatment (which might be considered a cost of that benefit) is attractive is problematic. It depends upon a number of variables, including assumptions as to tax rate (for both the annuity and the alternative), investment return rate, and, most importantly, how the money will eventually be distributed.

Many "annuity versus investment alternative" comparisons are pure accumulation scenarios. They reckon the worth of each side of the comparison in terms of an after tax future lump sum. In the authors' opinion, such an analysis is inherently faulty. The benefits of a deferred annuity include guaranteed annuity payout factors–assurances that, regardless of future investment conditions or life expectancies, the annuity owner is assured of receiving at least a specified income, every year (or more frequent payment interval), for each dollar that is annuitized. This benefit does come at a cost (which is part of the M&E charges of a variable annuity).

Whether the benefit is worth the cost is certainly arguable. There has (to the authors' knowledge) never been a time when the guaranteed payout rates contained in a deferred annuity have been as attractive as the payout rates available in single premium immediate annuity (SPIA) contracts. The holder of any non-annuity investment, wishing to convert his accumulated wealth to a guaranteed income stream could elect to purchase a SPIA. However, the success of this scenario (as compared to investing in a deferred annuity at the outset) depends upon two assumptions:

1.   That the payout rates in SPIA contracts will always be more attractive than those guaranteed in today's deferred contracts;

2.   That the after-tax value of the accumulated wealth (invested in the alternative being considered) will, when invested in the SPIA, produce a greater income than the annuitized deferred annuity. If the alternative investment contains any as-yet-untaxed capital gains, the tax on that gain must be paid on the surrender of the investment. By contrast, the entire future value of the deferred annuity (including all untaxed gain) could be available to purchase the same SPIA, if the deferred annuity is exchanged for the SPIA in a tax-free exchange under Code section 1035.[7] Or the deferred annuity could be annuitized using the then-current payout factors available for holders of that contract, if they are more attractive than those of every SPIA the investor might consider (a situation that is possible, but not likely).

A comparison of a variable annuity versus an investment alternative that concludes which alternative is better purely in terms of an after-tax future lump sum does not consider the potential advantages of such an exchange of annuities. Moreover, it does not allow for even the possibility that the guaranteed payout factors in the deferred annuity might be more attractive than future SPIA rates. Whatever one believes, as to the latter possibility, it should be taken into account. Any comparison that ignores a benefit that is contractually guaranteed by one alternative but is absent in the other, is hopelessly flawed, unless one is prepared to decree that benefit to be utterly worthless–now, and at every time in the future.

3.   Loss Due to Bankruptcy or Other Failure of the Institution Holding the Investment.

All investors are (or should be) concerned with the extent to which they may lose money as a result of the bankruptcy (or other failure) of the institution holding that money. Investors in annuities should be aware that the cash value in their contracts is not insured by the FDIC. Fixed annuities are backed by the general assets of the issuing insurer and are subject to the creditors of that insurer. The situation with variable annuities is somewhat different. The investments in the variable sub-accounts are not held by the insurer, are not protected from loss other than by operation of any living benefits elected by the annuity owner, and are not subject to the insurer's general creditors. However, the contractual guarantees—including annuity payout factors, guaranteed minimum death benefits and guaranteed living benefits—are, like the cash value of a fixed annuity, backed only by the financial resources of the issuing insurer. The advisor recommending—or even discussing—an annuity with a client should exercise special care to ensure that the client understands these limitations. That said, most alternative investments are not guaranteed against loss due to bankruptcy or insolvency, as many holders of stock and bond issues can attest. We mention the issue only because annuities are sometimes marketed by depository institutions whose regular accounts are insured, and because of frequently-cited regulatory concerns that the inapplicability of such insurance to annuities sold by those institutions—or by advisors not connected with such institutions—is not well understood by consumers.

That said, there exist, in all fifty states (as well as Puerto Rico and the District of Columbia) guarantee funds to reimburse owners of annuity and life insurance contracts from losses resulting from insurer insolvency. The coverage provisions and limits of these funds vary by state. Information on this topic is available at www.annuityadvantage.com/stateguarantee.htm.

4.   Loss to Judgment Creditors.

A serious concern, for many investors, is the extent to which their assets may be attached by judgment creditors. Many advisors are unaware of the special protections afforded annuities by the laws of many states. Unfortunately, the extent to which annuity cash values receive creditor protection and the limitations on such protection vary widely, and simple answers are, in this context, more than usually dangerous. Two sources of insightful information on this subject are the websites of the law firm of

Donlevy-Rosen and Rosen, www.protectyou.com (see, especially, www.protectyou.com/apn13-2-fr.html) and a marvelously informative and surprisingly humorous website devoted to estate planning and creditor protection scams, www.quatloos.com.

Distribution

The third leg of the planning stool is Distribution. Here, there are typically two goals involved:

1. During the investor's lifetime, to create income–in the amounts required–from accumulated capital.

2. At the investor's death, to ensure that the wealth passes, as efficiently as possible, to those intended.

How can a variable annuity help our investor to realize these goals?

Income

Annuities are particularly useful in meeting a goal of required income, because income is what annuities are all about. Their effectiveness as accumulation instruments notwithstanding, annuities were originally developed for one purpose–to produce income. When the desire is for an income that will, in any and all events, last as long as the life of the recipient–however long that may be–an annuity is arguably the perfect instrument, because it is the only instrument that is guaranteed to do so. All annuities can do so.

What a variable annuity can do, in this regard, that no other financial instrument can, is produce an income stream that (a) is guaranteed to last for the lifetime of the annuitant (assuming a life annuity payout option is elected) and (b) will fluctuate in amount (that is, the amount of each payment will vary), reflecting the performance of the underlying investments. This is the so-called "variable annuity payout" option in a variable deferred annuity contract and the basic structure of a variable immediate annuity.

Why is such a variable payout desirable? Well, it should be admitted that, for some investors, it is not. Some will wish a guarantee that annuity payments will never change. For those individuals, a fixed annuity payout is more appropriate.

This option is available in variable deferred annuity contracts, just as it is in their fixed cousins. However, many investors are concerned with the impact of inflation on their retirement income. They know that, whatever the nominal value of their income, it is the purchasing power that buys groceries.

Is a payout arrangement where the amount of each payment varies, not with the cost of living, but with the performance of the annuity investments, the best way to keep with inflation? If keeping pace with inflation is the sole objective, probably not. After all, the investments could suffer a loss–resulting in a decrease in the amount of the annuity payment–at the same time as inflation is increasing, further eroding the purchasing value of each dollar of that payment. A better solution would be a life annuity where the amount of each annual payment is adjusted in accordance with some index of inflation (such as the Consumer Price Index). Unfortunately, very few insurance companies offer such a contract. A few insurers offer fixed annuities where the amount of each year's payment will be increased by a specified percentage (typically, 1-3%; the authors know of no company offering, at the time of this writing, an annual adjustment of more than 5%). For the inflation fearful, a guaranteed increase of a few percentage points each year is better than nothing, but it is probably not what they would prefer. Of course, the initial payment of the increasing annuity will be lower than that of the level one. The greater the guaranteed annual increase, the greater this difference will be.

For those individuals, the choice, at the present time, comes down to purchasing a truly inflation-indexed annuity from an insurer that offers one (and the annuity may not contain all the features the investor wants) or electing a variable payout, in the hope that the performance of the annuity investments chosen will enable annuity payments to rise with (or even beyond) the rate of inflation. The authors hope that more insurers will choose to offer genuinely inflation indexed annuities, both as immediate contracts and as payout options in deferred ones.

The scenario described above is one in which the investor's goal is for an income that is guaranteed both to last a lifetime (or for the lifetime of investor and someone else) and to keep pace with inflation. But what if the goal is to outperform inflation? Many consumers (and probably all advisors) know that lifestyles are not carved in stone. Some retirees wish to "do better every year"–in real dollar terms. For these individuals, an inflation-indexed payout may not be so attractive. If they believe that a properly designed portfolio (probably consisting mostly of equities) is more likely than not to outperform inflation, a variable payout may make more sense. In any event, the guarantee that the income (whether level or varying with investment performance or inflation rate) cannot be outlived is a powerful benefit.

But annuity payout factors are not the only mechanism by which a variable annuity can generate income for the investor. "Living benefits" can do so as well. The guaranteed minimum income benefit (GMIB) guarantees a minimum income based on a guaranteed benefit base which is unaffected by any investment losses within the annuity. The cost of this benefit is, however, not only the contractual charge assessed, but the fact that the GMIB income stream usually requires annuitization using payout factors less attractive than those available to contract holders not electing this benefit (see Chapter 5).

The guaranteed partial withdrawal benefit also provides a guarantee of a minimum income, but it is really a guarantee of principal, irrespective of adverse investment performance, provided that principal (or benefit base, if higher) is accessed via withdrawals not exceeding a certain limit each year.

Passing Wealth to Those Intended

Annuity proceeds are paid to the contract owner's designated beneficiary. They generally pass outside of probate, avoiding the potential cost and time delays that may be associated with that process. In addition, annuity proceeds usually enjoy special creditor protection (the level of protection varying with state law).

Furthermore, special "restrictive beneficiary designations" offered by some carriers can allow the contract owner to limit the beneficiary's access to proceeds, either by requiring a fixed systematic withdrawal schedule or imposing limits on the amount that the insurer will release each year.[8]

The variable annuity, viewed strictly as an investment, is a remarkably potent vehicle. While many proponents and critics see it purely as an accumulation device, it offers benefits designed to address the needs implicit in all three legs of the financial and estate planning stool.

Chapter Endnotes

1. Two of the best demonstrations of this conclusion are "Making Retirement Distributions Last A Lifetime", by Ameriks, Veres, and Warshawsky, *Journal of Financial Planning*, Dec, 2001, and "Merging Asset Allocation and Longevity Insurance: An Optimal Perspective On Payout Annuities", by Chen and Milevsky *Journal of Financial Planning*, June 2003.

2. These variable sub-accounts are sometimes referred to as "separate accounts."

3. For purposes of projecting possible future values, the arithmetic mean is generally considered to be a better factor than the geometric mean. Published historical performance figures generally report the geometric mean, which is always equal or lower–often, significantly lower–than the arithmetic mean.

4. As noted earlier, most historical returns information, when including mean return, use the geometric mean (as that is the best measure of "average" performance in historical data). If that geometric mean is used as an input in an optimizer software program that expects the user to supply an arithmetic mean (a better measure of the average when forecasting future values), the results will be theoretically inaccurate.

5. "R-Squared" (R2) is a measure of the extent to which change in one variable can be explained by changes in another (the model). It is often said to be a measure of "goodness of fit."

6. Many contracts limit the number of transfers that may be made without cost per year. A few allow switching as often as daily.

7. Deferred annuities are commonly exchanged for SPIAs when the annuity owner decides to annuitize and the current payout factors in the deferred annuity are less attractive than those available from a SPIA. Because this practice is so common, the authors suggest that the often-cited statistic that "only about 2% of deferred annuities are ever annuitized" is probably misleading–perhaps very misleading. Any deferred annuity exchanged for a SPIA would be considered as not annuitized, although the result of the 1035 exchange produces that result.

8. Such options are particularly appealing for deferred annuity owners that do not necessarily want to deal with the cost and hassle of using a trust to accomplish the same goals. In addition, the use of an individual beneficiary (albeit with restrictions) may be more income-tax-favorable that naming a trust as a beneficiary.

Chapter 7

Index Annuities

In Chapter One, we observed that one of the ways to classify annuities is to distinguish how the cash value is invested–between fixed annuities and variable annuities. Some commentators suggest that there is a third type–index annuities. While this might seem reasonable–after all, index annuities certainly look different–it is not correct. An index annuity is a type of fixed annuity. It is, in every respect, a fixed annuity, because its value is expressed in dollars, not units which vary in value according to the underlying investments. It *is not*, in *any* respect, a *variable* annuity. To understand why, we must examine how it works.

But first, it is important to understand the sometimes troublesome matter of its name. Index annuities (IAs) are also referred to as equity index annuities (EIAs) or equity-linked index annuities (ELIAs). This is because the interest[1] credited to an IA is linked to an external index, which is usually (but not always), an equity index–typically (but not always), the S&P 500.[2] The nature of this linkage–that is, the extent to which changes in the index will be reflected in the amount of interest credited to the index annuity–varies (often greatly) from one IA product to another. There are several (or many, depending upon how closely one wishes to differentiate) basic index annuity designs and dozens of methods of crediting interest. But all of them link the interest to be credited to the annuity contract to changes in the index used for that contract.

A serious problem with the terms equity index annuity and equity-linked index annuity, according to Jack Marrion, probably the foremost expert in IAs, is that both imply a greater degree of correspondence between movement of the underlying index and interest credited to the index annuity than exists in any of the IA designs. Holders of IA contracts may, in attending to those two terms, come to expect the same level of returns (specifically, positive returns) that they could enjoy by holding a more nearly direct investment in the index (such as an index mutual fund or exchange traded fund such as the S&P 500 SPDR[3]). Moreover, both terms virtually ignore two of the most attractive benefits enjoyed by IA owners, by virtue of the fact that an IA is a fixed annuity—namely, (a) a guarantee of principal and (b) a guarantee (in most, but not all, IA contracts) of a minimum rate of interest.

For these reasons, Marrion prefers to use the term index annuity, or, better yet, fixed index annuity (FIA). In the authors' opinion, his concerns are valid. The last thing any advisor should want is a label for any savings or investment product that is misleading. So, we will dispense with both as equity index annuity and equity-linked index annuities. But, with all due respect to Jack, we'll stick with the term index annuity because it is in common usage. It's also shorter.

Basics of Index Annuities

An index annuity is a fixed deferred annuity. Like all fixed deferred annuities, it offers a guarantee of principal and a guaranteed minimum rate of interest.[4] However, unlike traditional fixed annuities, the IA offers the potential for excess interest based, not on whatever the insurer decides to declare, but on the performance of the underlying index. An index annuity gives the buyer some of the gains achieved by the stock index and none of the losses. What do we mean by some? The extent to which the annuity owner participates in the gains realized by the underlying index and when those gains are credited to the annuity (in the form of interest) depends upon the design of the annuity. We will examine the basic designs later in this chapter, but, first, we need to clarify some of the special terminology used in index annuities and to understand the various "moving parts" that go into the construction of these contracts.

Index Annuity Terminology[5]

Indexing Method

The indexing method is the approach used to calculate the change in the underlying index, for the purpose of determining the interest to be credited to the annuity.

Term (or Index Term)

The term or index term of an IA is the period over which index-linked interest is calculated. It is important to understand that "term" does not mean the duration of the annuity contract itself.

Participation Rate

The participation rate is a method (but not the only method) used to determine how much of the increase in the underlying index will be credited as interest to the annuity. For example, if the index growth, over the index term, was 10% and the participation rate is 70%, the interest credited will be 7% (10% x 70%). The participation rate may be guaranteed by the issuer for a period of time (from one year to the entire term) or may be changeable, by the insurer, at any time. Some contracts guarantee that this rate will never fall below a stated minimum. The participation rate is one of the "moving parts" in an index annuity, allowing the issuing insurer to adjust the interest crediting formula to reflect changes in interest rates and the cost of equity options[6] over the term period.

Yield Spread (or "Term Asset Fee")

The yield spread is another method of reducing the amount of index gain that will be credited as interest to the annuity, thus reducing the risk to the insurer (another of the "moving parts"). If the annualized growth of the index, over the index term, was 10% and the yield spread is 3%, the interest credited will be 7% (10% - 3%). Yield spread is simply another way of limiting the insurer's risk (and annuity owner's gain)–an alternative to the participation rate.

Cap Rate (or "Cap")

Some index annuities put a maximum value on either the interest rate that will be credited (interest rate cap) or the amount of index gain that will be recognized in calculating the equity-linked interest (index cap). The marketing material for some IAs that use a "cap" do not make entirely clear whether an interest rate cap or an index cap is being used. It is vitally important that the advisor, discussing an IA with a "cap," understand which method is being employed. Here's why. Assume the underlying index gains 20% in a given year:

1. An IA with a 70% participation rate and a 12% interest rate cap will credit 12%. (20% x 70% = 14%, but the "cap" limits the interest credited to 12%; therefore, the interest credited is 12%).

2. An IA with a 3% yield spread and a 12% interest rate cap will credit 12%. (20% - 3% = 17%, but the "cap" limits the interest credited to 12%; therefore, the interest credited is 12%).

3. An IA with a 70% participation rate and a 12% index cap will credit 8.4% interest. (The "cap" recognizes no more than 12% of the index movement. 12% x 70% = 8.4%).

4. An IA with a 3% yield spread and a 12% index cap will credit 9% interest. (The "cap" recognizes no more than 12% of the index movement. 12% - 3% = 9%).

Does this mean that IAs with index caps are not as good as those with interest rate caps? Not necessarily, because IAs with index caps frequently offer higher participation rates or lower yield spreads than contracts with interest rate caps. As Jack Marrion explains, "caps are used to boost participation rates or minimize yield spreads. Since they limit upside exposure, the cost [to the insurer] of providing the index-linked interest is less, so participation in caps up to the cap are higher. Caps enable one to get 'more of most' instead of 'less of more'"[7]

Index Annuity Designs

At the time of this writing, there are several different IA designs that are commonly used. However, as Marrion points out, "there are really only two ways to credit index-linked interest to an annuity. One can either measure index movement over a year or two–an annual reset method, or one can measure index movement over a period of years–a term end point method."

Annual Reset

Like a fixed rate annuity (a conventional fixed annuity) the annual reset, or annual ratchet, method credits interest each year. The amount of interest credited each year is based on the movement of the underlying index during that year, calculated from the ending balance of the index for the previous year. An essential characteristic of annual reset index annuities is that losses are ignored. If the index movement in any year is negative, the contract treats that loss as a zero percent gain and credits zero interest for that year. Another essential characteristic is that, because gain is measured from the index value at the end of the previous year, an annual reset IA can credit interest based on index gain even if the index value, after that gain, is less than it was at some earlier point in the contract.

The charts below illustrate the hypothetical performance of a $100,000 annual reset annuity with a 100% participation rate and a 12% interest rate cap. In the first year, the index gained 15.63% and the contract credited 12% interest (due to the cap), resulting in a cash value of $112,000. In the second year, the index lost 17.37%. The contract credited 0% interest, and the cash value remained at $112,000. In the third year, the index lost another 29.72%, but, again, that loss was not recognized, and the cash value stayed at $112,000.

In the fourth year, however, the index gained 31.55%, resulting in crediting of 12% interest to the annuity. That gain was credited, despite the fact that the index balance, at the end of the fourth year (90.19), was less than its value at the inception of the annuity (102.09). The fourth year gain merely re-traced prior years' losses. At the end of ten years, the index had gained 1.84%, while the annuity produced an annualized return of 5.94%. Does this mean that one can expect an annual reset IA (or any IA, for that matter) to outperform the underlying index? Definitely not. First, stocks in an equity index may produce dividends, which are not taken into account in IAs, but would be received by investors holding a mutual fund or exchange traded fund (ETF) based on that index. Moreover, this hypothetical illustration (which uses actual values of the

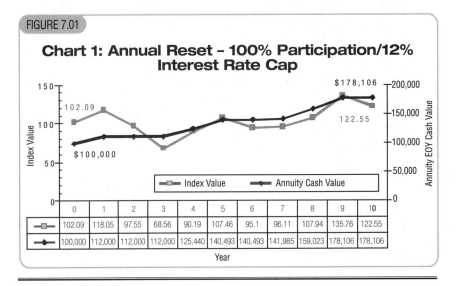

FIGURE 7.01

Chart 1: Annual Reset – 100% Participation/12% Interest Rate Cap

Year	0	1	2	3	4	5	6	7	8	9	10
Index Value	102.09	118.05	97.55	68.56	90.19	107.46	95.1	96.11	107.94	135.76	122.55
Annuity Cash Value	100,000	112,000	112,000	112,000	125,440	140,493	140,493	141,985	159,023	178,106	178,106

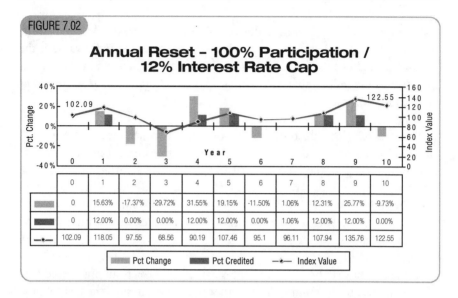

FIGURE 7.02

Annual Reset – 100% Participation / 12% Interest Rate Cap

	0	1	2	3	4	5	6	7	8	9	10
Pct Change	0	15.63%	-17.37%	-29.72%	31.55%	19.15%	-11.50%	1.06%	12.31%	25.77%	-9.73%
Pct Credited	0	12.00%	0.00%	0.00%	12.00%	12.00%	0.00%	1.06%	12.00%	12.00%	0.00%
Index Value	102.09	118.05	97.55	68.56	90.19	107.46	95.1	96.11	107.94	135.76	122.55

■ Pct Change   ■ Pct Credited   ◆ Index Value

S&P 500 index from 12/31/71 – 12/31/81) is of a highly volatile period. Annual reset index annuities do very well in such climates, if an investor should be lucky enough to be invested when one occurs.

Point-to-Point

The point-to-point (or term end point) design measures index movements over a period greater than one or two years and does not calculate or credit interest each year. The investor's return is not known, and cannot be estimated, until the end of the term period (which is typically 7–10 years). The index gain is calculated by dividing the index value at the end of the term by its value at the beginning and subtracting 1. For example, if the index is 100 at the outset of the contract, and 180 ten years later, the index gain is 80% ((180/100)-1). That gain is then adjusted by applying any participation rate and the resulting interest percentage is multiplied by the initial contract value to produce the interest to be credited. For example, at a 70% participation rate, the cumulative interest credited would be 56% (80% x 70%). Such an annuity, purchased for $100,000, would be worth $156,000 at the end of the ten years.

A variation of this design, called Term Yield Spread, works similarly, in that interest is neither calculated nor credited until the end of the period. However, the yield spread is not simply subtracted from the index gain, because the yield spread is an annual figure and the index gain is a cumulative one. Instead, the interest is credited by applying the yield spread to the annualized return of the index over the time period, using this formula: $R = (E/S)^{(1/n)} - 1$; Interest Credited $= R - Y$ (where E = Ending Index Value; S = Starting Index Value; n= number of years in period, R = Index Return (the annualized compound rate of return over the period); and Y = Yield Spread). Using the facts above and a yield spread of 3%, the interest credited would be 3.054% per year $[(180/100)^{(1/10)} - 1 = 6.054; 6.054 - 3.00 = 3.054]$. The annuity, at the end of ten years would be worth \$135,098 [100,000 x $(1 + .0354)^\wedge 10$]. What if the index were lower, at the end of ten years, than at the outset (or higher, but less than the guaranteed value)? Then the contract would not use that final index value, but would, instead, credit the guaranteed interest rate to the initial index value for each year of the term.

The Annual Reset and Point-to-Point designs are the two basic types of index annuities. However, there are many variations on those themes. We will not attempt to describe all the variations out there (for a thorough under-standing of these contracts, we recommend Jack Marrion's *Index Annuities: Power and Performance*, available at www.indexannuity.org), but we will look now at certain features that are common to several, or even all, index annu-ities.

"High Water Mark"

In this variation on the Term End Point design, index-linked interest (if any) is credited based on the difference between the starting index value and the highest value of the index (usually, at policy anniversaries) during the peri-od. Although some contracts credit interest only at the end of the term, Marrion observes that most annuities using this method (which he labels"term high point") vest "any index gains, a bit each year, so you could get some or most of any gains if you surrender early."[8] Moreover, Marrion points out this method locks in the highest anniversary level of the index, so late peri-od index losses are avoided.

Averaging

Another method to protect the annuity owner from the impact of a severe decline in the index value at the end of the term is averaging index values for the purpose of calculating index-based gains. Most index annuities today (Marrion estimates that more than 75%) average at least some portion of index values. Many point-to-point contracts will use the average of the last year's values, and most index annuities sold are annual reset contracts that use averaging. Averaging has the effect of driving numbers to the middle, and "smoothing" index performance, but its true impact on that performance is often misunderstood. Clearly, it prevents the annuity owner from finishing a year locked into the lowest index point of that year, but it also guarantees that he will never hit the highest point. Less obvious, however, is the fact that, while averaging always drives values to the middle, this "does not mean that index annuities using averaging will have half the return of an index annuity with a point-to-point design because averaging structures typically have higher rates or higher caps or lower spreads than unaveraged ones."[9] The bottom line, for the issuing insurer, is a simple choice. "If you do not use averaging in an index formula, you will either have a lower participation rate and/or need to use a cap to limit gains."[10]

Guaranteed Interest Rates

Some index annuities guarantee the crediting of a minimum amount of interest to the owner's entire investment. Others guarantee it to only a percentage (often, 80% or 90%) of that investment. The latter arrangement can produce confusion as to the minimum interest the annuity owner is guaranteed to receive. For example, many contracts guarantee 3% interest on 90% of the amount invested. This may appear to mean that the interest rate guaranteed is an annual compound rate of 2.7%, credited to the amount invested. This is not correct! The principal on which the 3% interest is credited is only 90 cents for each dollar invested. Thus, on a $100,000 single premium, the guaranteed future value, at the end of 10 years would be $FV=PV(1+I)^n$, or $90,000 * 1.03 \wedge 10 = $120,952$. The compound rate of return required to produce $120,952 at the end of 10 years, if one invests $100,000 today, is 1.92%. The effective guaranteed minimum rate on the entire amount invested is, thus, 1.92%, not 2.7%.

Will that guaranteed minimum interest be paid if the owner of the annuity surrenders the contract before the end of the term? According to Marrion, "guaranteed interest is almost always credited at the end of the surrender period and not each year."[11] The owner surrendering an annuity that is not an annual reset design, or one that otherwise "vests" interest (as some "high water mark" designs do), will generally receive no index-linked interest, if surrender occurs prior to the end of the term. In this case, the individual would simply receive a return of the original premiums paid, and any guaranteed interest payable if applicable. Moreover, surrender charges may apply.

Surrender Charges

Surrender charges in index annuities work just like the surrender charges in other annuity contracts. However, the size of the charges, and the length of time during which they apply, is generally higher in index annuities. Some IAs do not impose surrender charges as such, but base the surrender value on the guaranteed minimum amount (based on crediting of interest to less than the full investment). This has the same effect as a declining surrender charge over the first few years of the contract.

Free Withdrawals

As is typically the case with both conventional fixed and variable annuities, IAs usually permit withdrawals of up to a specified percentage of the cash value each year without imposing surrender charges.

However, if the client feels that there is a significant likelihood of a need to tap the money in the index annuity before the expiration of the surrender charge period, we suggest that the annuity may not be appropriate in the first place. As was noted, surrender charges in index annuities typically are higher and last longer than those in other annuity contracts, so an early distribution in excess of the amount permitted under the "free withdrawal" feature could be subjected to a stiff penalty. Moreover, any distribution, whether surrender charges apply or not, could be subject to the 10% early distribution penalty. Moreover, as discussed earlier, an early partial surrender could cause forfeiture of any accumulated equity-linked interest, or guaranteed minimum interest, to the extent attributable to the withdrawal taken. In short, the authors believe that annuities in general, and index annuities in particular, are of questionable appropriateness when liquidity is an issue.[12]

"Premium Bonus"

Many index annuities offer a premium bonus, whereby the contract owner is credited with an additional percentage of the premium actually paid, which will earn interest on the same basis as paid premium, provided that the contract is not surrendered before the end of the term. However, this bonus is not "free." Often, contracts offering a premium bonus require higher surrender charges or longer surrender charge periods or a lower participation rate, compared to contracts without the bonus. In some contracts, the difference is not reflected in lower benefits for the owner, but, rather, in a lower commission paid to the selling agent.

Required Annuitization

Some index annuities require the contract to be annuitized for certain benefits to be payable or provide lower levels of benefits (such as participation rate) for contracts that are surrendered for a lump sum–even if held to the end of the required term. The value of annuitization is, as will be discussed in a later chapter, a very controversial issue in the financial services community. The authors do not subscribe to the widespread belief that it is always a bad decision. However, it seems only logical to observe that, whatever value the annuity owner places on annuitization, an obligation to take proceeds in that form would not be attractive to a rational investor in the absence of some benefit not available without that requirement.

How Can the Insurance Company Do All This?

A question often asked by consumers is "How can the insurance company do all this?" (guarantee principal plus a minimum rate of interest and participation in exceptional upside movements in the underlying index). Where's the catch? When this question is asked, it usually means that the advisor has done a poor job of explaining how the index annuity works. It may look too good to be true. This is certainly true when the advisor has said something like "with this annuity, you get the upside of the equity market, but with no downside risk."

That is just not true! The index annuity owner does not "get the upside of the equity market", but only a portion of that growth. The portion of any index growth he or she gets is determined by the various limiting factors–the "moving parts"–in the contract design. These moving parts are essential for the issuing insurer to limit its loss exposure. After all, it is guaranteeing the purchaser's principal from any loss of principal and a minimum rate of return (if the contract is held for the full term).

Typically, the insurer purchases a combination of bonds and call options on the underlying index to guarantee the funds required to meet its obligations under the contract. The greatest part of the purchaser's premium is invested in bonds, in sufficient amount to provide the dollars needed to meet the insurer's minimum obligations. The remainder is used to buy those call options. The price of the call options (to fund the indexed-linked interest) and the cost and yield of bonds (to fund the contractual guarantees) together determine how many options the insurer can purchase with a given premium. If option prices, at a particular time, are low (because expected index volatility is low) and bond yields are high, it might be possible for the insurer, at that time, to purchase enough index options to provide the annuity owner with 100% of the performance of the index, in addition to guaranteeing principal and the minimum interest rate.

As of the time of this writing, such is not the case. Interest rates are near historic lows and option prices are relatively high (because index performance is expected to be more than "usually" volatile). So, at this time, insurers do not have enough left over, from an index annuity purchaser's premium, after purchasing the bonds required, to buy enough index options to give that purchaser 100% of the index performance, on the premium invested. For that reason, today's participation rates and cap rates are relatively low and yield spreads are relatively high. Issuers of index annuities are not–at this time–purchasing options for all possible growth–because they can't. But they don't need to–because today's participation rates, caps, and yield spreads limit the amount of that growth they're obliged to credit to their annuities.

This is precisely why, when an annuity owner is limited to a 70% participation rate or a cap of, say, 9%, and the index goes up 15%, the insurer does not "keep" the excess return above the 10.5% it would credit under a 70% participation rate or the 9% it would credit under the cap. It does not purchase enough options to get 100% of the growth on the entire amount of that annuity owner's premium. There is no need to do so, nor is there enough paid-in premium left over, after purchase of the bonds, to do so. The insurer does not keep that excess because it does not receive it.

But why can't the insurer guarantee the level of the various moving parts–the cap rate, participation rate, and yield spread, for example. It may guarantee some of these factors, but it cannot guarantee all of them and expect to remain in business. Why?

It is because financial markets change. Interest rates change, and, with them, the cost of the bonds the insurer will purchase to meet minimum contractual guarantees. So do the cost of index options. The cost of options increases with the volatility (or expected volatility) of the index and the length of time over which they are exercisable. If an insurer chooses to guarantee the participation rate, cap rate, or yield spread for the entire term, it cannot offer as high a participation rate and cap rate, or as low a yield spread, as if it reserves the right to adjust those factors periodically, because it will not be able to purchase as many options, because the cost of those options will be higher. For these reasons, nearly all index annuities do not guarantee all the moving parts for the entire term. This is particularly true of annual reset contracts, where the insurer will need to continue purchasing call options in the future at an unknown cost.

Because the issuing insurer can adjust these moving parts periodically, to reflect changing economic realities, it is essential that the advisor choose an insurer with a good record of renewing these rates so as to treat existing contract holders fairly. The authors strongly suggest that advisors ask the issuer of any index annuity (or fixed annuity, for that matter) they are considering for a history of renewal rates.

Which Index Annuity Design is Best?

Perhaps the most common question asked by advisors who are considering index annuities for their clients is "which kind is best?" In the authors' opinion, the only reasonable answer is: "It depends." As Jack Marrion points out in his book, "any crediting method can produce the best return for a given period."[13] There are, however, certain general observations that one can make, regarding index annuity policy designs.

Annual Reset

With an annual reset index annuity, the purchaser knows, at the end of each year, how much her annuity is worth. Interest is calculated, credited, and locked-in each year. Future decreases in the index will not reduce the annuity value. The biggest trade off to this is that the participation rate, cap rate, or yield spread is likely to be lower than in other designs. These contracts generally excel in markets with high volatility (although such volatility tends to increase option costs and reduce participation rate or increase yield spread).

High Water Mark

The high water mark design protects the annuity owner from a decline in the index at the end of the term, which could wipe out much (or even all) of the gain previously experienced (but not credited). However, the rates for the various moving parts are likely to be less attractive than for a contract with a point-to-point design with the same term.

Point-to-Point

The point-to-point design does not allow the purchaser to know the value of the annuity until the end of the term. However, the rates for the moving parts are likely to be greater than for other policy designs with the same term. In addition, because many or all of the bonds and call options are put in place when the contract is acquired, point-to-point contracts tend to have fewer moving parts that may be changed after the contract is initially acquired.

Chapter Endnotes

1. The gain realized in an index annuity is interest, not dividends or capital gains.

2. The S&P 500, or S&P 500 Composite Price Index, was created by the Standard & Poor's Company in 1923. The S&P 500 is "calculated using a base-weighted aggregate methodology, meaning the level of the Index reflects the total market value of all component stocks relative to a particular base period. Total market value is determined by multiplying the price of its stock by the number of shares outstanding." (Quoted from Standard & Poor's website.)

3. SPDR is the exchange symbol for the S&P 500 Index Fund, an exchange traded fund, and stands for Standard & Poor's Depository Receipt.

4. Some index annuities guarantee only a zero rate of return. Most guarantee a rate of at least 3%, which might be credited to only a percentage (such as 80% or 90%) of the premiums received.

5. Some of the material in this section was taken from the *Buyer's Guide To Equity-Indexed Annuities*, prepared by the National Association of Insurance Commissioners, reprinted by the Illinois Division of Insurance at www.ins.state.il.us/Life_Annuities/equityindex.htm.

6. Purchase of equity "call" options is the usual mechanism used by issuers of index annuities to guarantee the funds to pay the equity-linked interest. However, other methods may be used, or the insurer may "go naked" and self-insure that equity-linked interest payment liability (see Jack Marrion, "Index Annuities: Power & Protection" (Advantage Compendium, 2003), p. 107).

7. Jack Marrion, "Index Annuities: Power & Protection" (Advantage Compendium, 2003), p. 48

8. *Ibid*, p. 66.

9. *Ibid*, p. 81.

10. *Ibid*, p. 80.

11. *Ibid*, p. 30.

12. Annuities with no surrender charges are, arguably at least, a separate case. However, even without surrender charges, it is still important to understand that any uncredited gains may be lost by early withdrawals, to the extent of gains attributable to the withdrawal.

13. Marrion, p. 85.

Chapter 8

Annuities and Trusts

As a financial asset, an annuity is necessarily part of the overall financial and estate plan of its purchaser. However, it is sometimes not well coordinated with the other components. Indeed, the ownership and beneficiary arrangement of an annuity may be inconsistent with–or even in conflict with–the rest of a client's plan. Not uncommonly, this results from an advisor's decision to employ the annuity in connection with a trust without a full understanding of the rules governing both. In the following discussion, we will examine some of the problems advisors may encounter when annuities are owned by, or made payable to, a trust, and the rules–tax rules and the contractual provisions and administrative policies of annuity issuers–that are not well understood. For most of the following discussion, we will be concerned only with deferred annuities. Not only are most annuities sold of this type, but the Internal Revenue Code (IRC) provisions that cause most of the difficulties where annuities are owned by or payable to a trust–Section 72(u) and certain paragraphs of Section 72(s)–do not apply to immediate annuities. We will also be concerned only with non-qualified contracts, as qualified annuities (or annuities used to fund IRAs) cannot be owned by a trust, other than the trust for the type of plan being funded.

Problematic Annuity Structuring with Trusts

Problems can arise when a deferred annuity is –

- Owned by and payable to a trust

- Owned by a trust and payable to another party

- Payable to a trust and owned by another party

When an annuity is owned by a trust, the "holder" of the annuity is deemed, by IRC section 72(s)(6)(A),[1] to be the primary annuitant.[2] It is vital that the advisor understand that this provision applies with regard to distributions required to be made from the annuity upon death of the holder by Section 72(s), if the annuity is to be considered an annuity for income tax purposes. What if a particular annuity does not provide for payment upon the primary annuitant's death, when the annuity is owned by a trust? The result is a conflict–an incongruity. This incongruity can pose serious problems, as will be discussed later in this chapter.

Also, as was discussed in Chapter 2, an annuity owned by a trust (or other "non-natural person") will not be considered an annuity for income tax purposes unless the owning entity is acting as the "agent of a natural person."[3] This requirement, too, is a source of potential problems. Although many trusts qualify as such agents, not all do (see Chapter 2).

When a trust is the beneficiary of an annuity, that annuity is subject to distribution requirements different from those applying when the beneficiary is an individual (i.e., a "natural person"). These requirements apply whether or not the trust is also the holder of the annuity.

Annuity-Trust Situations

Where Trust Owns Annuity

1. The Annuity is Owned By a Revocable Living Trust

A curiosity that advisors frequently encounter is a deferred annuity contract owned by a client's Revocable Living Trust (hereafter referred to as "RLT"). It is curious, because there is often little reason for it. Sometimes, the annuity was transferred into the RLT because someone felt that "everything ought to be in the trust." But there can be some problems with this arrangement.

First, we should ask–what is to be gained by owning a deferred annuity inside an RLT? RLTs avoid probate, of course, which is often a main reason for establishing these trusts. But annuity death benefits pass to beneficiaries outside probate anyway, by operation of the annuity contract, so probate avoidance is not a good reason for putting an annuity in an RLT. Another, and better, reason might be a desire to have annuity death proceeds distributed under the terms of that trust, which terms can be far more flexible than a normal beneficiary designation. But that does not require that the annuity be owned by the trust, merely that it be payable to the trust. Another reason might be to avoid problems that could arise upon the annuity owner's becoming incompetent. Yet a properly drafted Durable Power of Attorney may suffice for this purpose.

Thus, nearly all of the benefits just described can be achieved by other means (or by virtue of the annuity itself), without inviting the problems connected with naming the RLT as the annuity owner.

2.   The Annuity is Transferred To Owner's Irrevocable Trust

A common reason for an owner to transfer ownership of a deferred annuity to his irrevocable trust is to remove its value from his taxable estate. Can this create problems? Perhaps. IRC section 72(e)(4)(C) says that:

If an individual who holds an annuity contract transfers it without full and adequate consideration, such individual shall be treated as receiving an amount equal to the excess of–

(I) the cash surrender value of such contract at the time of transfer, over

(II) the investment in such contract at such time,

under the contract as an amount not received as an annuity.

In other words, such a transfer will trigger recognition of all the gain in the contract. The only statutory exception to this rule is a gift to holder's spouse.[4]

But what if the receiving trust is a grantor trust? Under the grantor trust rules of IRC Sections 671-677, there is no income tax consequence to transfers from an individual to his grantor trust. And Section 72 is an income tax provision. Thus, under those rules, an individual holding a highly appreciated deferred annuity can transfer ownership of that annuity to a grantor trust and avoid income tax gain recognition, and the value of the annuity will also not be includible in the estate for federal estate tax purposes if the trust is otherwise not includable. Trusts that are not part of the transferor's estate for estate tax purposes while still considered grantor trusts for income tax purposes are generally called intentionally defective grantor trusts (IDGTs). Of course, such a transfer for less than adequate consideration is probably a gift (in the case of a IDGT), but the gift tax liability for such a transfer may, in some situations, be less onerous than the estate tax liability thus avoided (particularly if annual exclusion gifts are available).

An alternative might be the sale of the annuity to the trust, perhaps in exchange for a balloon note, private annuity, or self-canceling installment note (SCIN). Such a sale would still not trigger income tax consequences, under the grantor trust rules,[5] and would allow the owner to avoid gift tax consequences on the transfer in exchange for the cash flow and estate tax consequences of using such devices.

Would the transfer of an annuity to the owner's trust produce different results with regard to the death benefit of the annuity? If the annuity owner is also the annuitant, and will remain annuitant after the transfer of the annuity to the trust, the answer is no. But if the owner is not the annuitant, the answer may be a surprising–and possibly alarming–yes. We will examine this scenario, later, as we consider the implications of having a trust named as beneficiary of a non-qualified annuity.

Where Trust is Beneficiary of Annuity

Naming a trust as beneficiary of a non-qualified deferred annuity is even more common than naming the trust as owner of that annuity. As was noted above, the transfer is sometimes for no other reason than a belief that "everything should be in the trust." Often, however, the reason is deliberate–because trusts allow greater dispositive freedom. The settlement provisions of most annuity contracts are fairly standardized; a trust can provide far greater flexibility.

What is often not well understood–or, in some instances, understood at all–is that when an annuity is payable to a trust–or to any beneficiary other than a natural person–the Internal Revenue Code imposes special restrictions as to when and how distributions must be made and a special rule as to whose death will trigger such distributions. We noted, in Chapter 3, that IRC section 72(h) governs payments to beneficiaries of annuities and when those payment elections must be made. However, Section 72(h) is not the only sub-section that addresses beneficiary payments. As also mentioned in Chapter 3, IRC section 72(s) imposes its own requirements. So let's review the rules of Section 72(s) that apply to all payments of annuity proceeds to any beneficiaries.

IRC section 72(s) says that any annuity contract issued since January 18, 1985, in order to be considered an annuity in the first place, must provide that, upon the death of the annuity holder, proceeds will be distributed in accordance with the following rules:

Distribution Requirements for Annuity Contracts

Section 72(s)(1) discusses the basic provisions regarding annuity distributions that all annuity contracts must contain.

It says that if the death occurred after the annuity starting date (where the contract was an immediate annuity or a deferred annuity after annuitization commenced), the proceeds must be distributed "at least as rapidly as under the method of distributions being used as of the date of his death."[6]

But what if the deceased was holder of a deferred annuity and had not yet elected to annuitize? In that event, the proceeds must be distributed within five years of the holder's death.[7]

The next paragraph provides an exception to this rule, allowing the beneficiary to take proceeds over life expectancy (or a period not exceeding life expectancy).[8] However, this requires that the annuity be payable "to (or for the benefit of) a designated beneficiary."[9] And Section 72(s)(4) says, quite plainly, that "for purposes of this subsection, the term 'designated beneficiary' means any individual designated a beneficiary by the holder of the contract."

The key word, here, is "individual." An "individual" is a natural person. And a trust is not a natural person.

Section 72(s)(3) provides an even more liberal exception. If the designated beneficiary is the spouse of the holder, that spouse may elect to treat the annuity as her own, and continue tax deferral, with no mandatory distribution.

Trusts Under the Annuity Distribution Rules

So what happens if the deferred annuity is payable to a trust? A trust is not an individual, and, thus, cannot be a designated beneficiary. It certainly cannot be a spouse. Must a trust that is the beneficiary of a non-qualified annuity take proceeds within five years, with no opportunity for stretching out payments based on a life expectancy or for electing spousal continuation?

Some commentators believe that other alternatives are available. One argument asserts that because Section 72(s)(2)(A), in defining when the annuitization option of Section 72(s)(2)(B) will be permitted, requires only that the holder's interest be "payable to (*or for the benefit of*) [authors' emphasis] a designated beneficiary", then, if the trust is acting as the "agent of a natural person," and if that natural person is the sole beneficiary of the trust, it follows that the trust is acting "for the benefit of" that "designated beneficiary," and should be able to take proceeds over a period not exceeding the life expectancy of that designated beneficiary, so long as payments commence within one year of death.

However, the authors believe that the agency argument just stated, however elegant, avoids the fact that Section 72(s)(4) is really quite precise. It says:

> For purposes of this subsection, the term "designated beneficiary" means any individual designated a beneficiary by the holder of the contract.

There is no opportunity for agency here. To be a "designated beneficiary," an individual must be designated as such by the holder of the contract. He or she may not acquire that status by imputation—Section 72(s)(4) does not state that a designated beneficiary may be "any individual, or a non-natural agent for that individual." If the beneficiary shown in the annuity contract and appearing on the application for that annuity is a trust, the trust is the party designated as a beneficiary. But a trust cannot be a designated beneficiary, because that term, in the very specific context of Section 72(s)(4), must be an individual. As the trust, the only entity which was actually "designated" by the holder to be the beneficiary is not an individual, and, therefore, not a designated beneficiary, the annuity has no designated beneficiary. Therefore, the annuitization option of Section 72(s)(2) is unavailable.

Another argument for the availability of the Section 72(s)(2) option holds that Congress, in enacting Section 72(s), intended to provide parity between the rules governing distributions from qualified plans and IRAs, and those governing distributions from non-qualified annuities. The legislative history of Section 72 shows such intent, and the structure of that section certainly resembles that of Section 401(a)(9). Therefore, it is argued, it is only logical that we look through the trust to the individual trust beneficiaries in applying the required distribution rules, in the same manner that existing regulations permit a look through of a trust named as beneficiary of a qualified plan or IRA.

It may be logical for us to do so, but the authors do not believe that existing rules offer any authority for such a position, and, unfortunately, the IRS has not seen fit to provide much guidance in this area. In addition, it is important to note that the existing Treasury Regulations which allow look-through trust treatment are fairly new[10] in the context of a section of the Internal Revenue Code that has existed for much longer. Furthermore, the IRS has explicitly noted other situations where the provisions that apply to retirement accounts are intended to apply to annuities,[11] and their failure to announce any such parity regarding look-through trust treatment should inspire caution.

However, there is one holding[12] that affirms not only the availability of the annuitization option Section 72(s)(2), but also the spousal continuation option of Section 72(s)(3), where the beneficiary was a trust. However, the fact situation was extremely unusual. The surviving spouse/grantor/trustee had, according to the ruling, such "complete control and dominion" over the trust assets (which included two annuity contracts) that she was permitted to treat herself, individually, as the designated beneficiary of the annuities and exercise the spousal continuation option of Section 72(s)(3).[13]

What does this ruling suggest about the willingness of the IRS to ignore the existence of other trusts named as annuity beneficiaries and to look through to the trust beneficiaries in applying Section 72(s) rules? In the authors' opinion, very little. This ruling is an anomaly. The fact situation was, as we noted, very unusual. In a normal context, trusts established for other individuals will not allow complete dominion and control over the trust assets (otherwise, one might contend, why establish the trust in the first place?), and consequently will not be able to apply the facts of this ruling. Moreover, we have been unable to locate any other ruling regarding annuities that arrived at a similar conclusion. Despite arguments that Congress intended parity between the rules governing non-qualified annuities and qualified plans, and that a trust as a beneficiary is merely an agent acting for the benefit of individuals who should be deemed to be designated beneficiaries, existing law and rulings, in the authors' opinion, support only a conclusion that a trust named as beneficiary of a non-qualified will not be able to elect the annuitization option of Section 72(s)(2) or the spousal continuation option of Section 72(s)(3). Moreover, most insurance companies are unwilling to permit trust beneficiaries to elect these options.

At this point, the authors want to make clear–and to emphasize–that Section 72(s) does not say how death benefits will be paid from any particular annuity contract. The contract itself will govern. Section 72(s) merely dictates what provisions must be in an annuity contract (issued since January 18, 1985) if that contract is to qualify as an annuity for income tax purposes in the first place. It is entirely possible that an annuity contract may contain provisions that are perfectly legal and enforceable (i.e.; they do not violate principles of contract law, public policy, etc.), but that might violate the requirements of Section 72(s), such that the contract would not qualify as an annuity under that subsection.

Let's look at an example of such a potential conflict–specifically of the congruity or incongruity between when death distributions from an annuity owned by a trust must be made by law and when they will be made under terms of the annuity contract.

Annuities and Consistency with Section 72(s)

Annuity contracts issued since January 18, 1985 must require distribution of proceeds, in accordance with the rules of Section 72(s), upon the death of the holder. All annuities issued since that date require distribution of the annuity proceeds to the beneficiary upon the death of the owner of the annuity contract.[14] (These are called "owner driven" contracts). Some, but not all, annuities will also pay a death benefit upon the death of the annuitant. (These are called "annuitant-driven" contracts. Actually, they are both owner-driven and annuitant-driven).

When either type of annuity is owned by an individual, the death of the owner will always trigger payment of a death benefit[15] under the terms of the annuity contract (i.e., by the terms of a provision the annuity contract must contain under the death-of-holder rules of Section 72(s)). Here, owner and holder refer to the same individual, and when that individual dies and a payout occurs, the requirements of Section 72(s) that the owner's "entire interest in the contract" be distributed at the owner's death are satisfied.

But where the annuity is owned by a trust, the triggering event for the distribution required under Section 72(s) may not be the same as the event causing payment of any death benefit under the terms of the annuity contract. Section 72(s) mandates a distribution upon the death of the holder of an annuity. Where an annuity is owned by a trust (or other "non-natural person"), Section 72(s)(6)(A) deems the holder of the annuity to be the primary annuitant "for purposes of this subsection."[16] Thus, for Section 72(s) purposes (that is, for purposes of "Required Distributions Where Holder Dies Before

Entire Interest Is Distributed"), an annuity owned by a trust, must, by its terms, require that the entire interest in the annuity will be distributed upon the death of the annuitant.

The problem–the incongruity–is that some annuity contracts do not contain this requirement. Some annuities state that, where the contract is owned by a trust, the contract value (but not necessarily the guaranteed minimum death benefit) will be distributed upon the death of the primary annuitant. No problem here. But at least one contract the authors have read contains language that appears to contravene the rule stated above (that an annuity owned by a trust, must, by its terms, require that the entire interest in the annuity will be distributed upon the death of the annuitant). In the section on "Death Benefit" in the prospectus, it states -

> If the Annuity is owned by one or more natural persons, the Death Benefit is payable upon the first death of an Owner. If the Annuity is owned by an entity, the Death Benefit is payable upon the Annuitant's death, if there is no Contingent Annuitant. If a Contingent Annuitant was designated before the Annuitant's death and the Annuitant dies, then the Contingent Annuitant becomes the Annuitant and a Death Benefit will not be paid at that time. The person upon whose death the Death Benefit is paid is referred to below as the "decedent."

Note that, while this provision does direct that the death benefit be paid upon the death of the primary annuitant if no contingent annuitant had been named, it denies a payment when a contingent annuitant had been named (and elevates that contingent annuitant to the status of primary annuitant). Whatever the reason for this provision, the authors believe that it clearly violates the requirements of Section 72(s) and that the IRS could, as a consequence, declare that every annuity issued with these terms fails to qualify as "an annuity" for income tax purposes.[17] Is this likely? The contract in question has been marketed since 2000, and the IRS has not, to the authors' knowledge, raised this issue. Moreover, the legal department of the issuing insurance company evidently believes that the provision does not violate the Section 72(s) rules.

Is this merely nit-picking on the part of the authors of this book? Perhaps it is. But we believe it is more than that. Whether the contract provision cited above actually does violate the required distribution rules of Section 72(s) is just one issue, and perhaps the authors' conclusion is wrong. But that cited provision is also an example of another issue–one that is absolutely vital to the financial well being of financial advisors who sell or offer counsel about annuities and the clients of those advisors. That issue is this:

> The contractual provisions of every annuity you deal with will determine how the various benefits of that annuity will be provided or not provided. If you, the advisor, do not understand what those provisions say–and what they mean–you cannot tell your client when–or whether–he will receive those benefits.

Many advisors rely upon the marketing materials, home office marketing representatives, or external wholesalers of insurance companies for their understanding of those companies' insurance products. To be sure, these sources can be very helpful. But they may not be sufficient. And sometimes, they are either unclear or just plain wrong.[18] Those of us who are not licensed attorneys cannot, and should not, "practice law". But we can, should, and must exercise due care in our advisory activities. With regard to annuities, the authors strongly recommend that advisors consider the following caveats:

1.   Avoid naming a trust as annuity owner unless –

  a.   There is *very* good reason for doing so, and

  b.   You are sure of *all* of the results of the designation (including when the insurance company will pay a benefit and under what conditions any death benefit enhancements will be payable).

2.   Avoid naming a trust as beneficiary–for the same reasons.

3.   Avoid naming different individuals as owner and annuitant–for the same reasons.[19] This is a good rule to observe, whether a trust is involved or not.

4.   If the owner and annuitant will be two different individuals, know whether the contract you are considering is annuitant-driven or not.

The above list is not a complete recitation of "things to know, and avoid" about annuities, merely the authors' suggestions of the most vital caveats to consider when annuities and trusts are both involved. A better general caveat might be: "Be sure that you understand how, and under what conditions, the annuity you are considering will deliver, or not deliver, all the benefits provided by that annuity."

Chapter Endnotes

1. This provision applies to any annuity owned by an entity other than a "natural person," including a corporation, partnership, or trust.

2. "Primary annuitant" is defined by IRC Sec. 72(s)(6)(B) as "the individual, the events in the life of whom are of primary importance in affecting the timing or amount of the payout under the contract."

3. IRC Sec. 72(u).

4. IRC Sec. 72(e)(4)(C)(ii).

5. There are no income or gift tax consequences of transfers from a taxpayer to himself, whether by gift or sale.

6. IRC Sec. 72(s)(1)(A).

7. IRC Sec. 72(s)(1)(B).

8. IRC Sec. 72(s)(2).

9. IRC Sec. 72(s)(2)(A).

10. Amendments to Treas. Reg. §1.401(a)(9)-4 became effective on April 15, 2002.

11. For example, IRS Notice 2004-15 explicitly established cross-application of the rules under IRC Sec. 72(t)(2)(A)(iv) regarding substantially equal periodic payments from retirement accounts to the same type of payments under annuities and IRC Sec. 72(q)(2)(D).

12. Let. Rul. 200323012.

13. In addition, the spouse was permitted to make a tax-free exchange of the annuities, under IRC Sec. 1035, for new annuity contracts owned by herself.

14. An exception to this general rule exists where an annuity is jointly owned. See Chapter 3.

15. We have said "*a* death benefit", rather than "*the* death benefit" because annuitant-driven contracts typically pay the contractually-guaranteed *guaranteed* minimum (or "enhanced") death benefit only upon the death of the annuitant. In these contracts, the amount payable to the beneficiary upon the death of the owner is only the cash value of the annuity (and, in some contracts, a surrender charge may apply).

16. "This subsection" refers to IRC Sec. 72(s).

17. Presumably, the most immediate consequence would be that all these contracts were not in fact tax-deferred, and that income attributable to the contract for prior years should be declared as taxable income, with retroactive interest (and potential penalties) applicable to any years not closed by the statute of limitations.

18. Most experienced advisors have at least a few horror stories of home office marketing reps or wholesalers who made statements about the operation or tax treatment of an insurance product that were totally inaccurate. The authors have more than a few of these stories as well.

19. The potential problems resulting from different individuals named as the annuitant and owner are so common and serious that some insurance companies refuse to issue contracts on this basis.

Chapter 9

Annuities in Estate Planning

Chapter 8 examined the annuity as an investment, in the context of a 3-legged stool model. This chapter will focus on how various kinds of annuities can work in a more specific context – that of estate planning.

Avoidance of Probate

One of the estate planning reasons often cited for buying (or recommending) an annuity is that values in such contracts generally pass to beneficiaries directly, through the beneficiary designation, and are not subject to the probate process. This is true, but one does not need to purchase an annuity to achieve this result. Assets held in trust or taxable accounts titled as POD (payable on death) or TOD (transfer on death) also bypass probate.[1]

However, annuity beneficiary designations and the beneficiary designations permitted by state laws regulating POD and TOD accounts typically do not allow the degree of dispositive flexibility offered by a well-drafted trust. Moreover, values in an annuity may be includable, under state law, in the owner's augmented estate and subject to a surviving spouse's elective share.[2] If includable, an election by such spouse to take such share could cause the annuity value to be subject to probate, and to pass other than by the beneficiary designation to someone besides the named beneficiary. Whether this is an issue is a matter of state law, so advisors should check the rules in those jurisdictions in which they practice.

That said, the fact that annuity values do generally pass directly to named beneficiaries, outside of probate, is significant, and may be a valuable advantage for many clients.

Providing Guaranteed Income to Heirs

A principal goal of many estate plans is to provide income to the estate owner's heirs. This goal can often be achieved by using either immediate or deferred annuities. Where the goal is to provide heirs with an immediate income, an immediate annuity may be the ideal mechanism, especially if the income is to continue for the recipient's lifetime. The certainty afforded by such a contract is sometimes more important than the amount of each income payment or the fact that the annuity income does not preserve principal. This may be particularly appropriate to satisfy specific beneficiary lifetime income bequests from a portion of assets while the remainder passes to another beneficiary.[3]

Where the desire is for the heir's income to increase over time (perhaps to keep pace with inflation), an immediate annuity providing for known annual increases is often attractive. While most insurers do not offer immediate annuities with cost of living increases tied to some index such as the consumer price index, some do, and more are likely to be offering such contracts in the future in response to a demand that appears to be increasing. An additional attraction is that annuities enjoy creditor protection in most jurisdictions.

A disadvantage to immediate annuities, in this context (and others), is their inflexibility. Most immediate annuities, once begun, do not permit modification of the payment amount or commutation, although an increasing number of contracts do.

Purchase of a SPIA by a Credit Shelter Trust

One application of immediate annuities which may be of interest to estate planners is their use to solve the trustee's investment dilemma. Often, a trust (e.g., a credit shelter trust) is established to provide both an income to an income beneficiary (perhaps the surviving spouse) and growth of principal, for the benefit of remainder beneficiaries (perhaps the children and/or grandchildren). The dilemma for the trustee is satisfying the opposing desires of these beneficiaries. The income beneficiary wishes to receive as much income as possible, and would prefer that trust monies be invested to provide that goal. Remainder beneficiaries are interested in capital accumulation, and prefer that the trust be funded with growth investments. The problem, of course, is that investments which provide high current income rarely offer good long term growth – and vice versa.

This conflict has always presented problems for trustees. A possible solution might be for the trust to purchase an immediate annuity, naming the income beneficiary as annuitant, in an amount sufficient to provide the income the beneficiary requires (perhaps increasing over time), and to invest all remaining trust assets solely for growth – without regard for whether they produce any current income. Adverse results in the growth investments will have no effect upon the income beneficiary. This strategy does not always work, of course. Financially, its attractiveness may appear to be directly proportional to the age of the income beneficiary/annuitant – because, the older the annuitant, the greater the income that each dollar of premium will purchase (or, viewed another way, the less premium required to produce each dollar of income), assuming that the annuity is to continue for the annuitant's life. However, it's also arguable that older income beneficiaries are likely to die sooner, and that an annuity that expires without value at the beneficiary's death may be perceived as a bad deal. The existence of a refund element may reduce this objection.

Whether a refund feature should be included in the annuity is, however, problematic. A life only annuity will require a smaller premium than one providing a benefit to another beneficiary if the annuitant (the income beneficiary of the trust) should die prematurely. This would allow a greater percentage of the trust corpus to be allocated to growth investments, for the benefit of remainder beneficiaries. However, many people (including many advisors) find unacceptable an annuity that provides no further benefit if an annuitant dies shortly after income payments commence. The perception is that the insurance company keeps this extra money. This perception is false; the money is not retained by the insurer, but is paid out by that insurer to other members of the risk sharing pool – annuitants who lived longer than their expected lifetimes. That said, the perception may be its own reality. Most people will not buy a life only annuity and would probably prefer that such an annuity not be purchased for anyone of whom they might become remainder beneficiary.

Purchase of an Immediate Annuity for Heirs Outside a Trust

Sometimes, an estate owner's goals include providing a specific, and certain, income for specified heirs, apart from the overall dispositive provisions of the estate plan. Here, an immediate annuity is arguably the perfect instrument. Without the certainty of the annuity, a trustee or executor must take into account the market risk involved when invested assets must be accessed each year to make payments to the beneficiary. Thus, the use of an annuity may allow the trustee/executor to invest more money immediately on behalf of the other beneficiaries while still guaranteeing that the income beneficiary will receive all promised payments.

Purchase of a Deferred Annuity for Heirs

Where estate planning goals include providing a certain income for heirs to begin at some future time, a deferred annuity may make sense. Advantages include tax deferral of current gains, which can be of considerable importance if the annuity is owned by a trust subject to the compressed tax rates applicable to nongrantor trusts,[4] creditor protection (to the extent allowed by relevant law) where the annuity is owned outside a trust, and the risk management and investment characteristics of deferred annuities discussed at length in earlier chapters of this book. Disadvantages include the overhead cost of the annuity, which may be higher than that of alternative investments, surrender charges (if applicable), the fact that all distributions from an annuity are taxed at ordinary income rates, and the unavailability of a step-up in basis for annuities owned by a decedent.

Purchase of a SPIA by the Estate Owner for the Estate Owner (and Spouse)

Impact on the Attractiveness of Making Lifetime Gifts to Heirs

A primary goal of many (if not all) estate owners is to ensure income for themselves for their lifetimes. This goal often surfaces in discussions between clients and advisors when considering lifetime gifts. "I might need that money" is perhaps the most common objection raised by many clients to suggestions that they utilize the gift tax annual exclusion[5] in making lifetime gifts to heirs. To the extent that the estate owner is guaranteed that he or she (and his/her spouse, if applicable) can be assured of required income no matter what, annual gifts to heirs (whatever the reason for making them) may be far less worrisome. If, having secured this required income – perhaps by purchasing an immediate annuity – a client feels able to make more lifetime gifts than he or she otherwise would, the result can be both greater net wealth transferred to heirs (due to lower transfer tax and estate clearance costs) and greater emotional satisfaction. One can live to see his heirs enjoy lifetime gifts. One can also see how well such gifts are managed. For the parent or grandparent concerned that sizeable inheritances might spoil the kids, being able to see how well those kids deal with the money can be both gratifying and informing. If the kids mishandle such gifts, estate plans can be changed (perhaps by adding additional spendthrift provisions).

Implications for the Estate Owner's Asset Allocation Decisions

Even where lifetime gifts are not a concern, adequate income for the estate owner(s) is usually a key estate planning goal. "We want to provide for the kids and grandkids, but first we've got to take care of ourselves" is a refrain familiar to all estate planners. Allocating a portion of one's retirement portfolio to an instrument designed specifically to produce income can help one achieve this key planning objective, to the extent of making the allocation of remaining assets easier (or, at least, less worrisome). This can be done using either a deferred annuity or an immediate annuity.

Using the Guarantees in a Deferred Annuity to Provide Portfolio Insurance

A fixed deferred annuity provides three guarantees to its owner.

1. A guarantee of principal. The money invested in a fixed deferred annuity is guaranteed against loss by the insurer.

2. A guaranteed minimum rate of return.

3. Guaranteed annuity payout factors.

The first two guarantees provide a known minimum return, on the portion of one's portfolio allocated to the annuity, which has the effect of lowering the overall principal and interest rate risks of the entire portfolio. Moreover, the assurance that this known future value can be converted into an income stream that will provide at least a certain amount of money each year can make projections of one's future cash flows less problematic.

A variable deferred annuity does not offer the first two guarantees to the living policy owner (except to the extent that annuity values are invested in the fixed account). However, it provides others. The guaranteed death benefit always provides assurance that heirs (not the living policy owner) will receive, at a minimum, the amount originally invested or the account balance at death, if greater. Enhanced death benefit guarantees, common in newer variable contracts, can assure heirs of the greater of that original investment or account balance at death or some other potentially higher minimum amount (perhaps the account balance at some policy anniversary prior to death or the original investment, compounded at some specified rate of return). If the minimum amount that will pass to heirs is a serious estate planning concern, the guaranteed death benefit may be worth its cost.

The guaranteed living benefits in today's variable deferred annuities may provide even more comfort for the estate owner in making his asset allocation decisions, precisely because of the refrain noted earlier – namely: "We want to provide for the kids and grandkids, but first we've got to take care of ourselves." The guaranteed minimum income benefit, guaranteed minimum withdrawal benefit, guaranteed minimum accumulation benefit, and provisions combining all three features can assure the estate owner that, irrespective of the performance of the investments in the annuity, certain minimum income and/or future lump sum values will be available.

Many critics contend that the costs for these provisions outweigh the benefits that they are likely to provide. The mathematics supporting such a conclusion (if any are supplied) often rely upon historical averages and probable life expectancies. This is not to say that all such criticisms are invalid, or that the logic and mathematics are never valid or persuasive. They may be both. However, it is the authors' contention that the certainties that these riders provide can be very important to many estate owner clients on an emotional level – that these certainties, with regard to that part of a client's portfolio invested in annuities providing them, can enable him to make asset allocations with regard to that money that he might not otherwise feel comfortable making. In addition, it's important to note that even though the client may come out with less money in the long run on average, the client is still guaranteeing that a particular minimum amount will be available – which may be more consistent with a client's goals than merely having the most dollars at death by investing heavily in equities.

Many clients, especially older ones, are often wary of putting too much in the stock market, even though they know that equities have historically provided significantly better returns than fixed dollar investments such as CDs and bonds. To the extent that such a conservative (read: risk-intolerant) client's equity investments can be held in an investment account that guarantees minimum future lump sum and present and future income values, he may be willing to allocate more of his portfolio to such equities, and to remain invested in them longer, than if no such guarantees were available. For the client whose portfolio is not large enough to generate required income with reasonable certainty if invested very conservatively, this increased equity exposure might make the difference between an adequate income and just getting by – or even running out of money. Why might this be? Because that client might only be willing to invest substantially in equities if there are underlying guarantees, and would otherwise choose a much more conservative portfolio, with lower expected risk and return.

Using the Guaranteed Income of an Immediate Annuity to Reduce Retirement Portfolio Failure Rate

As noted, the risk management benefits of either a fixed or variable deferred annuity may allow some clients to invest their retirement portfolios (the portion invested in those annuities, but also, perhaps, more of the non-annuity portion) more aggressively, and with more confidence, than they might in the absence of these guarantees. The result of such a change in allocation should, over time, be an increase in the income produced, despite the expenses of the annuity. For retirees living on less than the amount their portfolios earn, this translates to greater capital accumulation – ultimately providing more wealth to transfer to heirs.

Yet many retirees do not live on less than what their investments earn. For all too many clients, the most important issue is not how much will be left to heirs after they die, but whether their portfolios will produce enough for them to live on, for as long as they live. Indeed, this uncertainty represents what one of the authors refers to as the one big risk in retirement income planning – a risk which can be stated in the form of a question – namely: "What are the chances that my account balance will fall to zero before my blood pressure does?" This risk can be managed, with considerable effectiveness, by use of immediate annuities. As was noted in the last chapter, there is mounting evidence that allocating a portion of one's retirement portfolio to a mechanism to provide immediate, certain income can produce a significant increase in the probability that the portfolio as a whole will be able to provide required income for the retiree's entire lifetime, however long that may be. The purchase of a life annuity, either for a level or an increasing annual benefit, can offset (to an extent proportional to the percentage of required retirement income provided by the annuity) the effects of negative dollar cost averaging (where more shares must be liquidated to provide a set amount of income after a decline in the value of those shares than would have had to be sold if the share price remained level or increased). But a life annuity is not the only way to implement this strategy. Laddered bonds or laddered period certain annuities may also be used. Whatever the implementation, this strategy can offset negative dollar cost averaging, decrease the probability that the retirement portfolio will be exhausted during retiree's lifetime (or produce declining income levels), and provide greater emotional comfort (although only an annuity guarantees that payments will continue even if an individual lives much longer than anticipated). In addition, this strategy may foster greater willingness to make life-time gifts to heirs and/or gifts (lifetime, testamentary, or both) to charities.

Using Annuities to Maintain Tax Deferral – and Control – From Beyond the Grave

Ensuring Tax Deferral of Gain Beyond the Annuity Owner's Lifetime

The income tax on annual gain in a deferred annuity is generally deferred until it is distributed (see Chapter 2). Distributees of annuity proceeds can benefit from even further tax deferral if those distributions are considered amounts received as an annuity (see Chapter 3). If so, a portion of each payment is excluded from tax as a return of principal under the regular annuity rules of IRC Section 72(b). This treatment applies to annuity payments whether made to an annuitant or to a beneficiary. Thus, if a deferred annuity is structured so as to ensure that the beneficiary or beneficiaries can – or perhaps must - take proceeds in the form of an annuity, the benefits of tax deferral will survive the annuity owner. This can be done utilizing a concept that has come to be known as the stretch annuity.

What is a stretch annuity? In its broadest sense, one might say that the term describes any annuity where the beneficiary designation allows (or requires) the beneficiary to stretch death proceeds (and the benefits of tax deferral of undistributed gain) over as long a period as possible. Deferred annuity contracts nearly always allow the beneficiary to take proceeds in the form of an annuity – either over lifetime or for a period of years. If the beneficiary is the surviving spouse of the owner, all deferred annuity contracts issued since 1985 contain a spousal continuation option, allowing the surviving spouse/beneficiary to elect to treat the contract as if it were his/her own from inception,[6] and to name new beneficiary(ies), who will, themselves, be able to choose to take proceeds as an annuity. Moreover, many contacts permit the owner to ensure that death proceeds will be eligible for the favorable tax treatment of the regular annuity rules by allowing the owner to require that death proceeds be taken by the beenficiary(ies) as an annuity. This election is usually made on the beneficiary designation form, or by election of a special contract option. Such election is usually revocable by the contract owner at any point before death, but not by the beneficiary after the owner dies.

However, election of a regular annuity payout option (whether by the owner or beneficiary) is not necessarily the only way to achieve this post-death tax deferral. As was noted in Chapter 3, the IRS has privately ruled that payment of annuity death benefits to a beneficiary where the amount of each payment is determined by the life expectancy fraction method, rather than by the payout factors of a regular annuity option, can satisfy the requirements of IRC Section 72(s) and that undistributed gain would not be constructively received (and would, therefore, enjoy tax deferral until it is distributed).[7] In other words, the private ruling allowed a beneficiary to take systematic withdrawals as the beneficiary of an annuity, without annuitizing, and still stretch the payments – and tax on the gain – over the beneficiary's lifetime.

In a subsequent letter ruling the Service went even further, to hold that, under certain circumstances, payout to a beneficiary using this method or the amortization or annuity factor methods[8] will qualify as amounts received as an annuity.[9] As such, the regular annuity rules of IRC Section 72(b) would be applicable, whereby a portion of each annuity payment is excluded from tax as a return of principal. It must be noted that the ruling that permitted this tax result did so on the basis of case-specific facts. Advisors should not assume that this result is available for any particular client without a ruling from the Internal Revenue Service. Moreover, many annuity contracts do not permit the life expectancy fraction method to be used.[10] Finally, insurers that do permit this option may issue a Form 1099-R to beneficiaries indicating that the payments made are amounts not received as an annuity. That is, they may not apply the regular annuity rules exclusion ratio, but will report such payments as fully taxable, to the extent of any remaining gain in the contract.

Of the three optional methods referred to above (amortization, annuity factor, and life expectancy fraction), the last offers the most stretch of tax deferral, because it permits smaller payments in the early payout years. It also offers beneficiaries the greatest flexibility. Most annuitizations are irrevocable. The beneficiary is stuck with the arrangement for the duration of the payout (which may be for that beneficiary's entire lifetime).

By contrast, the fractional method permits the beneficiary to take only the relatively small amounts required under that method and the freedom to take amounts over and above those required at any time. Moreover, undistributed proceeds will remain invested in the chosen sub-accounts and any gains earned will continue to enjoy the benefit of tax deferral.

As noted, the life expectancy fraction method of payout offers the most stretch. Thus, a more restrictive (but, in the authors' opinion, better) definition of stretch annuity is any annuity contract that guarantees to the beneficiaries the right to take proceeds according to this life expectancy fraction method. This definition might be refined even further, to include only contracts that waive surrender charge upon death.

A few caveats should be noted. First, as was noted above, few deferred annuity contracts allow the beneficiary to use the life expectancy fraction method (or, for that matter, the other two optional methods described in Notice 89-25). Most restrict the beneficiary to the use of regular annuity options. Second, not all contracts that do make the life expectancy fraction method payout arrangement available to beneficiaries permit the policy owner to restrict beneficiaries to using only that option. But is that necessarily a bad thing?

An annuity owner's right to restrict beneficiaries to some form of stretched payout of death proceeds does offer the benefit of post-death tax deferral. But it does so at the cost of flexibility. What if the beneficiary has extraordinary, unanticipated financial needs such as uninsured medical bills? An irrevocable annuity income will be of little help in meeting such expenses.[11]

Some flexibility and post-death control may be offered by the use of special beneficiary designations or contractual options. One key benefit of these is that annuity owners can place certain limitations on how beneficiaries receive the money after death, without having to go through the cost and trouble of having a lawyer draft a trust to accomplish that goal. Of course it should be noted that, a trust can provide much greater flexibility to accomplish goals than use of a beneficiary designation, which, no matter how special, cannot.

However, a nonqualified annuity payable to a trust will be required to make a full distribution under the five-year rule (as discussed in Chapter 2), while the same annuity payable to an individual beneficiary with a restricted beneficiary designation may provide for similar restrictions while still allowing the beneficiary to stretch withdrawals (and income tax consequences) over his/her lifetime. Consequently, as long as trusts cannot be designated beneficiaries, owners and their advisors must weigh the income tax consequences with the flexibility allowed by trusts in determining an appropriate course of action.

> *Example*: One major insurer offers a Predetermined Beneficiary Payout Option that permits the owner to restrict the beneficiary to a payout over his/her lifetime calculated only in accordance with the Single Life table of Treasury Regulation Section 1.401(a)(9)-9, Q&A 1,

and, upon reaching a specified age, access to any distributions above the minimum specified by that table.

However, most deferred annuities do not offer such provisions. It is essential that the advisor know what stretch provisions are permitted by the annuity contract being considered. Whether the law permits a payout option is a moot point if the issuing insurer does not offer it. It is also crucial that the advisor knows whose death will result in the payment of the contractually guaranteed death benefit of the annuity being considered. In annuitant-driven contracts, the death of a non-annuitant owner will force distribution (per the requirements of IRC Section 72(s), but any guaranteed death benefit exceeding the cash value in the contract will not be payable. (See Chapters 1 and 3.)

Using a Variable Annuity to Fund a Charitable Remainder Unitrust

One commonly used application of a variable annuity is in funding a charitable remainder unitrust (CRUT). In fact, the variable annuity has often been touted as the perfect funding instrument for the so-called spigot NIMCRUT – especially by those marketing variable annuities. Is it? The following discussion will examine the pros and cons of such a strategy. But, first, some terms need defined. What is a "spigot NIMCRUT"?

A CRUT is a type of charitable remainder trust (CRT) – a split-interest trust with a charitable remainder beneficiary and one or more noncharitable beneficiaries with rights to payments each year during the term of the trust. Often, the estate-owner client is the noncharitable beneficiary. The CRUT provides that the noncharitable beneficiaries will receive a unitrust amount each year (i.e., a certain percentage of the trust value, as revalued each year). (CRTs that pay specified amounts each year are called charitable remainder annuity trusts).

The NIM stands for net income with makeup. Net income means that each year the trust will pay the lesser of the net income or the payout percentage specified in the trust to the noncharitable beneficiary. The makeup part means that whenever net income is less than the payout percentage, the shortfall is credited to a makeup account, which can be tapped later on if the trust's net income exceeds the specified payout percentage (but only to the extent of that excess).

The spigot part means that the payment stream can be turned on and off – as with a spigot. Typically, this works by having a special independent trustee instruct the trust administrator to turn the payment stream on or off, as needed by the noncharitable beneficiary.

Proponents of the variable annuity-funded spigot NIMCRUT sometimes assert that only with a variable annuity can the noncharitable beneficiary be sure of being able to tap the makeup account (which may have been created deliberately, by having the trust invest in the early trust years in vehicles which produce only capital gains, but no trust income).

This is not necessarily true. First, the Principal and Income Act of the state in which the trust is sited may permit allocation of post-contribution capital gains as either income or principal, each year, as the trustee sees fit. Secondly, there are certain types of investments that can produce income on demand, so to speak, such as a limited liability company (LLC). Some commentators have described a one person LLC as the ideal spigot NIMCRUT instrument, where state law permits such entities.

There are also some fundamental disadvantages to using variable annuities to fund this type of CRT. First, there's the fact that, beneficiaries of a CRT are generally taxed under a four-tier system in which trust income is deemed to be (1) ordinary income, (2) realized capital gains, (3) tax-exempt income, or (4) principal, in WIFO order (worst in, first out). But all distributions from an annuity are always ordinary income. A CRT funded with an annuity can never receive capital gains treatment on any gains from that annuity.

A second disadvantage is that a variable annuity owned by a NIMCRUT is not considered to be owned as an agent for a natural person.[12] Consequently, annual gain in the annuity – even if not distributed – is taxable. Although the NIMCRUT itself is a tax-deferred entity, insurance companies have recently adopted the practice of issuing a Form 1099-R to the CRT/owner, showing the annuity gain to be currently taxable. (Previously, many insurers did not issue a Form 1099-R to report undistributed gain if the contract owner was a CRT, since it is already a tax-exempt entity). For this reason, and because charitable trust accounting is very complex, advisors recommending or considering a variable annuity to fund a NIMCRUT should be aware that the services of an accountant experienced in charitable trust accounting will be essential.

A third disadvantage is the wrapper cost of the annuity, which was discussed earlier. These overhead costs can serve as a drag on investment performance – especially if the insurance charges produce benefits only for the charitable remainder beneficiary and if the client's interest in benefiting the charity is secondary. (It should be mentioned, here, that the first word in the term charitable remainder trust is charitable, and that advisors – and clients – probably ought to keep that in mind).

Critics of using variable annuities to fund spigot NIMCRUTs often harp on these disadvantages, often without acknowledging that there might be advantages in the bargain. This is neither fair nor accurate.

Ordinary trust accounting rules treat realized capital gains as additions to trust corpus, not as income. However, a CRT can be drafted so as to allow the trustee to treat capital gains as income. Regardless of which rule is applicable, if the trust investments include, say, a stock which has appreciated in value in the trust, but which is now performing poorly, the trustee (or a special trustee) of a spigot NIMCRUT may have an unpleasant decision to make if the income beneficiary doesn't happen to want income at the time. If the stock is sold, the gains are additions to principal, which will not benefit the income beneficiary; or, the trustee treats the capital gain as income – but at a time when the beneficiary doesn't want income.

On the other hand, a spigot NIMCRUT funded by an annuity can be drafted so as to define distributable income as "any distribution from the annuity" used to fund the trust, provided state law permits such language. Buys and sells within the annuity aren't income unless actually distributed. When income is desired, the distribution may be taken in the amount desired (limited, of course, by the actual gain the annuity has produced), provided that there is gain in the annuity. There can be no distributable income from the annuity unless its value exceeds its basis (the amount originally invested). If no gain exists in the annuity, no income exists to be distributed to the income beneficiary, because of how trust accounting rules define income. This last point is all too often not fully understood by clients – or advisors.

It's also important to understand that when a spigot NIMCRUT defines distributable income, that definition of income (or the definition under the state's Principal and Income Act) may be different than taxable income earned by the trust. This is specifically applicable when a NIMCRUT owns a variable annuity, because the trust's non-natural person ownership causes annual gains on the contract to be taxable. Consequently, even when a NIMCRUT receives a Form 1099-R for taxable income attributable to annual gains on the contract, it does not necessarily mean that the trust must distribute that amount of income under its net income requirements, if the definition of income states otherwise.

The bottom line answer – to the question of whether a variable annuity is the best funding instrument for a spigot NIMCRUT or not – is, as one might expect, it depends on several factors, including: what the client's state Principal & Income Act permits; how flexible a spigot the client requires; and on the size of the annuity wrapper costs, just to name three factors. An excellent software tool is available to assist planners who regularly deal with the issue of whether or not to fund a NIMCRUT with an annuity, versus some alternative investment. It's an Excel®-based program called *WealthMaster®*, a component of the *WealthTec Suite®* (www.wealthtec.com), and it incorporates several dozen focused modules, including the NIMCRUT planner. Using this tool, a planner can vary assumptions as to investment returns, tax rates, annuity charges, and funding and distribution patterns to compare funding a hypothetical NIMCRUT with a deferred annuity versus an alternative investment.

Chapter Endnotes

1. POD and TOD are types of financial accounts with designated beneficiaries, where account values pass directly to those beneficiaries, generally bypassing the probate process. POD accounts are often bank accounts, while securities or investment accounts are typically TOD.

2. That share which, by state law, is the surviving spouse's by right, regardless of decedent spouse's provisions to the contrary.

3. For example, a decedent wants to leave $50,000/year, for life, to one beneficiary while leaving the remaining estate assets to other beneficiaries (e.g., children).

4. Such tax deferral is possible only if the trust owning the annuity can qualify as an agent of a natural person. See Chapter 2.

5. IRC Sec. 2503(b).

6. For the tax implications of this decision, see Chapter 3.

7. PLR 200151038.

8. These are the three methods set forth in Q&A-12 of Notice 89-25, 1989-1 CB 662, 666, as modified by Rev. Rul. 2002-62, 2002-2 CB 710.

9. PLR 200313016.

10. According to Rick Bueter [www.rickbueter.com], an industry expert on stretch annuities, only a fraction of contracts currently available permit the use of the life expectancy fraction option.

11. It should be noted that firms exist that will purchase an annuitant's right to an annuity income (or a structured settlement) for a lump sum, but the lump sum is usually discounted at a rate of interest much greater than the rate used to create that income stream. Moreover, such a purchase may be barred by contractual provisions or local law.

12. PLR 9009047.

Chapter 10

The Great Debate: Are Annuities Good or Bad? (Part One: Arguments in Favor of Annuities)

Annuities have, for many years, been the subject of considerable debate among financial planners, insurance agents, financial journalists, and academics. While some of this discussion is dispassionate, a surprising amount of it is not. Much of what is written on the subject–especially by those opposed to annuities–is outright polemic. The debate has become, for many, a feud–as if one must either be for annuities or against them.

This is both unfortunate and absurd. It is unfortunate because the tone and level of discussion regarding the appropriateness and value of annuities in financial planning often sinks to the point of mere diatribe, in which the search for genuine understanding is abandoned for the sake of making one's case. In that sort of debate, as in war, the first casualty is truth. It is absurd because it rests upon an absurd premise–that an annuity, which is simply a financial tool, can be, in and of itself, inherently good or bad.

The authors of this book are neither in favor of, nor opposed to, annuities. They view, and strongly encourage the reader to view, an annuity–any annuity–as a tool, the appropriateness and value of which necessarily depends upon how well it does the job to be done, how well it accomplishes the planning objectives compared to other tools that are available. In these final two chapters we will evaluate some of the more commonly advanced arguments for and against annuities and attempt to supply some balance.

Arguments in Favor of Deferred Annuities

The Benefits of Tax Deferral

Many proponents of deferred annuities point to tax-deferral as a great advantage of these instruments. Indeed, many commentators have stated, flatly, that tax deferral is the main attraction of deferred annuities (implying that it must be the main reason for purchasing one). Others have argued that the real value to such deferral is the control it gives the contract owner. Because there are no required minimum distributions applicable to deferred annuities, and because the contract owner can decide when, and in what amounts, to take distributions, the deferred annuity has been labeled by some as the perfect tax control device.

Certainly, tax deferral has value. Some commentators have observed that it enhances, even further, the "miracle" of compound interest. Jack Marrion refers to this enhancement as "triple interest crediting."

> Money that remains inside an annuity grows free from current income taxes. Not only does the principal earn interest (simple interest at work), and the interest earns interest (compound interest at work), but the money that would have gone to Uncle Sam also earns interest (tax-advantaged interest at work).[1]

Moreover, the control over the timing of taxation of gain enjoyed by the owner of a deferred annuity is unquestionably worthwhile. The annuity owner may choose to take distributions in years of unusually low income or when such distributions can be netted against ordinary income losses. Moreover, the income earned in an annuity, but not yet distributed, is not countable for purposes of the alternative minimum tax or the taxability of Social Security benefits.

Yet the tax deferral and tax control provided by a deferred annuity are not entirely free. There are costs to these benefits, and the costs are not always acknowledged by those who proclaim the benefits. What are these costs?

Insurance Charges (applies only to variable annuities) – The insurance charges (the sum of the mortality and expense (M&E) charge and any separate Administrative Expense charge) are usually the largest component of the "overhead cost" in a variable annuity. These charges are discussed in detail in Chapter 4.

Surrender Charges – Many deferred annuities assess surrender charges for distributions exceeding a specified amount or a percentage of the account value, if taken during the surrender charge period. These charges are a limitation upon the control the annuity owner enjoys over the money invested in his annuity.

Early Distribution Penalty – In addition to any contractual surrender charges, the Internal Revenue Code imposes a penalty tax on distributions taken from a non qualified annuity by an annuity owner who is under age 59½, unless the distributions qualify under certain very specific exceptions (see Chapter 2). The penalty is equal to 10% of the taxable amount of such distributions.[2] Like surrender charges, this penalty tax is a limitation on the tax control enjoyed by the annuity owner.

Ordinary Income Treatment – All distributions from an annuity are taxed as ordinary income. The preferential tax treatment of long term capital gains, enjoyed by many other investment alternatives, is not applicable to the gain in an annuity. This is true for all distributions–partial withdrawals, total contact surrenders, or death benefits–to the extent that there is gain in the contract, and applies whether a distribution is taken as a lump sum or in the form of annuity income.

Does ordinary income treatment constitute a disadvantage of deferred annuities? If someone is comparing a deferred variable annuity to investments such as stocks, commodities, or mutual funds, the answer might be yes. Much of the gain derived from these investments will, if the investment is held for at least one year, qualify for long term capital gains rates, which are significantly lower than ordinary income rates–especially for high-income investors. In addition, "qualified" dividends on stocks (or mutual funds holding stocks) may also be eligible for preferential tax treatment lower than ordinary income tax rates. The difference in net, after-tax, accumulated wealth and upon net after-tax income, wrought by the differential between these two tax regimes, can be profound.

That said, when comparing a deferred fixed annuity to investments such as certificates of deposit or bonds, the ordinary income treatment of annuity distributions may not represent a disadvantage, simply because the interest earned on CDs and bonds is taxed in exactly the same way.

It should be noted that the benefit of tax deferral in a deferred annuity is not limited to the accumulation phase (that is: the period from contract inception to the point where the owner begins taking distributions). Distributions taken as an annuity are taxable only to the extent that the annuity payment exceeds the excludible portion (calculated according to the annuity rules of Section 72(b)). Gain not yet received, by this method, continues to enjoy tax-deferral until all gain has been distributed (which occurs when the annuitant reaches life expectancy or the end of a period certain term).

This opportunity for tax deferral of annuity growth, even during the distribution phase of a deferred annuity is often overlooked by critics of annuities, who often compare the annuity to some investment alternative assuming that both will be surrendered at some future point in a lump sum. The advantage of continuing tax deferral during the distribution period can be very substantial, as was noted in a study conducted in 2002 by Price Waterhouse Cooper, entitled "The Value of Lifetime Annuitization."[3]

No Step up in Basis for Inherited Annuities – As was noted above, the gain in a deferred annuity is always taxed as ordinary income, even when distributed to a beneficiary as death proceeds. When received by a beneficiary, such gain is considered income in respect of a decedent. Most investments held by a decedent enjoy, under current law, a treatment known as "step-up in basis," in which the cost basis, for income tax purposes, of the investment passing to an heir is "stepped up" to its value as of the date of decedent's death. Thus, a stock, which the decedent paid $1,000 for, but which is worth $2,000 at his death, passes to his heir with an income tax cost basis of $2,000. If that heir subsequently sells the stock for $2,500, he will pay tax only on a gain of $500.

If, however, the decedent had bought a deferred annuity for $1,000 and died without taking any distributions, when the annuity was worth $2,000, the beneficiary would be liable for the tax on the entire $1,000 of untaxed gain, at ordinary income rates.[4]

The tax treatment just described applies to property of decedents dying prior to the year 2010. Under current law, the "step-up in basis" applicable to property owned by decedents dying in the year 2010 would be subject to certain limits. It is unclear whether it will apply in years after 2010. Current law would reinstate the present "step-up in basis" rules for years after 2010, but, at the time of this writing, Congress is considering estate tax legislation that may result in some other regime. We simply do not know, at this point, what the rules will be in future years. But we can say that, under the current rules, the lack of "step-up in basis", as applied to deferred annuities, represents a disadvantage for those clients whose goals include passing as much net wealth to heirs as possible.

The authors suggest that, where net wealth passing to heirs is a major planning goal, far better instruments than a deferred annuity may be available For example, life insurance offers far better tax treatment, if the individual is insurable. The beneficiary of a life insurance policy can receive, free of income tax, not just the full cash value of the policy, but the greater (often, far greater) death benefit.

An Annuity is the Only Vehicle That Can GUARANTEE an Income for Life

One of the most commonly advanced arguments in favor of an annuity states that an annuity is the only vehicle which can guarantee, for a given amount invested, an income which (a) is certain as to amount and (b) cannot be outlived. Strictly speaking, this is not true. Perpetual Bonds guarantee an interest rate in perpetuity, in addition to invested principal, but these bonds are sufficiently rare as to qualify as exotic investments. Ordinary bonds cannot guarantee an income indefinitely, because all ordinary bonds have a fixed duration. Most instruments considered by investors desiring a certain income either have fixed durations or generate income only through dividends or interest that are not absolutely guaranteed. Deferred annuities also have a maximum maturity date, by which the owner must either surrender or annuitize the contract, so the claim stated above really applies only to immediate annuities or deferred annuities that will be annuitized.

That being said, there is a huge difference between the income generated by an immediate annuity (or a deferred annuity that has been annuitized) and that produced by any non-annuity alternative. By definition, an annuity is an income stream representing both earnings and the systematic liquidation of principal. To compare the income produced by an annuity with the income produced by some alternative using only earnings on principal is to compare totally dissimilar instruments. Unless it is made clear that one alternative preserves principal while the other exhausts it, such a comparison is utterly misleading.

Yet if income is the only goal for a particular investor, the fact that no principal will remain at the annuitant's death (or at the end of the annuity period, if a period certain payout is contemplated) may not be as important as the amount of the income. For older clients, the annual annuity payment may be significantly greater than that realistically obtainable from any alternative, given the same lump sum investment. The additional income may, for these clients, be worth the cost of "spending the kids' inheritance." Moreover, a comparison of a life annuity with an alternative investment need not contemplate that all of the investor's capital will be placed under either alternative. Allocating part of someone's assets to a life annuity might, in some situations, produce an income that is both certain (with all the emotional satisfaction that certainty provides) and sufficiently larger than might otherwise be achievable. The investor then might feel comfortable allocating his remaining assets to more conservative investments (to reduce investment risk) or to more aggressive ones (to achieve even greater total income or final wealth). In either scenario, the annuity would be performing, not only as an investment, but also (the authors would say primarily) as a risk management tool.

If one grants the advantages to annuitization just described, there remains the question of when the annuity needs to be purchased to achieve these advantages. Would it not make sense for our investor to put his money into some instrument that offers more growth opportunity than a fixed annuity or lower overhead costs than a variable one and simply sell that instrument to purchase an immediate annuity when the time comes to begin taking income?

Many commentators and advisors will answer "yes." Supporting this conclusion is the fact that the annuity payout factors guaranteed in a deferred annuity have never (to the authors' knowledge) been as attractive as the payout factors available in the immediate annuity marketplace. Moreover, many investment alternatives may be taxed at long-term capital gains (LTCG) rates and may even enjoy some degree of tax deferral. For example, the profit from an investment in a non-dividend-paying growth stock will be taxed only when that stock is sold, and, then, at LTCG rates.

These are valid points. Tax deferral is not the sole province of annuities, and annuities never get capital gains treatment. However, the guarantee of principal and of a minimum rate of return in fixed annuities and the guaranteed living benefits available in today's variable contracts provide a degree of downside risk protection that should not be overlooked. Whether that protection is worth the tradeoffs involved is a question well worth serious consideration. But it is not actually an investment question, even though most critics view it as such. It is really a risk management question.

As to whether investing in some alternative (that perhaps offers LTCG tax treatment) during someone's wealth accumulation phase and then surrendering that investment to purchase an immediate annuity is preferable to locking in guaranteed annuity rates that have never been all that attractive, we should consider that question in the light of longevity trends. Americans are living longer with each passing decade. Is it not possible that medical breakthroughs may so lengthen the life expectancy of the average American that immediate annuity rates, decades hence, will be less attractive than those payout rates guaranteed in today's deferred annuity contracts? If so–and, especially, if those future annuity payout factors are significantly lower than today's guaranteed ones–the result could be a significantly lower income, for every year of the investor's retirement, for each dollar annuitized.

Can we know which scenario is more likely? Not unless we have a functioning crystal ball. Absent that, we can either make a bet that future SPIA rates will be at least as attractive as today's guaranteed rates and that the risk management features of the deferred annuity will cost us more than the benefits they guarantee, or we can insure against those risks.

Furthermore, it is important to remember that if the alternative investment has created substantial gains over the years, a tax liability will be due upon the conversion of that asset from its non-annuity form to an annuitized payout. This foregoes the opportunity for additional tax deferral. Consequently, it may be more beneficial to accumulate funds within an annuity with the plan of future annuitization, because of the tax-deferral achieved not only during the accumulation phase, but also the tax further deferred by spreading the income recognition treatment across a lifetime of annuity payments.

The Guaranteed Death Benefit in a Variable Annuity Provides Protection Alternative Investments Do Not Offer

A feature of modern variable deferred annuity contracts often cited by their proponents is the guaranteed death benefit. It offers the annuity investor assurance of a minimum amount that will pass to his heirs, regardless of the performance of the underlying investment sub-accounts. If the annuity owner happens to pass away after a severe market decline, the beneficiaries will not suffer from that decline, but will receive a guaranteed minimum amount. The standard minimum death benefit is typically the greater of (a) the account balance at death or (b) the amount originally invested (less cumulative withdrawals). Most contracts also offer an enhanced death benefit for an additional charge. The enhanced death benefit may provide that the beneficiary will receive the greater of (a) the amount originally invested (less any withdrawals); (b) the account balance at death; (c) the original investment (less withdrawals), compounded at some specified rate of interest; or (d) the highest account balance at any of certain specified prior policy anniversaries. Some contracts will include only one of the last two factors.

For investors who are greatly concerned with maximizing the amount passing to their heirs, this guarantee may be very important. It is further argued that this investor might, having the assurance of the minimum death benefit guarantee, allocate his investments more aggressively than he would without that guarantee. If so (the argument goes), the historical "risk premium" of equities investments (the amount by which equities returns have exceeded returns on more conservative investments to compensate their owners for the additional risk involved) should offer opportunity both for a greater death benefit (because the guarantee typically is the largest of the account balance at death or other specified amounts) and greater wealth accumulation for the annuity owner during his lifetime.

The authors believe that this argument has merit. However, fairness obliges us to point out that the same objective could be accomplished with life insurance. If the investor is able to obtain life insurance, of a type that is likely to be in force when death occurs, the cost for the coverage could be less than the cost of the guaranteed minimum death benefit. Moreover, the life insurance death proceeds will be payable regardless of how the annuity (or other investment alternative) performs. If the alternative investment never experiences a decline in value, the combination of a life insurance policy and the investment will pay both the face amount of the insurance plus the (appreciated) value of the investment. The premium for the life insurance will always produce more wealth passing to heirs than would be the case if no insurance were purchased (assuming that the insurance death benefit exceeds the total premiums paid into the policy).[5]

By contrast, the annuity death benefit guarantee is not certain to produce more money for the owner's beneficiaries than they would receive without it. If the account balance at death is greater than the other factors taken into account in the guarantee (e.g., the amount contributed to the annuity, that amount compounded at a certain rate of interest, or account balance at some prior policy anniversary), the beneficiaries will receive "only" the accumulated account balance. The presence of the guaranteed minimum death benefit will produce no additional value, unless the owner happened to achieve a greater return with higher risk (and return) investments because of the presence of the guarantee.

Some critics of variable annuity death benefit guarantees believe that the historical "upside bias" of equity investments means that if the annuity is held long enough, the probability that the death benefit guarantee will exceed the account balance at death is too small to justify the cost of that guarantee. "Over the long haul," it is sometimes said, equity investments have returned an average of, say, 10% per year. Even after reducing that average return by, say, 2.5% (to reflect the total expense ratio, including sub-account expenses, of a typical variable annuity), the result is an average return of 7.5%. That should (so the argument goes) produce an account balance at death greater than the original contribution compounded at the 5% or 6% rate typically used in a VA guaranteed death benefit formula, and far greater than the original contribution. Thus, the argument concludes, the cost of the death benefit guarantee is merely wasted money, nothing more than an annual drag on investment performance.

In the authors' opinion, there are two serious flaws to this argument. First, it amounts to the notion that "the market always goes up...eventually." It is certainly true that the long-term trend of equities markets has generally been upward. However, prolonged bear markets happen, and one cannot be certain that one will not die during, or at the end of, one of them. Second, many death benefit guarantee formulas include as a factor (of which the highest will be paid to beneficiaries) the account balance as of certain prior policy anniversaries. Even the most bullish critic must concede that the upward trend of equities markets is not constant. Corrections happen, and markets often take years to return to a prior high point. A death benefit guarantee that locks in a prior all time high may be of significant value, especially in a period of high market volatility.

With regard to the cost of the guaranteed death benefit provisions in today's variable annuity contracts, one criticism that is rarely voiced, but which deserves the advisor's serious attention, is how that cost is calculated. Most (but not all) contracts assess the charge for both the standard and enhanced death benefit against the accumulated account balance in the annuity.[6] The additional charge for the enhanced death benefit is typically in the range of 10-30 basis points per year, as a percentage of account balance. As the account balance increases, so does the cost for the guaranteed minimum death benefit. Yet, as the account balance (and the amount of gain in the contract) increases, the probability that the beneficiary will receive more than that account balance from one of the death benefit guarantees decreases. This occurs because the more that the account balance grows beyond the amount originally invested, the less chance there is that it will fall below that amount. The same is true (though to a lesser degree) of the chance that the account balance will fall below the value of that original investment, accumulated at the rate of return specified in the death benefit guarantee (for death benefits that have this option). To the extent that the annual growth in the annuity exceeds this specified rate, the accumulated value will exceed the death benefit guaranteed using that rate. The greater this excess, the less likelihood that the account balance will later fall below that future "contributions, accumulated at N%" value. Thus, in a situation where the annuity performs well, the contract owner will incur an increasing annual cost for a benefit increasingly unlikely to be payable. The cost/benefit ratio actually decreases with the annuity value.

This pattern does not hold true, however, for the "account balance at a prior policy anniversary" component. If someone believes that the magnitude of a possible market decline (and, thus, a decline in the value of the annuity value) increases with the size of the account balance ("the higher the market goes, the bigger the correction is likely to be"), the reverse may even be true.

When considering the enhanced death benefit as a whole, however, the fact that the cost of the death benefit guarantee is based on the account balance, rather than upon the value guaranteed, appears (to the authors, at least) to be unattractive, from a cost/benefit perspective. A few insurers have recognized this, and now offer guaranteed death benefit provisions where the cost is more directly related to the amount at risk.

Whether the guaranteed death benefit in a variable annuity (either standard or enhanced) is worth its cost is, ultimately, a risk management question. Regrettably, many critics of annuities insist upon treating it as an investment one, where the cost of what is clearly an insurance feature is seen simply as an overhead cost. In the authors' view, this makes sense only if the insurance benefits are dismissed as valueless–or, at the very least, unimportant.

They may, for some investors, be just that. For the client who has no heirs (or who dislikes those he has), a guaranteed minimum death benefit is likely to be of little or no interest, and the cost of that benefit would, indeed, be merely a drag on investment performance. For this individual, a variable annuity–because it charges for insurance he does not want or need–is arguably a poor choice.

The Case for Guaranteed Living Benefits in Variable Annuities

In recent years, the emergence of guaranteed living benefits has made variable annuities increasingly attractive to many investors. As guaranteed death benefits offer beneficiaries the assurance of minimum values, irrespective of the performance of the underlying investment sub-accounts, living benefits guarantee minimum values (no matter how the annuity investments perform) to living contract owners. Three basic types are currently available –

1. Guaranteed Minimum Income Benefit;

2. Guaranteed Minimum Accumulation Benefit; and

3. Guaranteed Minimum Withdrawal Benefit

These guaranteed living benefits (described extensively in Chapter 5) assure different things. The first guarantees a minimum income. The second guarantees a minimum future lump sum value. The third guarantees that the contract owner will be able to receive the amount invested, in installments, while enjoying the potential for further growth on undistributed amounts. A fourth type, combining features of all three benefits,[7] was introduced in 2005, and has become very popular.

While the mechanics and specific guarantees offered by these provisions vary widely from contract to contract, two generalizations may be made about them: (1) they are complicated and (2) they are risk management features.

They are Complicated

The values guaranteed by these living benefit provisions are often the result of formulas and conditions. Rarely can one point to a dollar figure and say "this is the amount guaranteed by this benefit." Moreover, the terms under which the guaranteed amounts are payable can also be quite complicated. The result is a serious potential for misunderstanding and confusion–both by those purchasing these contracts and by those selling them.

For example, a Guaranteed Minimum Income Benefit (GMIB) provision may apply a guaranteed interest rate of 6% to amounts invested, to produce a "benefit base" from which GMIB payments will be calculated. This does not mean that the contract owner is guaranteed a minimum of a 6% return on his investment (as would be the case if the guaranteed cash value of the contract could never be less than contributions compounded at 6%). Yet one of the authors has heard this provision explained in just that way on several occasions–not only by policy owners, but also by professional advisors. Clearly, these individuals had no idea how the GMIB provision they were describing actually worked. Other living benefit provisions, especially the recently introduced "combination living benefit" riders, are even more complex, and offer an even greater opportunity for confusion.

In the authors' view, this is potentially a very serious problem, both for advisors and for their clients. Any competent decision as to whether a guaranteed living benefit is worth, to a particular client, what the insurer charges for it necessarily requires that all parties to that decision fully understand what they are assessing. Some insurers, recognizing this, have instituted special training programs to ensure that those recommending these complex products understand them. Yet many (if not most) professional advisors who will, at one point or another, deal with these complex instruments will never attend even one of these sessions. For those advisors, this leaves only the marketing materials provided by the annuity issuer (augmented, perhaps, by an explanation by a marketing representative of the company) and a reading of the annuity contract itself as the sole sources of information regarding how these provisions work–and don't work. The authors strenuously recommend a serious study, both of the marketing brochures and the actual contract language describing guaranteed living benefits, to anyone who intends to purchase a variable annuity with these provisions. We also recommend that any advisor who intends to sell, or offer advice concerning, these benefits to take advantage of special training classes on the subject.

They are Risk Management Features

The most important thing to know about guaranteed living benefits is that they are not investment features, designed to maximize profit, but risk management features, designed to control loss. In a best case scenario (e.g., where the investment sub-accounts produce double-digit returns in each and every year), living benefits can never be worth their cost, because those benefits will never be triggered. In other scenarios, the costs of the living benefits may increase (because the account balance increases) in all but the final year or two of the contract, but the benefits themselves, when triggered, will be comparatively small. In these scenarios, someone might view these costs, from a purely investment perspective, as excessive, or even wasted money.

In the authors' opinion, such a view is mistaken because it applies a perspective that is inappropriate. A variable annuity–especially one that provides guaranteed living benefits–is not purely an investment and should not be analyzed as if it were. The purpose of guaranteed living benefits is not to maximize wealth or investment success (or future account balance) but to minimize the chance of failure (that the future account balance will be insufficient to meet a client's needs). Electing these benefits is a choice, by the client, to give up some potential excess return as a cost of insurance against the risk that the returns will produce less than the amounts guaranteed. It is a prudent choice for the client who assigns a greater economic value to the risks that are shifted to the insurance company than to the total annual costs for the transfer–including the opportunity cost of those dollars. One might also argue that there is also economic value to peace of mind, quite apart from mathematical probabilities of failure or success.

The Guaranteed Minimum Withdrawal Benefit assures that the contract owner will be able to recover his investment (by periodic withdrawals), irrespective of adverse investment performance, and be able to participate in investment gains earned by funds not withdrawn. If that guarantee of return of principal is worth the drag on investment performance represented by its cost, electing it makes sense.

The Guaranteed Minimum Income Benefit assures a minimum amount of income (for whatever payout period is elected, including lifetime), based on the greater of the actual future account balance or a guaranteed minimum balance. If that guarantee of minimum income is worth the cost,[8] electing it makes sense.

The Guaranteed Minimum Accumulation Benefit assures the contract owner of a minimum future lump sum account balance, even if actual investment performance produces a lower one. If this assurance is worth the cost, electing it makes sense.

Whatever the decision with regard to these options, it must be understood that they are insurance options, not investment ones and that their costs will necessarily produce a lower future account balance, on average, than would result from the same annuity's performance if these options were not elected (and the costs for them not incurred). This is because the issuing insurance company has expenses associated with its operations, and prices its products to make a profit. For the entire risk pool of contract holders with access to these living benefits, the insurer knows that the premiums paid for them should, over time, be greater than the benefits the insurer will pay out. However, this actuarial certainty has no application to a single individual. For the contract owner concerned about having too small a future account balance, or too little income, or losing principal due to investment losses, the experience of his or her account is all that matters. That the cost of these insurance benefits makes the contract offering them less optimal as a purely investment vehicle may be less worrisome than the prospect of not having those benefits.

The authors suggest that what really matters is not whether the advisor thinks the guarantees represent a good deal, but whether the client (assisted by the advisor in making an informed and educated choice) feels that they provide a good value for the client's goals and the desire to ensure those goals are achieved.

Arguments in Favor of Immediate Annuities

An Annuity is the Only Device That Can GUARANTEE a Stated Income For a Stated Period or For Life

An annuity is the only financial instrument that can guarantee a stated level of income for a specific time period or for the life of the recipient. This point was discussed earlier in this chapter.

The Income Produced By an Immediate Annuity is Greater Than That Achievable From Any Investment Alternative, on a Guaranteed Basis.

Because an annuity consists both of earnings and the systematic amortization of principal, the amount of income produced by an annuity is virtually certain to exceed that of an investment alternative producing an income consisting solely of earnings or interest. Conceivably, there may be some device guaranteeing an interest rate high enough that its interest income would exceed an immediate annuity payout over the same guarantee period, but it is exceedingly unlikely. For example, one insurer, as of this writing, guarantees a monthly income of $971 for a 10 Year Period Certain annuity, on an investment of $100,000. The yield required to produce this same level of income, while preserving principal, is 11.65%. That same company guarantees $654 per month for a life annuity (with no refund feature) for a 65-year-old male, for the same $100,000 investment. The yield required to produce that income for as long as the recipient lives, while preserving principal, is about 8%. No investment (that the authors are aware of) available at the time of this writing offers such returns. Although a rise in future interest rates might be able to produce such income-only returns, the payments from the above annuity examples would be expected to increase as well, perpetuating the difference.

Of course, principal is not preserved in an immediate annuity payment stream. To equate the income produced by an immediate annuity with that produced solely from earnings is not a valid comparison, unless the only factor of importance is the amount of income. While this would not likely be the case in the first example described above (where the investment horizon is 10 years), it might be so in the second–where the income is to last for the recipient's entire remaining lifetime. For example, suppose a 79-year-old widow, having that same $100,000 to invest, could receive an income of $957 per month from an immediate life only annuity, of which approximately 91% will be excluded from taxable income until she has recovered her entire investment tax-free. Suppose also that a tax-free bond offers a rate of 6.5%. That bond would produce an income to her of about $540 per month. The bond would provide her heirs with $100,000 (assuming it is valued at par at her death). If having as much income as possible on an absolutely certain basis, for as long as she lives is this woman's chief concern, the huge difference in the income of which she can be certain may, to this woman, be worth the tradeoffs (loss of access to principal, "spending the kids' inheritance"). In addition, the woman also faces the risk that the tax-free bond may eventually mature, forcing her to reinvest at potentially lower future interest rates; the immediate annuity's guaranteed payment stream does not face any such reinvestment risk.

The Certain Income of an Annuity May Allow a Client to Act Differently With Regard to His Other Assets

One of the curiosities of the "Great Debate" over annuities is that it often presumes an either-or scenario. Consider, for example, the following two assertions:

- Don't invest your retirement money in an immediate annuity.

- An immediate annuity is the ideal retirement investment.

The unspoken implication in both statements is that it applies to a person's entire retirement portfolio–that one should either avoid buying an immediate annuity with any of that money or that one should do so with every dollar. Neither necessarily makes good sense.

What often does make sense is the purchase of an immediate annuity with part of a retirement portfolio. There are several benefits to this strategy:

1. The estate owner who wishes to use lifetime gifting may be more willing to do so having the assurance of a certain income for life.

2. A risk averse investor, having invested a portion of his retirement portfolio in an immediate annuity to secure income, may be more com-

fortable allocating more of the rest of his portfolio to higher return (but higher risk) instruments than he would in the absence of those annuity guarantees.

3. For the client concerned with outliving his retirement portfolio, annuitizing a portion of it may increase the probability that the portfolio as a whole will provide a required income level given the uncertainties of future market performance.

4. The emotional value of a certain income for life is not necessarily limited to that calculable by investment algebra. The confidence that such a client gains from the certainty of his annuity income, like the peace of mind many homeowners gain by paying off the mortgage, may be worth more than a computation of return on investment would indicate.

Chapter Endnotes

1. Jack Marrion, "*Index Annuities: Power and Protection*" (Advantage Compendium, 2003), p. 193.
2. IRC Sec. 72(q).
3. Available from www.navanet.org.
4. An itemized income tax deduction for the Federal Estate Tax attributable to this gain is available to the beneficiary, under IRC Sec. 691(c).
5. One might argue (and the authors do) that this statement is strictly true only if the insurance proceeds exceed the total premiums paid, accumulated at an appropriate Time Value of Money.
6. The standard death benefit guarantee is usually a part of the standard mortality and expense charge.
7. One insurer offering this combination provision refers to it as the "All In One" benefit.
8. The cost of the Guaranteed Minimum Income Benefit should be considered to include the reduced annuity payout factors that are often applicable to its exercise, as well as any annuitization age setback required. See Chapter 5.

Chapter 11

The Great Debate: Are Annuities Good or Bad? (Part Two: Arguments Against Annuities)

They're Too Expensive

Perhaps the most common argument heard against deferred annuities is that they are too expensive. Usually, this criticism refers to variable contracts, as most fixed annuities assess no front-end or annually recurring charges.[1] We have seen in Chapter 10 how the costs for the insurance offered by the guaranteed living benefits of variable annuities can be (and often are) seen as excessive, and that this judgment may result from the application of investment analysis methodology to an insurance problem.[2]

One example of this misapplication that appears frequently in the financial press is the so-called "side by side" comparison of a variable annuity with a mutual fund, assuming both the same assumed gross investment return and that the investor will liquidate the investment in a lump sum at the end of a specified period. Even where the analyst attempts to be fair and reasonable with income tax assumptions (e.g., taking into account the turnover rate in the mutual fund portfolio and the fact that not all distributions are taxed at long term capital gains rates), assuming that both alternatives will earn a specific positive rate of return each year renders the death benefit guarantees of the annuity inoperative. Moreover, the stipulation that the investor will cash out both alternatives in a lump sum obviates the tax advantages of the taxation of annuitized proceeds and assumes that the annuity payout factors guaranteed in the annuity can never be of any value. The costs for these insurance features are taken into account, each year, by reducing the gross return assumed on the annuity by the mortality and expense charge, but the potential benefits purchased by those costs are precluded from ever being realized. Such a comparison may be side by side, but it is not truly apples to apples.

An even more egregious example of unfairness occurs when the comparison pits a fully commissionable variable annuity (VA) against a no load mutual fund. On the VA side of the ledger, the costs include compensation to the financial advisor, including ongoing renewal commissions. These commissions pay, not simply for the advisor's selling the annuity, but for the financial counsel that the advisor renders to the investor as part of the sale (including the initial asset allocation and ongoing servicing, portfolio rebalancing, etc.). On the mutual fund side, there are no commission costs–which necessarily implies that the investor is receiving no financial advice. In the authors' opinion, such an analysis is no more fair than a comparison of the bill presented to a client by a competent estate planning attorney with the cost of do it yourself legal software such as Quicken Family Lawyer®. The product in both cases may be valid legal instruments, but the attorney's documents were informed by individual professional counseling and the attorney's client will have recourse for liabilities caused by errors or problems through the attorney's actions or work.

If the investor does not want or need any counsel, he should not be required to pay for it. But where advice is both wanted and needed–where it has clear value–both the benefit of that advice and its cost should be reflected on both sides of the comparison. Thus, if the mutual fund considered (hypothetically, of course) is a no load product and where the annuity cost includes compensation to the investment advisor, fairness would require that the mutual fund side of the ledger include a separate cost for advice. That sort of comparison is rarely seen.

Annuities Should Never Be Used to Fund an IRA or Qualified Plan

A generalization often made about annuities claims that they should never be used to fund an IRA or qualified plan. This sweeping pronouncement has met with surprisingly wide acceptance among financial journalists, attorneys, accountants, and many financial planners. It has become virtually accepted wisdom for many, despite the facts that (a) it ignores the huge differences that exist between immediate and deferred annuities and between the fixed and variable varieties of the latter and (b) the arguments most commonly made in its support are grievously and obviously flawed.

Those who argue that annuities are inappropriate instruments for funding IRAs or qualified plans are almost always referring to deferred annuities, and, usually, to variable deferred annuities. The three most common of these are –

1. "You're paying for tax deferral you're not getting." This is simply nonsense. While it is true that an annuity offers no additional tax advantages over any other investment vehicle, when used to fund an IRA or qualified, no annuity assesses any charge for the benefit of tax deferral. To be sure, variable deferred annuities impose charges that alternatives such as mutual funds do not, but those are, as we have seen, insurance charges. They have absolutely nothing, whatsoever, to do with the tax treatment enjoyed by the annuity. The tax treatment of an annuity used to fund an IRA or qualified plan is identical to that applicable to any other IRA investment. The treatment that would apply to a deferred annuity, if it were not used to fund such a plan, is irrelevant when the annuity is so used.

    The insurance charges of a variable deferred annuity may or may not be worthwhile to a particular investor, based upon that investor's need for the risk management benefits that the charges pay for, but this is true whether the annuity is funding an IRA or is a non-qualified annuity. If the insurance benefits are not worth the cost to a particular client, then they should not be paid for, whether the money in question is qualified or not.

2. "The tax deferral of an annuity used to fund an IRA is wasted." This one is doubly flawed. First, because the tax deferral enjoyed by non-qualified annuities flows from provisions of the Internal Revenue Code that apply only to non-qualified annuities. That deferral cannot be wasted by an IRA annuity because it does not apply to an IRA annuity. Second, the argument rests upon an assumption that the tax treatment that a particular type of investment property would enjoy if it were held in a taxable account is somehow relevant to whether it is an appropriate funding vehicle for an IRA or qualified account. To illustrate the absurdity of this assumption, let us consider the question of whether small cap growth stocks, or a fund investing in these stocks, might be appropriate for an IRA. The investment returns produced by these stocks (or funds) will generally be taxed at long term capital gain (LTCG) rates if held for longer than one year. LTCG rates are, of course, significantly lower than the rates for ordinary income. Inasmuch as all

non-Roth IRAs and qualified plans (except for "basis") are taxed at higher ordinary income rates, it would follow (if the argument we are examining is sound) that funding an IRA with small cap growth stocks (or a fund investing in the same) would be a waste of capital gains treatment. Obviously, the appropriateness of a small cap growth stock for an IRA or qualified plan has nothing to do with how it would be taxed if it were held otherwise. The same holds true for an annuity.

Furthermore, a small cap growth stock held in a taxable account receives the same tax-deferral benefit as one held in a retirement account, if you assume that it is held until some future point when it is sold or liquidated for a lump sum (as is commonly the case with annuity comparisons). Although individual stocks can be held indefinitely, with no recognition of annual gain until liquidation (not unlike a non-qualified annuity), one rarely sees arguments that stocks are an inappropriate investment for retirement accounts–despite the fact that the tax benefit of holding individual stocks outside of a retirement account is even more beneficial than that applying to a non-qualified annuity, because the stock receives preferential tax treatment (through the application of LTCG rates) and the opportunity for a step-up in basis if held until death. To the extent that it is clearly inappropriate to suggest that retirement accounts should not hold individual stocks because of the benefits foregone by not purchasing them in taxable accounts, the same holds true for annuities.

3.   "They're Too Expensive." As we have said, if the insurance benefits of the annuity–which are the source of the excessive costs cited by critics–are neither needed nor wanted, they should not be purchased. A deferred annuity–especially a deferred variable annuity with guaranteed death and living benefits–is chiefly a risk management tool. If the risk management features are not desired, an instrument providing and charging for them is, indeed, too expensive. If they are desired, the charges for them must be viewed for what they are–insurance costs.

Annuities are Sold Mostly Because of the High Commissions They Pay

This argument may be accurate to some degree, but it is also an ad hominem logical fallacy. It is true that the commissions paid on deferred annuities are often higher than those paid on mutual funds, and common sense suggests that a commissioned advisor, in choosing among alternatives to recommend to a client, will be influenced by the amount of compensation each alternative provides him. However, the benefit of any investment to its owner consists in what can be realized from it. The value of that investment must, of course, be reckoned by relating the benefits received to the cost paid. If a deferred annuity offers benefits not available from alternatives, but its cost to purchase and maintain is higher, the value of that contract depends upon whether the additional benefits are worth the additional cost.

A particular annuity contract that pays 3.5% of the investor's contribution to one selling agent, but 6% to another (because those agents have different contracts with their respective broker/dealers) will have the same value to the purchaser (assuming that the advisors are equally competent and diligent). The agents' commissions will be of significance to those agents, and, arguably, may affect their recommendations. But the value of that annuity to its purchaser will be the same, whichever agent makes the sale.

The value of the annuity relative to its costs depends on the features and benefits of the contract, and the costs to the client, regardless of where or how those costs may be subsequently allocated. As an extreme (and entirely imaginary) example, consider an investment that charges the purchaser an overhead cost of 5% per year, but provides a guaranteed return of between 15%-25%. Although the annual cost of the investment is absurdly high, so is the return. This would probably be an extremely good investment–if it existed. Moreover, the decision as to whether this is or is not a good investment depends solely on the costs and benefits of the contract. Whether the issuer uses the 5% per year it collects from the purchaser to compensate a salesman with 2%, 5%, 10%, or 20% of the purchase price has no bearing on the value of the investment to the client.

Some annuities do not pay commissions, and generally offer lower charges as a result. These "low load" contracts account for only a small fraction of the annuities sold each year. Does this mean that most annuity purchasers are being abused? That conclusion does not follow, for two reasons:

1. The guaranteed death benefits and–especially–the guaranteed living benefits offered by low load deferred annuity contracts are generally less attractive (though, of course, less costly) than those offered by fully loaded annuities. Where these guarantees are important to the client, the lesser benefits offered by low load contracts may be unattractive, even at a lower annual cost.[3]

2.   Non-commissionable products are sold chiefly by advisors who charge a fee for advisory services ("fee-based" or "fee-only" advisors). Adding the advisory fee to the annual cost of a low load annuity, the resulting total annual cost, while it may (or may not) be less than the annual cost of a fully-commissionable contract, may still be unattractive, as the benefit of that cost will be limited to the generally less attractive guarantees of the low load annuity.

Only 2% (or Some Other Low Percentage) of Deferred Annuities are Ever Annuitized

There are two flaws implicit in this argument. First, the right to annuitize is just that–a right. It is not an obligation. The opportunity to avail oneself of either the payout factors currently available to holders of a deferred annuity or to elect annuitization using the factors guaranteed in the contract, is just that, an opportunity–a choice, and a risk management decision (much more than an investment one). A decision not to exercise an option does not make the option valueless.

An even more serious flaw to this argument is that it is a statistic that is utterly unreliable. Even conceding the accuracy of data on annuitized contracts, the flaw lies in the definition of "annuitized." That term means an election, by the owner of a deferred annuity contract, to accept an annuitization option in that contract. In that literal sense, the statistic (of 2% or whatever percentage one happens to use) of "contracts that are annuitized" may be accurate, but it is entirely meaningless as an indication of how many owners of deferred annuity contracts have chosen to convert their accumulated value to an income stream.

One of the authors has been selling annuities for over thirty years and has never recommended that a client exercise any annuity option in his contract. He has recommended to many clients that they exchange an existing deferred annuity for a single premium immediate annuity from whatever highly rated insurer happened, at the time, to offer the highest annuity payout rate for the option chosen. As it happened, the issuer of the deferred annuity was never, in any of these instances, the company offering the best rate.

This procedure, of going shopping for annuity rates on behalf of a client and recommending a tax-free exchange of that client's existing deferred annuity for an immediate annuity is a very common practice. It could be argued that the failure to offer this option to a client constitutes a breach of advisor responsibility, as the client cannot, by accepting a payout rate higher than the one guaranteed in his deferred contract, fail to benefit so long as the issuer of the immediate annuity is at least as financially strong and viable as the issuer of the deferred contract. These exchanges are done every day both because they are in the client's interest and because the agent selling the immediate annuity earns a commission. But they are not reflected in the statistic quoted above. It is certain that the total number of annuity contract holders electing to convert a deferred annuity to an income stream–a number that must include both annuitizations and exchanges of deferred annuities for immediate ones–is far higher than the 2% or so reported. How much higher is anyone's guess.

Arguments Against Immediate Annuities

Those who argue against the purchase of immediate annuities usually do so for one or more of the following reasons:

1. **Inflexibility.** Nearly all immediate annuities are inflexible. Once begun, the arrangement may not be modified, nor may remaining payments be commuted to a lump sum. This is certainly a valid concern. The inability of a planning strategy to adapt to changing goals and circumstances is, by definition, a disadvantage. Moreover, an irrevocable annuitization has an emotional component. One loses *control* over that part of one's wealth that has been annuitized. The *feeling* of this loss may exact a price not measurable in investment terms. That said, a few newer immediate annuity contracts allow for some modification in the payout arrangement, including commutation of remaining payments. There is, of course, a cost to this benefit (perhaps in the form of a lower initial payout than would be offered without it). Many consumers will find this flexibility worth the price.

    The authors suggest that an alternative might be to consider a conventional immediate annuity (without the flexibility benefits or the cost for same) only for that portion of one's portfolio that one is prepared to "lock into" an income stream. As noted earlier, the decision whether or not to purchase an immediate annuity need not be "all or nothing".

2. **Immediate Annuities "Lock In" Low Interest Rates.** This argument is usually advanced during periods of low prevailing interest rates, but it has merit at any time. The interest rate used to compute the amount

of payments in an immediate annuity contract are always conservative. They have to be, for the issuing insurer must make those payments regardless of future changes in the returns the insurer will earn on invested premiums and of how long the annuitant lives (in the case of life annuities). When interest rates change, so do annuity payout rates. Although immediate annuities with longer payout periods do not necessarily experience the same level of decline as those with longer period payouts, a decline in the general interest rate environment will generally reduce the current payout factors of all annuities.

That said, the argument that the buyer of an immediate annuity is "locking in" low interest rates for the duration of the annuity period misses the whole point. The point – the whole purpose – of an immediate annuity is not to earn a return on invested principal, but to *convert* that invested principal into *income* which is certain as to amount *and* duration (in the case of life annuities, for as long as the annuitant lives). It is those *certainties* that constitute the real benefit, not the rate of return used to compute the payments. An immediate annuity is an *insurance* vehicle that *transfers risks* from the contract owner to the issuing insurer. The risks transferred are (a) the risk that future changes in the financial markets might cause future income payments to decline and (b) the risk that the annuitant might outlive the income payments. If an investor is willing to *assume* those risks, other investments offer someone considering a life annuity potentially higher income (from potentially higher interest rates or investment yields), at the costs of no assurance of either the amount of income or its duration. For someone considering a *period certain* annuity (for a specified period of years, whether the annuitant outlives that period or not), alternatives may not provide the same *initial* level of income, but offer access to principal, and potentially higher returns in later years (due to principal growth). In the end, if the guarantees offered by the annuity produce the *actual dollars needed to secure one's goals*, the fact that interest rates or investment returns may be higher in the future is not necessarily even relevant to the client.

3. **No Inflation Protection.** Most immediate annuities are fixed in amount. Although a few contracts offer the option of either a fixed amount or an annuity increasing at a set percentage each year (usually no more than 3-5%), most do not. For those that do, the amount of the first year's annuity payment will be less than that of contracts with-

out this option. The greater the guaranteed annual increase, the lower the initial payment, for any amount invested. No contract the authors are aware of provides that annuity payments will vary directly with the unknown future fluctuations in the rate of inflation (as measured by an index such as the Consumer Price Index). Why such a contract has not yet been introduced is a puzzlement. The authors have heard, repeatedly, that there is no market for this type of product, which seems unpersuasive, given the almost universal recognition of the devastating impact that inflation can have on those living on a fixed income. To be sure, the first year's income from an inflation-adjusted annuity–especially an annuity guaranteed for the life of the annuitant–will necessarily be less (possibly, a great deal less) than that guaranteed by an un-indexed product, and it may be that most consumers would not be willing to accept that trade-off. Nevertheless, in the authors' opinion at least, a contract offering the purchase a choice between fixed payments and payments that will keep pace with inflation ought to be attractive.

Chapter Endnotes

1. This does not mean, of course, that there are no annual expenses in fixed annuities, but only that those expenses are paid for out of the interest rate spread, rather than by direct charges to the contract owner. See Chapter 4.

2. While a few critics arrive at the conclusion that insurance costs in VAs are too high from a risk management analysis (comparing the death benefit guarantee cost to term life insurance rates, for example), most (inappropriately, in the authors' opinion) treat these costs as investment overhead.

3. It is quite possible that some low load deferred annuity contracts will begin offering both guaranteed living and guaranteed death benefits comparable to their fully loaded cousins. However, this will increase, substantially, the cost of these contracts. As the chief appeal of low load annuities appears to be access to the annuity "wrapper" (and the tax treatment that goes with it) at the least annual cost, providers of low load contracts may be reluctant to increase costs of those contracts, particularly those companies that offer both commissionable and non-commissionable products.

Chapter 12

Overview: The Annuity as a Planning Tool

We have examined, in this and preceding chapters, how annuities work, how they are taxed, their special provisions, and some of the arguments made in favor of, and in opposition to, the use of annuities in financial, estate, and retirement planning. The authors have tried to treat the subject fairly, and to present the pros and cons of annuities, as planning tools, as objectively as we know how. It is, of course, up to the reader to decide whether we have been successful in that effort.

The authors are neither "for" nor "against" annuities. Annuities are merely tools, and are appropriate or inappropriate to the extent that they do the job better or worse than available alternatives. The value of any annuity, as a planning tool, depends upon the planning objective. Where that objective involves managing certain risks, the annuity may well be the right tool, for an annuity is not only an investment, but a risk management instrument. As such, its performance should be assessed in the light of how well it performs in both areas. If a particular investor has no want or need for some of the risk management features of an annuity, the cost for those features can reasonably be considered to be investment overhead cost. However, where the benefits provided by these features have value to the investor, the cost of those benefits should not be charged against investment performance (as is often done), especially when the annuity is compared to an instrument that neither provides these benefits nor charges for them. The risk management benefits, to the extent that they are wanted and needed, should be related to the charges for that benefit and a cost/benefit decision should be made. If, for example, the guaranteed death benefit in a variable annuity costs 25 basis points per year, its value might be ascertained by the consumer asking "would I rather have the investment performance of the contract without this benefit, and risk leaving my heirs with whatever the account balance happens to be on the day I die, or is having the guaranteed values I've just examined worth my giving up one-quarter of one percent of investment returns every year?"

This procedure can be done with each of the risk management features of the annuity that are not offered by an alternative investment. Where the benefit is perceived to be worth less than its contractual cost, that difference may be viewed as additional cost of the annuity. However, where the investor values the benefit, and has determined that it is worth so many basis points per year in reduced returns, a proper comparison of the annuity with an alternative would require that the return for that alternative be reduced by the cost of the valued benefit (which is not provided for on the alternative side of the ledger). On the other hand, the assumption, by many marketers of annuities, that the risk management features of these contracts are worth the charges imposed for them is no more valid than the assumptions of critics that such features are of little or no value.

Regrettably, many comparisons of annuities with investment alternatives either assume that the special annuity benefits are worth their cost or that they are not. Some proponents of annuities assume that tax deferral is always better than "as earned" taxation even when the trade-off is the unavailability of capital gains taxation. Often, the unattractive tax implications for beneficiaries of non-qualified annuities are either ignored or dismissed as unimportant. Critics of annuities frequently assume that the investor will take his accumulated money in a lump sum at the end of the comparison period, which implicitly condemns both the guaranteed payout factors as worthless and obviates the rule regarding the taxation of annuitized benefits. Even worse, many comparisons contain serious analytical errors, including "stacking the deck" by applying one set of assumptions on the annuity side of the ledger and different assumptions on the other side. One celebrated annuity proponent does this in his book comparing annuities with mutual funds.[1]

The great problem with "The Great Annuity Debate" is that it is, all too often, less a debate than a feud. Balance and logic give way to mere polemic, and the result is not analysis, but diatribe. No one benefits by this–least of all, the consumer seeking honest and impartial advice and a decent understanding.

Chapter Endnotes

1. John Huggard, "Investing With Variable Annuities: Fifty Reasons Why Variable Annuities Are Better Than Mutual Funds." Moreover, some of his analyses are just plain wrong, such as his comparison examples in which the returns on the mutual fund alternative are taxed twice.

Appendix A

Actuarial Tables for Taxing Annuities

As referenced in various places throughout the text of this publication, the tables used for taxing annuities appear on the following pages. Included here are gender-based Tables I, II, IIA, and III and unisex Tables V, VI, VIA, and VII. The gender-based tables are to be used if the investment in the contract does not include a post-June 30, 1986 investment in the contract. The unisex tables are to be used if the investment in the contract does include a post-June 30, 1986 investment in the contract.

However, even if there is no investment in the contract after June 30, 1986, an annuitant receiving annuity payments after June 30, 1986 (regardless of when they first began) may elect to treat his entire investment in the contract as post-June 30, 1986 and apply Tables V-VII. This election may be made for any taxable year in which such amounts are received by the taxpayer; it is irrevocable and applies with respect to all amounts the taxpayer receives as an annuity under the contract in the taxable year for which the election is made or in any subsequent tax year.

If investment in the contract includes both a pre-July 1986 investment and a post-June 1986 investment, an election may be made to make separate computations with respect to each portion of the aggregate investment in the contract using with respect to each portion the tables applicable to it. The amount excludable is the sum of the amounts determined under the separate computations. However, the election is not available (i.e., the entire investment must be treated as post-June 1986 investment) if the annuity starting date is after June 30, 1986 and the contract provides an option (whether or not it is exercised) to receive amounts under the contract other than in the form of a life annuity. Reg. §1.72-6(d).

Treasury regulations extend some of the tables to higher and lower ages, but the partial tables contained here are adequate for all practical purposes. The multiples in Tables I, II, and IIA or V, VI, and VIA need not be adjusted for monthly payments. For quarterly, semi-annual or annual payments, they must be adjusted according to the Frequency of Payment Adjustment Table, below. Table III and Table VII multiples, giving the percentage value of refund features, are never adjusted.

All tables are entered with the age of the annuitant at his or her birthday nearest the annuity starting date.

Frequency of Payment Adjustment Table

If the number of whole months from the annuity starting date to the first payment date is	0-1	2	3	4	5	6	7	8	9	10	11	12
And payments under the contract are to be made:												
Annually	+0.5	+0.4	+0.3	+0.2	+0.1	0	0	-0.1	-0.2	-0.3	-0.4	-0.5
Semiannually	+ .2	+ .1	0	0	- .1	- .2	....	....	....	....	....	....
Quarterly	+ .1	0	- .1	....	....	....	....	....	....	....	....	....

Example. Ed Black bought an annuity contract on January 1 which provides him with an *annual* payment of $4,000 payable on December 31st of each year. His age on birthday nearest the annuity starting date (January 1) is 66. The multiple from Table V for male age 66, is 19.2. This multiple must be adjusted for annual payment by subtracting .5 (19.2 - .5 = 18.7). Thus, his total expected return is $74,800 (18.7 x $4,000). See Treas. Reg. §1.72-5(a)(2).

Table I — Ordinary Life Annuities — One Life — Expected Return Multiples

Male	Female	Multiples	Male	Female	Multiples
6	11	65.0	59	64	18.9
7	12	64.1	60	65	18.2
8	13	63.2	61	66	17.5
9	14	62.3	62	67	16.9
10	15	61.4	63	68	16.2
11	16	60.4	64	69	15.6
12	17	59.5	65	70	15.0
13	18	58.6	66	71	14.4
14	19	57.7	67	72	13.8
15	20	56.7	68	73	13.2
16	21	55.8	69	74	12.6
17	22	54.9	70	75	12.1
18	23	53.9	71	76	11.6
19	24	53.0	72	77	11.0
20	25	52.1	73	78	10.5
21	26	51.1	74	79	10.1
22	27	50.2	75	80	9.6
23	28	49.3	76	81	9.1
24	29	48.3	77	82	8.7
25	30	47.4	78	83	8.3
26	31	46.5	79	84	7.8
27	32	45.6	80	85	7.5
28	33	44.6	81	86	7.1
29	34	43.7	82	87	6.7
30	35	42.8	83	88	6.3
31	36	41.9	84	89	6.0
32	37	41.0	85	90	5.7
33	38	40.0	86	91	5.4
34	39	39.1	87	92	5.1
35	40	38.2	88	93	4.8
36	41	37.3	89	94	4.5
37	42	36.5	90	95	4.2
38	43	35.6	91	96	4.0
39	44	34.7	92	97	3.7
40	45	33.8	93	98	3.5
41	46	33.0	94	99	3.3
42	47	32.1	95	100	3.1
43	48	31.2	96	101	2.9
44	49	30.4	97	102	2.7
45	50	29.6	98	103	2.5
46	51	28.7	99	104	2.3
47	52	27.9	100	105	2.1
48	53	27.1	101	106	1.9
49	54	26.3	102	107	1.7
50	55	25.5	103	108	1.5
51	56	24.7	104	109	1.3
52	57	24.0	105	110	1.2
53	58	23.2	106	111	1.0
54	59	22.4	107	112	.8
55	60	21.7	108	113	.7
56	61	21.0	109	114	.6
57	62	20.3	110	115	.5
58	63	19.6	111	116	.0

Table II — Ordinary Joint Life and Last Survivor Annuities — Two Lives — Expected Return Multiples

Male	Female	35 / 40	36 / 41	37 / 42	38 / 43	39 / 44	40 / 45	41 / 46	42 / 47	43 / 48	44 / 49	45 / 50	46 / 51	47 / 52
35	40	46.2	45.7	45.3	44.8	44.4	44.0	43.6	43.3	43.0	42.6	42.3	42.0	41.8
36	41	...	45.2	44.8	44.3	43.9	43.5	43.1	42.7	42.3	42.0	41.7	41.4	41.1
37	42	...	...	44.3	43.8	43.4	42.9	42.5	42.1	41.8	41.4	41.1	40.7	40.4
38	43	...	...	...	43.3	42.9	42.4	42.0	41.6	41.2	40.8	40.5	40.1	39.8
39	44	...	...	...	...	42.4	41.9	41.5	41.0	40.6	40.2	39.9	39.5	39.2
40	45	...	...	...	...	...	41.4	41.0	40.5	40.1	39.7	39.3	38.9	38.6
41	46	...	...	...	...	...	...	40.5	40.0	39.6	39.2	38.8	38.4	38.0
42	47	...	...	...	...	...	...	...	39.6	39.1	38.7	38.2	37.8	37.5
43	48	...	...	...	...	...	...	...	...	38.6	38.2	37.7	37.3	36.9
44	49	...	...	...	...	...	...	...	...	...	37.7	37.2	36.8	36.4
45	50	...	...	...	...	...	...	...	...	...	...	36.8	36.3	35.9
46	51	...	...	...	...	...	...	...	...	...	...	...	35.9	35.4
47	52	...	...	...	...	...	...	...	...	...	...	...	...	35.0

Male	Female	48 / 53	49 / 54	50 / 55	51 / 56	52 / 57	53 / 58	54 / 59	55 / 60	56 / 61	57 / 62	58 / 63	59 / 64	60 / 65
35	40	41.5	41.3	41.0	40.8	40.6	40.4	40.3	40.1	40.0	39.8	39.7	39.6	39.5
36	41	40.8	40.6	40.3	40.1	39.9	39.7	39.5	39.3	39.2	39.0	38.9	38.8	38.6
37	42	40.2	39.9	39.6	39.4	39.2	39.0	38.8	38.6	38.4	38.3	38.1	38.0	37.9
38	43	39.5	39.2	39.0	38.7	38.5	38.3	38.1	37.9	37.7	37.5	37.3	37.2	37.1
39	44	38.9	38.6	38.3	38.0	37.8	37.6	37.3	37.1	36.9	36.8	36.6	36.4	36.3
40	45	38.3	38.0	37.7	37.4	37.1	36.9	36.6	36.4	36.2	36.0	35.9	35.7	35.5
41	46	37.7	37.3	37.0	36.7	36.5	36.2	36.0	35.7	35.5	35.3	35.1	35.0	34.8
42	47	37.1	36.8	36.4	36.1	35.8	35.6	35.3	35.1	34.8	34.6	34.4	34.2	34.1
43	48	36.5	36.2	35.8	35.5	35.2	34.9	34.7	34.4	34.2	33.9	33.7	33.5	33.3
44	49	36.0	35.6	35.3	34.9	34.6	34.3	34.0	33.8	33.5	33.3	33.0	32.8	32.6
45	50	35.5	35.1	34.7	34.4	34.0	33.7	33.4	33.1	32.9	32.6	32.4	32.2	31.9
46	51	35.0	34.6	34.2	33.8	33.5	33.1	32.8	32.5	32.2	32.0	31.7	31.5	31.3
47	52	34.5	34.1	33.7	33.3	32.9	32.6	32.2	31.9	31.6	31.4	31.1	30.9	30.6
48	53	34.0	33.6	33.2	32.8	32.4	32.0	31.7	31.4	31.1	30.8	30.5	30.2	30.0
49	54	...	33.1	32.7	32.3	31.9	31.5	31.2	30.8	30.5	30.2	29.9	29.6	29.4
50	55	...	...	32.3	31.8	31.4	31.0	30.6	30.3	29.9	29.6	29.3	29.0	28.8
51	56	...	...	...	31.4	30.9	30.5	30.1	29.8	29.4	29.1	28.8	28.5	28.2
52	57	...	...	...	...	30.5	30.1	29.7	29.3	28.9	28.6	28.2	27.9	27.6
53	58	...	...	...	...	...	29.6	29.2	28.8	28.4	28.1	27.7	27.4	27.1
54	59	...	...	...	...	...	...	28.8	28.3	27.9	27.6	27.2	26.9	26.5
55	60	...	...	...	...	...	...	...	27.9	27.5	27.1	26.7	26.4	26.0
56	61	...	...	...	...	...	...	...	...	27.1	26.7	26.3	25.9	25.5
57	62	...	...	...	...	...	...	...	...	...	26.2	25.8	25.4	25.1
58	63	...	...	...	...	...	...	...	...	...	...	25.4	25.0	24.6
59	64	...	...	...	...	...	...	...	...	...	...	...	24.6	24.2
60	65	...	...	...	...	...	...	...	...	...	...	...	...	23.8

Table II — Ordinary Joint Life and Last Survivor Annuities — Two Lives —
Expected Return Multiples — Continued

Ages Male / Female	61 / 66	62 / 67	63 / 68	64 / 69	65 / 70	66 / 71	67 / 72	68 / 73	69 / 74	70 / 75	71 / 76	72 / 77	73 / 78
35 / 40	39.4	39.3	39.2	39.1	39.0	38.9	38.9	38.8	38.8	38.7	38.7	38.6	38.6
36 / 41	38.5	38.4	38.3	38.2	38.2	38.1	38.0	38.0	37.9	37.9	37.8	37.8	37.7
37 / 42	37.7	37.6	37.5	37.4	37.3	37.3	37.2	37.1	37.1	37.0	36.9	36.9	36.9
38 / 43	36.9	36.8	36.7	36.6	36.5	36.4	36.4	36.3	36.2	36.2	36.1	36.0	36.0
39 / 44	36.2	36.0	35.9	35.8	35.7	35.6	35.5	35.5	35.4	35.3	35.3	35.2	35.2
40 / 45	35.4	35.3	35.1	35.0	34.9	34.8	34.7	34.6	34.6	34.5	34.4	34.4	34.3
41 / 46	34.6	34.5	34.4	34.2	34.1	34.0	33.9	33.8	33.8	33.7	33.6	33.5	33.5
42 / 47	33.9	33.7	33.6	33.5	33.4	33.2	33.1	33.1	33.0	33.0	32.9	32.8	32.7
43 / 48	33.2	33.0	32.9	32.7	32.6	32.5	32.4	32.3	32.2	32.1	32.0	31.9	31.9
44 / 49	32.5	32.3	32.1	32.0	31.8	31.7	31.6	31.5	31.4	31.3	31.2	31.1	31.1
45 / 50	31.8	31.6	31.4	31.3	31.1	31.0	30.8	30.7	30.6	30.5	30.4	30.4	30.3
46 / 51	31.1	30.9	30.7	30.5	30.4	30.2	30.1	30.0	29.9	29.8	29.7	29.6	29.5
47 / 52	30.4	30.2	30.0	29.8	29.7	29.5	29.4	29.3	29.1	29.0	28.9	28.8	28.7
48 / 53	29.8	29.5	29.3	29.2	29.0	28.8	28.7	28.5	28.4	28.3	28.2	28.1	28.0
49 / 54	29.1	28.9	28.7	28.5	28.3	28.1	28.0	27.8	27.7	27.6	27.5	27.4	27.3
50 / 55	28.5	28.3	28.1	27.8	27.6	27.5	27.3	27.1	27.0	26.9	26.7	26.6	26.5
51 / 56	27.9	27.7	27.4	27.2	27.0	26.8	26.6	26.5	26.3	26.2	26.1	25.9	25.8
52 / 57	27.3	27.1	26.8	26.6	26.4	26.2	26.0	25.8	25.7	25.5	25.4	25.2	25.1
53 / 58	26.8	26.5	26.2	26.0	25.8	25.6	25.4	25.2	25.0	24.8	24.7	24.6	24.4
54 / 59	26.2	25.9	25.7	25.4	25.2	25.0	24.7	24.6	24.4	24.2	24.0	23.9	23.8
55 / 60	25.7	25.4	25.1	24.9	24.6	24.4	24.1	23.9	23.8	23.6	23.4	23.3	23.1
56 / 61	25.2	24.9	24.6	24.3	24.1	23.8	23.6	23.4	23.2	23.0	22.8	22.6	22.5
57 / 62	24.7	24.4	24.1	23.8	23.5	23.3	23.0	22.8	22.6	22.4	22.2	22.0	21.9
58 / 63	24.3	23.9	23.6	23.3	23.0	22.7	22.5	22.2	22.0	21.8	21.6	21.4	21.3
59 / 64	23.8	23.5	23.1	22.8	22.5	22.2	21.9	21.7	21.5	21.2	21.0	20.9	20.7
60 / 65	23.4	23.0	22.7	22.3	22.0	21.7	21.4	21.2	20.9	20.7	20.5	20.3	20.1
61 / 66	23.0	22.6	22.2	21.9	21.6	21.3	21.0	20.7	20.4	20.2	20.0	19.8	19.6
62 / 67	...	22.2	21.8	21.5	21.1	20.8	20.5	20.2	19.9	19.7	19.5	19.2	19.0
63 / 68	...	...	21.4	21.1	20.7	20.4	20.1	19.8	19.5	19.2	19.0	18.7	18.5
64 / 69	...	...	...	20.7	20.3	20.0	19.6	19.3	19.0	18.7	18.5	18.2	18.0
65 / 70	...	...	...	...	19.9	19.6	19.2	18.9	18.6	18.3	18.0	17.8	17.5
66 / 71	...	...	...	...	...	19.2	18.8	18.5	18.2	17.9	17.6	17.3	17.1
67 / 72	...	...	...	...	...	...	18.5	18.1	17.8	17.5	17.2	16.9	16.7
68 / 73	...	...	...	...	...	...	...	17.8	17.4	17.1	16.8	16.5	16.2
69 / 74	...	...	...	...	...	...	...	...	17.1	16.7	16.4	16.1	15.8
70 / 75	...	...	...	...	...	...	...	...	...	16.4	16.1	15.8	15.5
71 / 76	...	...	...	...	...	...	...	...	...	...	15.7	15.4	15.1
72 / 77	...	...	...	...	...	...	...	...	...	...	...	15.1	14.8
73 / 78	...	...	...	...	...	...	...	...	...	...	...	...	14.4

Ages Male / Female	74 / 79	75 / 80	76 / 81	77 / 82	78 / 83	79 / 84	80 / 85	81 / 86	82 / 87	83 / 88	84 / 89	85 / 90
35 / 40	38.6	38.5	38.5	38.5	38.4	38.4	38.4	38.4	38.4	38.4	38.3	38.3
36 / 41	37.7	37.6	37.6	37.6	37.6	37.6	37.5	37.5	37.5	37.5	37.5	37.4
37 / 42	36.8	36.8	36.7	36.7	36.7	36.7	36.6	36.6	36.6	36.6	36.6	36.6
38 / 43	36.0	35.9	35.9	35.8	35.8	35.8	35.8	35.8	35.7	35.7	35.7	35.7
39 / 44	35.1	35.1	35.0	35.0	35.0	34.9	34.9	34.9	34.9	34.8	34.8	34.8
40 / 45	34.3	34.2	34.2	34.1	34.1	34.1	34.1	34.0	34.0	34.0	34.0	34.0
41 / 46	33.4	33.4	33.3	33.3	33.3	33.2	33.2	33.2	33.2	33.1	33.1	33.1
42 / 47	32.6	32.6	32.5	32.5	32.4	32.4	32.4	32.3	32.3	32.3	32.3	32.3
43 / 48	31.8	31.8	31.7	31.7	31.6	31.6	31.5	31.5	31.5	31.5	31.4	31.4
44 / 49	31.0	30.9	30.9	30.8	30.8	30.8	30.7	30.7	30.7	30.6	30.6	30.6
45 / 50	30.2	30.1	30.1	30.0	30.0	30.0	29.9	29.9	29.8	29.8	29.8	29.8
46 / 51	29.4	29.4	29.3	29.2	29.2	29.2	29.1	29.1	29.0	29.0	29.0	28.9
47 / 52	28.7	28.6	28.5	28.5	28.4	28.4	28.3	28.3	28.2	28.2	28.2	28.1
48 / 53	27.9	27.8	27.8	27.7	27.6	27.6	27.5	27.5	27.5	27.4	27.4	27.4
49 / 54	27.2	27.1	27.0	26.9	26.9	26.8	26.8	26.7	26.7	26.6	26.6	26.6
50 / 55	26.4	26.3	26.3	26.2	26.1	26.1	26.0	26.0	25.9	25.9	25.8	25.8
51 / 56	25.7	25.6	25.5	25.5	25.4	25.3	25.3	25.2	25.2	25.1	25.1	25.0
52 / 57	25.0	24.9	24.8	24.7	24.7	24.6	24.5	24.5	24.4	24.4	24.3	24.3
53 / 58	24.3	24.2	24.1	24.0	23.9	23.9	23.8	23.7	23.7	23.6	23.6	23.5
54 / 59	23.6	23.5	23.4	23.3	23.2	23.2	23.1	23.0	23.0	22.9	22.9	22.8
55 / 60	23.0	22.9	22.8	22.7	22.6	22.5	22.4	22.3	22.3	22.2	22.2	22.1
56 / 61	22.3	22.2	22.1	22.0	21.9	21.8	21.7	21.6	21.6	21.5	21.5	21.4
57 / 62	21.7	21.6	21.5	21.3	21.2	21.1	21.1	21.0	20.9	20.8	20.8	20.7
58 / 63	21.1	21.0	20.8	20.7	20.6	20.5	20.4	20.3	20.2	20.2	20.1	20.0
59 / 64	20.5	20.4	20.2	20.1	20.0	19.9	19.8	19.7	19.6	19.5	19.5	19.4
60 / 65	19.9	19.8	19.6	19.5	19.4	19.3	19.1	19.0	19.0	18.9	18.8	18.7
61 / 66	19.4	19.2	19.1	18.9	18.8	18.7	18.5	18.4	18.3	18.3	18.2	18.1
62 / 67	18.8	18.7	18.5	18.3	18.2	18.1	18.0	17.8	17.7	17.7	17.6	17.5
63 / 68	18.3	18.1	18.0	17.8	17.6	17.5	17.4	17.3	17.2	17.1	17.0	16.9
64 / 69	17.8	17.6	17.4	17.3	17.1	17.0	16.8	16.7	16.6	16.5	16.4	16.3
65 / 70	17.3	17.1	16.9	16.7	16.6	16.4	16.3	16.2	16.0	15.9	15.8	15.8
66 / 71	16.9	16.6	16.4	16.3	16.1	15.9	15.8	15.6	15.5	15.4	15.3	15.2
67 / 72	16.4	16.2	16.0	15.8	15.6	15.4	15.3	15.1	15.0	14.9	14.8	14.7
68 / 73	16.0	15.7	15.5	15.3	15.1	15.0	14.8	14.6	14.5	14.4	14.3	14.2
69 / 74	15.6	15.3	15.1	14.9	14.7	14.5	14.3	14.2	14.0	13.9	13.8	13.7
70 / 75	15.2	14.9	14.7	14.5	14.3	14.1	13.9	13.7	13.6	13.4	13.3	13.2
71 / 76	14.8	14.5	14.3	14.1	13.8	13.6	13.5	13.3	13.1	13.0	12.8	12.7
72 / 77	14.5	14.2	13.9	13.7	13.5	13.2	13.0	12.9	12.7	12.5	12.4	12.3
73 / 78	14.1	13.8	13.6	13.3	13.1	12.9	12.7	12.5	12.3	12.1	12.0	11.8
74 / 79	13.8	13.5	13.2	13.0	12.7	12.5	12.3	12.1	11.9	11.7	11.6	11.4
75 / 80	...	13.2	12.9	12.6	12.4	12.2	11.9	11.7	11.5	11.4	11.2	11.0
76 / 81	...	...	12.6	12.3	12.1	11.8	11.6	11.4	11.2	11.0	10.8	10.7
77 / 82	...	...	...	12.1	11.8	11.5	11.3	11.1	10.8	10.7	10.5	10.3
78 / 83	...	...	...	...	11.5	11.2	11.0	10.7	10.5	10.3	10.1	10.0
79 / 84	...	...	...	...	...	11.0	10.7	10.5	10.2	10.0	9.8	9.6
80 / 85	...	...	...	...	...	...	10.4	10.2	10.0	9.7	9.5	9.3
81 / 86	...	...	...	...	...	...	...	9.9	9.7	9.5	9.3	9.1
82 / 87	...	...	...	...	...	...	...	...	9.4	9.2	9.0	8.8
83 / 88	...	...	...	...	...	...	...	...	...	9.0	8.7	8.5
84 / 89	...	...	...	...	...	...	...	...	...	...	8.5	8.3
85 / 90	...	...	...	...	...	...	...	...	...	...	...	8.1

Table IIA—Annuities for Joint Life Only — Two Lives — Expected Return Multiples

Ages Male	Female	35 40	36 41	37 42	38 43	39 44	40 45	41 46	42 47	43 48	44 49	45 50	46 51	47 52
35	40	30.3	29.9	29.4	29.0	28.5	28.0	27.5	27.0	26.5	26.0	25.5	24.9	24.4
36	41		29.5	29.0	28.6	28.2	27.7	27.2	26.7	26.2	25.7	25.2	24.7	24.2
37	42	...	...	28.6	28.2	27.8	27.3	26.9	26.4	25.9	25.5	25.0	24.4	23.9
38	43	...	...		27.8	27.4	27.0	26.5	26.1	25.6	25.2	24.7	24.2	23.7
39	44	...	...	...		27.0	26.6	26.2	25.8	25.3	24.8	24.4	23.9	23.4
40	45	...	...	...	...		26.2	25.8	25.4	25.0	24.5	24.1	23.6	23.1
41	46	...	...	...	...	...		25.4	25.0	24.6	24.2	23.8	23.3	22.9
42	47	...	...	...	...	...	...		24.6	24.2	23.8	23.4	23.0	22.6
43	48	...	...	...	...	...	...	...		23.9	23.5	23.1	22.7	22.2
44	49	...	...	...	...	...	...	...	...		23.1	22.7	22.3	21.9
45	50	...	...	...	...	...	...	...	...	...		22.4	22.0	21.6
46	51	...	...	...	...	...	...	...	...	...	...		21.6	21.2
47	52	...	...	...	...	...	...	...	...	...	...	...		20.9

Ages Male	Female	48 53	49 54	50 55	51 56	52 57	53 58	54 59	55 60	56 61	57 62	58 63	59 64	60 65
35	40	23.8	23.3	22.7	22.1	21.6	21.0	20.4	19.8	19.3	18.7	18.1	17.5	17.0
36	41	23.6	23.1	22.5	22.0	21.4	20.8	20.3	19.7	19.1	18.6	18.0	17.4	16.9
37	42	23.4	22.9	22.3	21.8	21.2	20.7	20.1	19.6	19.0	18.4	17.9	17.3	16.8
38	43	23.2	22.6	22.1	21.6	21.1	20.5	20.0	19.4	18.9	18.3	17.8	17.2	16.7
39	44	22.9	22.4	21.9	21.4	20.9	20.3	19.8	19.3	18.7	18.2	17.7	17.1	16.6
40	45	22.7	22.2	21.7	21.2	20.7	20.1	19.6	19.1	18.6	18.0	17.5	17.0	16.5
41	46	22.4	21.9	21.4	20.9	20.4	19.9	19.4	18.9	18.4	17.9	17.4	16.9	16.3
42	47	22.1	21.6	21.2	20.7	20.2	19.7	19.2	18.7	18.2	17.7	17.2	16.7	16.2
43	48	21.8	21.4	20.9	20.5	20.0	19.5	19.0	18.6	18.1	17.6	17.1	16.6	16.1
44	49	21.5	21.1	20.6	20.2	19.8	19.3	18.8	18.4	17.9	17.4	16.9	16.4	15.9
45	50	21.2	20.8	20.4	19.9	19.5	19.1	18.6	18.1	17.7	17.2	16.7	16.3	15.8
46	51	20.9	20.5	20.1	19.7	19.2	18.8	18.4	17.9	17.5	17.0	16.6	16.1	15.6
47	52	20.5	20.1	19.8	19.4	19.0	18.5	18.1	17.7	17.3	16.8	16.4	15.9	15.5
48	53	20.2	19.8	19.4	19.1	18.7	18.3	17.9	17.5	17.1	16.6	16.2	15.7	15.3
49	54	...	19.5	19.2	18.8	18.4	18.0	17.6	17.2	16.8	16.4	16.0	15.5	15.1
50	55	...	...	18.8	18.4	18.1	17.7	17.3	16.9	16.6	16.2	15.8	15.3	14.9
51	56	...	...	...	18.1	17.8	17.4	17.0	16.7	16.3	15.9	15.5	15.1	14.7
52	57	...	...	...	...	17.4	17.1	16.8	16.4	16.0	15.7	15.3	14.9	14.5
53	58	...	...	...	...	...	16.8	16.4	16.1	15.8	15.4	15.1	14.7	14.3
54	59	...	...	...	...	...	...	16.1	15.8	15.5	15.1	14.8	14.4	14.1
55	60	...	...	...	...	...	...	...	15.5	15.2	14.9	14.5	14.2	13.9
56	61	...	...	...	...	...	...	...	...	14.9	14.6	14.3	13.9	13.6
57	62	...	...	...	...	...	...	...	...	...	14.3	14.0	13.7	13.4
58	63	...	...	...	...	...	...	...	...	...	...	13.7	13.4	13.1
59	64	...	...	...	...	...	...	...	...	...	...	...	13.1	12.8
60	65	...	...	...	...	...	...	...	...	...	...	...	...	12.6

Ages Male	Female	61 66	62 67	63 68	64 69	65 70	66 71	67 72	68 73	69 74	70 75	71 76	72 77	73 78
35	40	16.4	15.8	15.3	14.7	14.2	13.7	13.1	12.6	12.1	11.6	11.1	10.7	10.2
36	41	16.3	15.8	15.2	14.7	14.1	13.6	13.1	12.6	12.1	11.6	11.1	10.6	10.2
37	42	16.2	15.7	15.1	14.6	14.1	13.6	13.0	12.5	12.0	11.5	11.1	10.6	10.1
38	43	16.1	15.6	15.1	14.5	14.0	13.5	13.0	12.5	12.0	11.5	11.0	10.6	10.1
39	44	16.0	15.5	15.0	14.5	13.9	13.4	12.9	12.4	11.9	11.5	11.0	10.5	10.1
40	45	15.9	15.4	14.9	14.4	13.9	13.4	12.9	12.4	11.9	11.4	11.0	10.5	10.0
41	46	15.8	15.3	14.8	14.3	13.8	13.3	12.8	12.3	11.8	11.4	10.9	10.5	10.0
42	47	15.7	15.2	14.7	14.2	13.7	13.2	12.7	12.3	11.8	11.3	10.9	10.4	10.0
43	48	15.6	15.1	14.6	14.1	13.6	13.1	12.7	12.2	11.7	11.3	10.8	10.4	9.9
44	49	15.5	15.0	14.5	14.0	13.5	13.1	12.6	12.1	11.7	11.2	10.8	10.3	9.9
45	50	15.3	14.8	14.4	13.9	13.4	13.0	12.5	12.0	11.6	11.1	10.7	10.3	9.8
46	51	15.2	14.7	14.2	13.8	13.3	12.9	12.4	12.0	11.5	11.1	10.6	10.2	9.8
47	52	15.0	14.6	14.1	13.7	13.2	12.8	12.3	11.9	11.4	11.0	10.6	10.1	9.7
48	53	14.9	14.4	14.0	13.5	13.1	12.6	12.2	11.8	11.3	10.9	10.5	10.1	9.7
49	54	14.7	14.3	13.8	13.4	13.0	12.5	12.1	11.7	11.3	10.8	10.4	10.0	9.6
50	55	14.5	14.1	13.7	13.3	12.8	12.4	12.0	11.6	11.2	10.7	10.3	9.9	9.5
51	56	14.3	13.9	13.5	13.1	12.7	12.3	11.9	11.5	11.1	10.7	10.3	9.9	9.5
52	57	14.1	13.7	13.3	12.9	12.5	12.1	11.7	11.3	10.9	10.6	10.2	9.8	9.4
53	58	13.9	13.6	13.2	12.8	12.4	12.0	11.6	11.2	10.8	10.5	10.1	9.7	9.3
54	59	13.7	13.4	13.0	12.6	12.2	11.9	11.5	11.1	10.7	10.3	10.0	9.6	9.2
55	60	13.5	13.2	12.8	12.4	12.1	11.7	11.3	11.0	10.6	10.2	9.9	9.5	9.1
56	61	13.3	12.9	12.6	12.2	11.9	11.5	11.2	10.8	10.5	10.1	9.8	9.4	9.0
57	62	13.0	12.7	12.4	12.1	11.7	11.4	11.0	10.7	10.3	10.0	9.6	9.3	8.9
58	63	12.8	12.5	12.2	11.8	11.5	11.2	10.9	10.5	10.2	9.8	9.5	9.2	8.8
59	64	12.6	12.3	11.9	11.6	11.3	11.0	10.7	10.4	10.0	9.7	9.4	9.1	8.7
60	65	12.3	12.0	11.7	11.4	11.1	10.8	10.5	10.2	9.9	9.6	9.3	8.9	8.6
61	66	12.0	11.8	11.5	11.2	10.9	10.6	10.3	10.0	9.7	9.4	9.1	8.8	8.5
62	67	...	11.5	11.2	11.0	10.7	10.4	10.1	9.8	9.6	9.3	9.0	8.7	8.4
63	68	...	...	11.0	10.7	10.5	10.2	9.9	9.7	9.4	9.1	8.8	8.5	8.2
64	69	...	...	...	10.5	10.2	10.0	9.7	9.5	9.2	8.9	8.7	8.4	8.1
65	70	...	...	...	...	10.0	9.8	9.5	9.3	9.0	8.8	8.6	8.3	8.0
66	71	...	...	...	...	...	9.5	9.3	9.1	8.8	8.6	8.3	8.1	7.8
67	72	...	...	...	...	...	...	9.1	8.9	8.6	8.4	8.1	7.9	7.7
68	73	...	...	...	...	...	...	...	8.6	8.4	8.2	8.0	7.7	7.5
69	74	...	...	...	...	...	...	...	...	8.2	8.0	7.8	7.6	7.3
70	75	...	...	...	...	...	...	...	...	...	7.8	7.6	7.4	7.2
71	76	...	...	...	...	...	...	...	...	...	...	7.4	7.2	7.0
72	77	...	...	...	...	...	...	...	...	...	...	...	7.0	6.8
73	78	...	...	...	...	...	...	...	...	...	...	...	...	6.7

Table IIA — Annuities for Joint Life Only — Two Lives —
Expected Return Multiples — Continued

Ages Male	Male Female	74 79	75 80	76 81	77 82	78 83	79 84	80 85	81 86	82 87	83 88	84 89	85 90	86 91
35	40	9.7	9.3	8.9	8.5	8.1	7.7	7.3	6.9	6.6	6.2	5.9	5.6	5.3
36	41	9.7	9.3	8.9	8.4	8.0	7.7	7.3	6.9	6.6	6.2	5.9	5.6	5.3
37	42	9.7	9.3	8.8	8.4	8.0	7.6	7.3	6.9	6.5	6.2	5.9	5.6	5.3
38	43	9.7	9.2	8.8	8.4	8.0	7.6	7.2	6.9	6.5	6.2	5.9	5.6	5.3
39	44	9.6	9.2	8.8	8.4	8.0	7.6	7.2	6.9	6.5	6.2	5.9	5.6	5.3
40	45	9.6	9.2	8.8	8.4	8.0	7.6	7.2	6.9	6.5	6.2	5.9	5.5	5.2
41	46	9.6	9.2	8.7	8.3	7.9	7.6	7.2	6.8	6.5	6.2	5.8	5.5	5.2
42	47	9.5	9.1	8.7	8.3	7.9	7.5	7.2	6.8	6.5	6.2	5.8	5.5	5.2
43	48	9.5	9.1	8.7	8.3	7.9	7.5	7.2	6.8	6.5	6.1	5.8	5.5	5.2
44	49	9.5	9.0	8.6	8.2	7.9	7.5	7.1	6.8	6.4	6.1	5.8	5.5	5.2
45	50	9.4	9.0	8.6	8.2	7.8	7.5	7.1	6.8	6.4	6.1	5.8	5.5	5.2
46	51	9.4	9.0	8.6	8.2	7.8	7.4	7.1	6.7	6.4	6.1	5.8	5.5	5.2
47	52	9.3	8.9	8.5	8.1	7.8	7.4	7.1	6.7	6.4	6.1	5.8	5.5	5.2
48	53	9.3	8.9	8.5	8.1	7.7	7.4	7.0	6.7	6.4	6.0	5.7	5.4	5.1
49	54	9.2	8.8	8.4	8.1	7.7	7.3	7.0	6.7	6.3	6.0	5.7	5.4	5.1
50	55	9.1	8.8	8.4	8.0	7.7	7.3	7.0	6.6	6.3	6.0	5.7	5.4	5.1
51	56	9.1	8.7	8.3	8.0	7.6	7.3	6.9	6.6	6.3	6.0	5.7	5.4	5.1
52	57	9.0	8.6	8.3	7.9	7.6	7.2	6.9	6.6	6.2	5.9	5.6	5.4	5.1
53	58	8.9	8.6	8.2	7.9	7.5	7.2	6.9	6.5	6.2	5.9	5.6	5.3	5.1
54	59	8.9	8.5	8.2	7.8	7.5	7.1	6.8	6.5	6.2	5.9	5.6	5.3	5.0
55	60	8.8	8.4	8.1	7.7	7.4	7.1	6.8	6.4	6.1	5.8	5.6	5.3	5.0
56	61	8.7	8.4	8.0	7.7	7.3	7.0	6.7	6.4	6.1	5.8	5.5	5.3	5.0
57	62	8.6	8.3	7.9	7.6	7.3	7.0	6.7	6.4	6.1	5.8	5.5	5.2	5.0
58	63	8.5	8.2	7.9	7.5	7.2	6.9	6.6	6.3	6.0	5.7	5.5	5.2	4.9
59	64	8.4	8.1	7.8	7.5	7.1	6.8	6.5	6.3	6.0	5.7	5.4	5.2	4.9
60	65	8.3	8.0	7.7	7.4	7.1	6.8	6.5	6.2	5.9	5.6	5.4	5.1	4.9
61	66	8.2	7.9	7.6	7.3	7.0	6.7	6.4	6.1	5.9	5.6	5.3	5.1	4.8
62	67	8.1	7.8	7.5	7.2	6.9	6.6	6.4	6.1	5.8	5.5	5.3	5.0	4.8
63	68	8.0	7.7	7.4	7.1	6.8	6.6	6.3	6.0	5.7	5.5	5.2	5.0	4.7
64	69	7.8	7.6	7.3	7.0	6.7	6.5	6.2	5.9	5.7	5.4	5.2	4.9	4.7
65	70	7.7	7.4	7.2	6.9	6.6	6.4	6.1	5.9	5.6	5.4	5.1	4.9	4.7
66	71	7.6	7.3	7.1	6.8	6.5	6.3	6.0	5.8	5.5	5.3	5.1	4.8	4.6
67	72	7.4	7.2	6.9	6.7	6.4	6.2	6.0	5.7	5.5	5.2	5.0	4.8	4.6
68	73	7.3	7.0	6.8	6.6	6.3	6.1	5.9	5.6	5.4	5.2	4.9	4.7	4.5
69	74	7.1	6.9	6.7	6.4	6.2	6.0	5.8	5.5	5.3	5.1	4.9	4.7	4.5
70	75	7.0	6.8	6.5	6.3	6.1	5.9	5.7	5.4	5.2	5.0	4.8	4.6	4.4
71	76	6.8	6.6	6.4	6.2	6.0	5.8	5.6	5.3	5.1	4.9	4.7	4.5	4.3
72	77	6.6	6.4	6.3	6.1	5.9	5.7	5.5	5.3	5.0	4.9	4.7	4.5	4.3
73	78	6.5	6.3	6.1	5.9	5.7	5.5	5.3	5.1	5.0	4.8	4.6	4.4	4.2
74	79	6.3	6.1	6.0	5.8	5.6	5.4	5.2	5.0	4.9	4.7	4.5	4.3	4.1
75	80	..	6.0	5.8	5.6	5.5	5.3	5.1	4.9	4.8	4.6	4.4	4.2	4.1
76	81	..	..	5.6	5.5	5.3	5.2	5.0	4.8	4.7	4.5	4.3	4.1	4.0
77	82	..	..	..	5.3	5.2	5.0	4.9	4.7	4.5	4.4	4.2	4.1	3.9
78	83	..	..	..	..	5.0	4.9	4.7	4.6	4.4	4.3	4.1	4.0	3.8
79	84	..	..	..	..	..	4.7	4.6	4.5	4.3	4.2	4.0	3.9	3.7
80	85	..	..	..	..	..	..	4.5	4.4	4.2	4.1	3.9	3.8	3.6
81	86	..	..	..	..	..	..	..	4.2	4.1	4.0	3.8	3.7	3.6
82	87	..	..	..	..	..	..	..	..	4.0	3.9	3.8	3.6	3.5
83	88	..	..	..	..	..	..	..	..	..	3.7	3.6	3.5	3.4
84	89	..	..	..	..	..	..	..	..	..	..	3.5	3.4	3.3
85	90	..	..	..	..	..	..	..	..	..	..	..	3.3	3.2
86	91	..	..	..	..	..	..	..	..	..	..	..	..	3.1

Table III — Percent Value of Refund Feature

| Ages | | Duration of guaranteed amount | | | | | | | | | | | |
Male	Female	1 Yr %	2 Yrs %	3 Yrs %	4 Yrs %	5 Yrs %	6 Yrs %	7 Yrs %	8 Yrs %	9 Yrs %	10 Yrs %	11 Yrs %	12 Yrs %
6	11									1	1	1	1
7	12									1	1	1	1
8	13								1	1	1	1	1
9	14								1	1	1	1	1
10	15								1	1	1	1	1
11	16								1	1	1	1	1
12	17								1	1	1	1	1
13	18								1	1	1	1	1
14	19								1	1	1	1	1
15	20								1	1	1	1	1
16	21								1	1	1	1	1
17	22								1	1	1	1	1
18	23								1	1	1	1	1
19	24								1	1	1	1	1
20	25								1	1	1	1	1
21	26								1	1	1	1	1
22	27							1	1	1	1	1	1
23	28							1	1	1	1	1	1
24	29							1	1	1	1	1	1
25	30							1	1	1	1	1	1
26	31						1	1	1	1	1	1	1
27	32						1	1	1	1	1	1	1
28	33						1	1	1	1	1	1	1
29	34						1	1	1	1	1	1	1
30	35					1	1	1	1	1	1	1	2
31	36					1	1	1	1	1	1	1	2
32	37					1	1	1	1	1	1	2	2
33	38				1	1	1	1	1	1	2	2	2
34	39				1	1	1	1	1	1	2	2	2
35	40				1	1	1	1	1	2	2	2	2
36	41				1	1	1	1	1	2	2	2	2
37	42			1	1	1	1	1	2	2	2	2	3
38	43			1	1	1	1	1	2	2	2	2	3
39	44			1	1	1	1	2	2	2	2	3	3
40	45			1	1	1	1	2	2	2	3	3	3
41	46			1	1	1	1	2	2	2	3	3	3
42	47			1	1	1	2	2	2	2	3	3	4
43	48		1	1	1	1	2	2	2	3	3	3	4
44	49		1	1	1	1	2	2	2	3	3	4	4
45	50		1	1	1	1	2	2	3	3	4	4	5
46	51		1	1	1	2	2	2	3	3	4	4	5
47	52		1	1	1	2	2	3	3	4	4	5	5
48	53		1	1	2	2	2	3	3	4	4	5	6
49	54		1	1	2	2	3	3	4	4	4	5	6
50	55		1	1	2	2	3	3	4	4	5	5	7
51	56		1	1	2	3	3	4	4	5	5	6	7
52	57	1	1	2	2	3	3	4	4	5	6	6	8
53	58	1	1	2	2	3	4	4	5	5	6	7	8
54	59	1	1	2	2	3	4	4	5	6	6	7	9
55	60	1	1	2	3	3	4	5	5	6	7	8	9
56	61	1	1	2	3	4	4	5	6	7	8	9	10
57	62	1	1	2	3	4	5	6	7	8	9	10	11
58	63	1	2	2	3	4	5	6	7	8	9	10	12
59	64	1	2	3	4	5	6	7	8	9	10	11	12
60	65	1	2	3	4	5	6	7	8	10	11	12	13
61	66	1	2	3	4	5	6	8	9	10	12	13	14
62	67	1	2	3	4	6	7	8	10	11	12	14	15
63	68	1	2	4	5	6	7	9	10	12	13	15	16
64	69	1	3	4	5	7	8	9	11	13	14	16	17
65	70	1	3	4	6	7	9	10	12	13	15	17	19
66	71	1	3	4	6	8	9	11	13	14	16	18	20
67	72	2	3	5	6	8	10	12	14	15	17	19	21
68	73	2	3	5	7	9	11	13	14	16	18	21	23
69	74	2	4	6	7	9	11	13	16	18	20	22	24
70	75	2	4	6	8	10	12	14	17	19	21	23	26
71	76	2	4	6	9	11	13	15	18	20	22	25	27
72	77	2	5	7	9	12	14	16	19	21	24	26	29
73	78	2	5	7	10	12	15	18	20	23	25	28	30
74	79	3	5	8	11	13	16	19	22	24	27	30	32
75	80	3	6	8	11	14	17	20	23	26	29	31	34
76	81	3	6	9	12	15	18	21	24	27	30	33	36
77	82	3	7	10	13	16	20	23	26	29	32	35	38
78	83	4	7	11	14	17	21	24	28	31	34	37	40
79	84	4	8	11	15	19	22	26	29	33	36	39	42
80	85	4	8	12	16	20	24	27	31	34	38	41	44
81	86	4	9	13	17	21	25	29	33	36	40	43	46
82	87	5	9	14	18	23	27	31	35	38	42	45	48
83	88	5	10	15	19	24	28	33	37	40	44	47	50
84	89	5	11	16	21	26	30	34	38	42	46	49	52
85	90	6	11	17	22	27	32	36	41	44	48	51	55

Table III — Percent Value of Refund Feature — Continued

Ages Male	Female		13 Yrs %	14 Yrs %	15 Yrs %	16 Yrs %	17 Yrs %	18 Yrs %	19 Yrs %	20 Yrs %	21 Yrs %	22 Yrs %	23 Yrs %	24 Yrs %
6	11		1	1	1	1	1	1	1	1	1	1	1	2
7	12		1	1	1	1	1	1	1	1	1	1	1	2
8	13		1	1	1	1	1	1	1	1	1	1	1	2
9	14		1	1	1	1	1	1	1	1	1	1	1	2
10	15		1	1	1	1	1	1	1	1	1	1	2	2
11	16		1	1	1	1	1	1	1	1	1	1	2	2
12	17		1	1	1	1	1	1	1	1	1	1	2	2
13	18		1	1	1	1	1	1	1	1	1	2	2	2
14	19		1	1	1	1	1	1	1	1	1	2	2	2
15	20		1	1	1	1	1	1	1	1	1	2	2	2
16	21		1	1	1	1	1	1	1	1	2	2	2	2
17	22		1	1	1	1	1	1	1	1	2	2	2	2
18	23		1	1	1	1	1	1	1	2	2	2	2	2
19	24		1	1	1	1	1	1	2	2	2	2	2	2
20	25		1	1	1	1	1	1	2	2	2	2	2	2
21	26		1	1	1	1	1	2	2	2	2	2	2	2
22	27		1	1	1	1	1	2	2	2	2	2	2	3
23	28		1	1	1	1	2	2	2	2	2	2	2	3
24	29		1	1	1	2	2	2	2	2	2	2	3	3
25	30		1	1	1	2	2	2	2	2	2	3	3	3
26	31		1	1	2	2	2	2	2	2	3	3	3	3
27	32		1	2	2	2	2	2	2	3	3	3	3	3
28	33		1	2	2	2	2	2	3	3	3	3	3	4
29	34		2	2	2	2	2	2	3	3	3	3	4	4
30	35		2	2	2	2	2	3	3	3	3	4	4	4
31	36		2	2	2	2	3	3	3	3	4	4	4	5
32	37		2	2	2	3	3	3	3	4	4	4	5	5
33	38		2	2	3	3	3	3	4	4	4	5	5	5
34	39		2	3	3	3	3	4	4	4	5	5	5	6
35	40		2	3	3	3	4	4	4	5	5	5	6	6
36	41		3	3	3	4	4	4	5	5	5	6	6	7
37	42		3	3	3	4	4	4	5	5	6	6	7	7
38	43		3	3	4	4	4	5	5	6	6	7	7	8
39	44		3	4	4	4	5	5	6	6	7	7	8	8
40	45		4	4	4	5	5	6	6	7	7	8	8	9
41	46		4	4	4	5	6	6	7	7	8	8	9	9
42	47		4	5	5	5	6	6	7	8	8	9	9	10
43	48		4	5	5	6	6	7	7	8	8	9	10	11
44	49		5	5	6	6	7	7	8	9	9	10	11	12
45	50		5	6	6	7	7	8	9	9	10	11	12	12
46	51		5	6	7	7	8	9	9	10	11	12	12	13
47	52		6	7	7	8	9	9	10	11	12	12	13	14
48	53		6	7	8	8	9	10	11	12	12	13	14	15
49	54		7	8	8	9	10	11	11	12	13	14	15	16
50	55		7	8	9	10	11	11	12	13	14	15	16	17
51	56		8	9	10	10	11	12	13	14	15	16	17	18
52	57		8	9	10	11	12	13	14	15	16	17	18	20
53	58		9	10	11	12	13	14	15	16	17	19	20	21
54	59		10	11	12	13	14	15	16	17	18	20	21	22
55	60		10	11	13	14	15	16	17	18	20	21	22	24
56	61		11	12	13	15	16	17	18	20	21	22	24	25
57	62		12	13	14	16	17	18	20	21	22	24	25	27
58	63		13	14	15	17	18	19	21	22	24	25	27	28
59	64		14	15	16	18	19	21	22	24	25	27	28	30
60	65		15	16	18	19	20	22	24	25	27	28	30	32
61	66		16	17	19	20	22	23	25	27	28	30	32	33
62	67		17	18	20	22	23	25	27	28	30	32	33	35
63	68		18	20	21	23	25	26	28	30	32	33	35	37
64	69		19	21	23	24	26	28	30	32	33	35	37	39
65	70		20	22	24	26	28	30	32	33	35	37	39	41
66	71		22	24	26	28	29	31	33	35	37	39	41	43
67	72		23	25	27	29	31	33	35	37	39	41	43	45
68	73		25	27	29	31	33	35	37	39	41	43	45	47
69	74		26	28	30	33	35	37	39	41	43	45	47	48
70	75		28	30	32	34	37	39	41	43	45	47	49	50
71	76		29	32	34	36	39	41	43	45	47	49	51	52
72	77		31	34	36	38	41	43	45	47	49	51	53	54
73	78		33	35	38	40	43	45	47	49	51	53	55	56
74	79		35	37	40	42	45	47	49	51	53	55	57	58
75	80		37	39	42	44	47	49	51	53	55	55	57	60
76	81		39	41	44	46	49	51	53	55	57	59	60	62
77	82		41	43	46	48	51	53	55	57	59	61	62	64
78	83		43	45	48	50	53	55	57	59	61	62	64	65
79	84		45	48	50	53	55	57	59	61	63	64	66	67
80	85		47	50	52	55	57	59	61	63	64	66	67	69
81	86		49	52	54	57	59	61	63	65	66	68	69	70
82	87		51	54	56	59	61	63	65	66	68	69	71	72
83	88		53	56	58	61	63	65	66	68	70	71	72	73
84	89		55	58	60	63	65	67	68	70	71	73	74	75
85	90		57	60	62	65	67	68	70	71	73	74	75	76

Table III — Percent Value of Refund Feature — Continued

Ages		Duration of guaranteed amount										
Male	Female	25 Yrs %	26 Yrs %	27 Yrs %	28 Yrs %	29 Yrs %	30 Yrs %	31 Yrs %	32 Yrs %	33 Yrs %	34 Yrs %	35 Yrs %
6	11	2	2	2	2	2	2	2	2	2	2	2
7	12	2	2	2	2	2	2	2	2	2	2	3
8	13	2	2	2	2	2	2	2	2	2	2	3
9	14	2	2	2	2	2	2	2	2	2	3	3
10	15	2	2	2	2	2	2	2	2	3	3	3
11	16	2	2	2	2	2	2	2	2	3	3	3
12	17	2	2	2	2	2	2	2	3	3	3	3
13	18	2	2	2	2	2	2	2	3	3	3	3
14	19	2	2	2	2	2	2	3	3	3	3	3
15	20	2	2	2	2	2	3	3	3	3	3	3
16	21	2	2	2	2	3	3	3	3	3	3	4
17	22	2	2	2	2	3	3	3	3	3	4	4
18	23	2	2	2	3	3	3	3	3	4	4	4
19	24	2	2	3	3	3	3	3	4	4	4	4
20	25	2	3	3	3	3	3	4	4	4	4	5
21	26	3	3	3	3	3	4	4	4	4	5	5
22	27	3	3	3	3	4	4	4	4	5	5	5
23	28	3	3	3	3	4	4	4	5	5	5	5
24	29	3	3	3	4	4	4	5	5	5	5	6
25	30	3	3	4	4	4	5	5	5	6	6	6
26	31	3	4	4	4	5	5	5	6	6	6	7
27	32	4	4	4	5	5	5	6	6	6	7	7
28	33	4	4	5	5	5	6	6	6	7	7	8
29	34	4	5	5	5	6	6	6	7	7	8	8
30	35	5	5	5	6	6	6	7	7	8	8	9
31	36	5	5	6	6	6	7	7	8	8	9	9
32	37	5	6	6	7	7	7	8	8	9	10	10
33	38	6	6	7	7	7	8	8	9	10	10	11
34	39	6	7	7	8	8	9	9	10	10	11	12
35	40	7	7	8	8	9	9	10	10	11	12	12
36	41	7	8	8	9	9	10	10	11	12	13	13
37	42	8	8	9	9	10	11	11	12	13	13	14
38	43	8	9	9	10	11	11	12	13	13	14	15
39	44	9	9	10	11	11	12	13	14	14	15	16
40	45	9	10	11	11	12	13	14	15	15	16	17
41	46	10	11	11	12	13	14	15	16	16	17	18
42	47	11	12	12	13	14	15	16	17	18	18	19
43	48	12	12	13	14	15	16	17	18	19	20	21
44	49	12	13	14	15	16	17	18	19	20	21	22
45	50	13	14	15	16	17	18	19	20	21	22	23
46	51	14	15	16	17	18	19	20	21	22	24	25
47	52	15	16	17	18	19	20	21	23	24	25	26
48	53	16	17	18	19	20	22	23	24	25	26	28
49	54	17	18	19	21	22	23	24	25	27	28	29
50	55	18	20	21	22	23	24	26	27	28	29	31
51	56	20	21	22	23	25	26	27	28	30	31	32
52	57	21	22	23	25	26	27	29	30	31	33	34
53	58	22	24	25	26	28	29	30	32	33	34	36
54	59	24	25	26	28	29	31	32	33	35	36	38
55	60	25	26	28	29	31	32	34	35	36	38	39
56	61	27	28	29	31	32	34	35	37	38	40	41
57	62	28	30	31	33	34	36	37	39	40	41	43
58	63	30	31	33	34	36	37	39	40	42	43	45
59	64	31	33	35	36	38	39	41	42	44	45	47
60	65	33	35	36	38	40	41	43	44	46	47	48
61	66	35	37	38	40	41	43	44	46	47	49	50
62	67	37	38	40	42	43	45	46	48	49	51	52
63	68	39	40	42	44	45	47	48	50	51	52	54
64	69	41	42	44	46	47	49	50	52	53	54	55
65	70	42	44	46	47	49	50	52	53	55	56	57
66	71	44	46	48	49	51	52	54	55	56	58	59
67	72	46	48	50	51	53	54	56	57	58	59	61
68	73	48	50	52	53	55	56	57	59	60	61	62
69	74	50	52	53	55	56	58	59	60	62	63	64
70	75	52	54	55	57	58	60	61	62	63	64	65
71	76	54	56	57	59	60	61	63	64	65	66	67
72	77	56	58	59	60	62	63	64	65	66	67	68
73	78	58	59	61	62	64	65	66	67	68	68	70
74	79	60	61	63	64	65	66	67	68	69	70	71
75	80	62	63	64	66	67	68	69	70	71	72	72
76	81	63	65	66	67	68	69	70	71	72	73	..
77	82	65	66	68	69	70	71	72	73	74	..	..
78	83	67	68	69	70	71	72	73	74	..	..	..
79	84	68	70	71	72	73	74	75	..	..	..	..
80	85	70	71	72	73	74	75	..	..	..	..	..
81	86	72	73	74	75	75	..	..	..	..	..	..
82	87	73	74	75	76	..	..	..	..	..	..	..
83	88	74	75	76	..	..	..	..	..	..	..	..
84	89	76	77	..	..	..	..	..	..	..	..	..
85	90	77	..	..	..	..	..	..	..	..	..	..

Table V — Ordinary Life Annuities — One Life — Expected Return Multiples

Age	Multiple	Age	Multiple	Age	Multiple
5	76.6	42	40.6	79	10.0
6	75.6	43	39.6	80	9.5
7	74.7	44	38.7	81	8.9
8	73.7	45	37.7	82	8.4
9	72.7	46	36.8	83	7.9
10	71.7	47	35.9	84	7.4
11	70.7	48	34.9	85	6.9
12	69.7	49	34.0	86	6.5
13	68.8	50	33.1	87	6.1
14	67.8	51	32.2	88	5.7
15	66.8	52	31.3	89	5.3
16	65.8	53	30.4	90	5.0
17	64.8	54	29.5	91	4.7
18	63.9	55	28.6	92	4.4
19	62.9	56	27.7	93	4.1
20	61.9	57	26.8	94	3.9
21	60.9	58	25.9	95	3.7
22	59.9	59	25.0	96	3.4
23	59.0	60	24.2	97	3.2
24	58.0	61	23.3	98	3.0
25	57.0	62	22.5	99	2.8
26	56.0	63	21.6	100	2.7
27	55.1	64	20.8	101	2.5
28	54.1	65	20.0	102	2.3
29	53.1	66	19.2	103	2.1
30	52.2	67	18.4	104	1.9
31	51.2	68	17.6	105	1.8
32	50.2	69	16.8	106	1.6
33	49.3	70	16.0	107	1.4
34	48.3	71	15.3	108	1.3
35	47.3	72	14.6	109	1.1
36	46.4	73	13.9	110	1.0
37	45.4	74	13.2	111	.9
38	44.4	75	12.5	112	.8
39	43.5	76	11.9	113	.7
40	42.5	77	11.2	114	.6
41	41.5	78	10.6	115	.5

Table VI — Ordinary Joint Life and Last Survivor Annuities — Two Lives — Expected Return Multiples

AGES	35	36	37	38	39	40	41	42	43	44	45	46	47	48	49	50
35	54.0	...	...	...	...	...	...	...	...	...	...	...	...	...	...	...
36	53.5	53.0	...	...	...	...	...	...	...	...	...	...	...	...	...	...
37	53.0	52.5	52.0	...	...	...	...	...	...	...	...	...	...	...	...	...
38	52.6	52.0	51.5	51.0	...	...	...	...	...	...	...	...	...	...	...	...
39	52.2	51.6	51.0	50.5	50.0	...	...	...	...	...	...	...	...	...	...	...
40	51.8	51.2	50.6	50.0	49.5	49.0	...	...	...	...	...	...	...	...	...	...
41	51.4	50.8	50.2	49.6	49.1	48.5	48.0	...	...	...	...	...	...	...	...	...
42	51.1	50.4	49.8	49.2	48.6	48.1	47.5	47.0	...	...	...	...	...	...	...	...
43	50.8	50.1	49.5	48.8	48.2	47.6	47.1	46.6	46.0	...	...	...	...	...	...	...
44	50.5	49.8	49.1	48.5	47.8	47.2	46.7	46.1	45.6	45.1	...	...	...	...	...	...
45	50.2	49.5	48.8	48.1	47.5	46.9	46.3	45.7	45.1	44.6	44.1	...	...	...	...	...
46	50.0	49.2	48.5	47.8	47.2	46.5	45.9	45.3	44.7	44.1	43.6	43.1	...	...	...	...
47	49.7	49.0	48.3	47.5	46.8	46.2	45.5	44.9	44.3	43.7	43.2	42.6	42.1	...	...	...
48	49.5	48.8	48.0	47.3	46.6	45.9	45.2	44.5	43.9	43.3	42.7	42.2	41.7	41.2	...	...
49	49.3	48.5	47.8	47.0	46.3	45.6	44.9	44.2	43.6	42.9	42.3	41.8	41.2	40.7	40.2	...
50	49.2	48.4	47.6	46.8	46.0	45.3	44.6	43.9	43.2	42.6	42.0	41.4	40.8	40.2	39.7	39.2
51	49.0	48.2	47.4	46.6	45.8	45.1	44.3	43.6	42.9	42.2	41.6	41.0	40.4	39.8	39.3	38.7
52	48.8	48.0	47.2	46.4	45.6	44.8	44.1	43.3	42.6	41.9	41.3	40.6	40.0	39.4	38.8	38.3
53	48.7	47.9	47.0	46.2	45.4	44.6	43.9	43.1	42.4	41.7	41.0	40.3	39.7	39.0	38.4	37.9
54	48.6	47.7	46.9	46.0	45.2	44.4	43.6	42.9	42.1	41.4	40.7	40.0	39.3	38.7	38.1	37.5
55	48.5	47.6	46.7	45.9	45.1	44.2	43.4	42.7	41.9	41.2	40.4	39.7	39.0	38.4	37.7	37.1
56	48.3	47.5	46.6	45.8	44.9	44.1	43.3	42.5	41.7	40.9	40.2	39.5	38.7	38.1	37.4	36.8
57	48.3	47.4	46.5	45.6	44.8	43.9	43.1	42.3	41.5	40.7	40.0	39.2	38.5	37.8	37.1	36.4
58	48.2	47.3	46.4	45.5	44.7	43.8	43.0	42.1	41.3	40.5	39.7	39.0	38.2	37.5	36.8	36.1
59	48.1	47.2	46.3	45.4	44.5	43.7	42.8	42.0	41.2	40.4	39.6	38.8	38.0	37.3	36.6	35.9
60	48.0	47.1	46.2	45.3	44.4	43.6	42.7	41.9	41.0	40.2	39.4	38.6	37.8	37.1	36.3	35.6
61	47.9	47.0	46.1	45.2	44.3	43.5	42.6	41.7	40.9	40.0	39.2	38.4	37.6	36.9	36.1	35.4
62	47.9	47.0	46.0	45.1	44.2	43.4	42.5	41.6	40.8	39.9	39.1	38.3	37.5	36.7	35.9	35.1
63	47.8	46.9	46.0	45.1	44.2	43.3	42.4	41.5	40.6	39.8	38.9	38.1	37.3	36.5	35.7	34.9
64	47.8	46.8	45.9	45.0	44.1	43.2	42.3	41.4	40.5	39.7	38.8	38.0	37.2	36.3	35.5	34.8
65	47.7	46.8	45.9	44.9	44.0	43.1	42.2	41.3	40.4	39.6	38.7	37.9	37.0	36.2	35.4	34.6
66	47.7	46.7	45.8	44.9	44.0	43.1	42.2	41.3	40.4	39.5	38.6	37.8	36.9	36.1	35.2	34.4
67	47.6	46.7	45.7	44.8	43.9	43.0	42.1	41.2	40.3	39.4	38.5	37.7	36.8	36.0	35.1	34.3
68	47.6	46.7	45.7	44.8	43.9	42.9	42.0	41.1	40.2	39.3	38.4	37.6	36.7	35.8	35.0	34.2
69	47.6	46.6	45.7	44.8	43.8	42.9	42.0	41.1	40.2	39.3	38.4	37.5	36.6	35.7	34.9	34.1
70	47.5	46.6	45.7	44.7	43.8	42.9	41.9	41.0	40.1	39.2	38.3	37.4	36.5	35.7	34.8	34.0
71	47.5	46.6	45.6	44.7	43.8	42.8	41.9	41.0	40.1	39.1	38.2	37.3	36.5	35.6	34.7	33.9
72	47.5	46.5	45.6	44.7	43.7	42.8	41.9	40.9	40.0	39.1	38.2	37.3	36.4	35.5	34.6	33.8
73	47.5	46.5	45.6	44.7	43.7	42.8	41.8	40.9	40.0	39.0	38.1	37.2	36.3	35.4	34.6	33.7
74	47.5	46.5	45.6	44.7	43.7	42.7	41.8	40.9	39.9	39.0	38.1	37.2	36.3	35.4	34.5	33.6
75	47.4	46.5	45.5	44.7	43.7	42.7	41.8	40.8	39.9	39.0	38.0	37.1	36.2	35.3	34.5	33.6
76	47.4	46.5	45.5	44.7	43.6	42.7	41.7	40.8	39.9	38.9	38.0	37.1	36.2	35.3	34.4	33.5
77	47.4	46.5	45.5	44.7	43.6	42.7	41.7	40.8	39.8	38.9	38.0	37.1	36.2	35.3	34.4	33.5
78	47.4	46.4	45.5	44.5	43.6	42.6	41.7	40.7	39.8	38.9	38.0	37.0	36.1	35.2	34.3	33.4
79	47.4	46.4	45.5	44.5	43.6	42.6	41.7	40.7	39.8	38.9	37.9	37.0	36.1	35.2	34.3	33.4
80	47.4	46.4	45.5	44.5	43.6	42.6	41.7	40.7	39.8	38.8	37.9	37.0	36.1	35.1	34.2	33.4
81	47.4	46.4	45.5	44.5	43.5	42.6	41.6	40.7	39.8	38.8	37.9	37.0	36.0	35.1	34.2	33.3
82	47.4	46.4	45.4	44.5	43.5	42.6	41.6	40.7	39.7	38.8	37.9	36.9	36.0	35.1	34.2	33.3
83	47.4	46.4	45.4	44.5	43.5	42.6	41.6	40.7	39.7	38.8	37.9	36.9	36.0	35.1	34.2	33.3
84	47.4	46.4	45.4	44.5	43.5	42.6	41.6	40.7	39.7	38.8	37.8	36.9	36.0	35.0	34.1	33.2
85	47.4	46.4	45.4	44.5	43.5	42.6	41.6	40.7	39.7	38.8	37.8	36.9	36.0	35.0	34.1	33.2
86	47.3	46.4	45.4	44.5	43.5	42.5	41.6	40.6	39.7	38.8	37.8	36.9	36.0	35.0	34.1	33.2
87	47.3	46.4	45.4	44.5	43.5	42.5	41.6	40.6	39.7	38.7	37.8	36.9	35.9	35.0	34.1	33.2
88	47.3	46.4	45.4	44.5	43.5	42.5	41.6	40.6	39.7	38.7	37.8	36.9	35.9	35.0	34.1	33.2
89	47.3	46.4	45.4	44.4	43.5	42.5	41.6	40.6	39.7	38.7	37.8	36.9	35.9	35.0	34.1	33.2
90	47.3	46.4	45.4	44.4	43.5	42.5	41.6	40.6	39.7	38.7	37.8	36.9	35.9	35.0	34.1	33.2

Table VI — Ordinary Joint Life and Last Survivor Annuities — Two Lives — Expected Return Multiples

AGES	51	52	53	54	55	56	57	58	59	60	61	62	63	64	65	66
51	38.2	...	...	...	...	...	...	...	...	...	...	...	...	...	...	...
52	37.8	37.3	...	...	...	...	...	...	...	...	...	...	...	...	...	...
53	37.3	36.8	36.3	...	...	...	...	...	...	...	...	...	...	...	...	...
54	36.9	36.4	35.8	35.3	...	...	...	...	...	...	...	...	...	...	...	...
55	36.5	35.9	35.4	34.9	34.4	...	...	...	...	...	...	...	...	...	...	...
56	36.1	35.6	35.0	34.4	33.9	33.4	...	...	...	...	...	...	...	...	...	...
57	35.8	35.2	34.6	34.0	33.5	33.0	32.5	...	...	...	...	...	...	...	...	...
58	35.5	34.8	34.2	33.6	33.1	32.5	32.0	31.5	...	...	...	...	...	...	...	...
59	35.2	34.5	33.9	33.3	32.7	32.1	31.6	31.1	30.6	...	...	...	...	...	...	...
60	34.9	34.2	33.6	32.9	32.3	31.7	31.2	30.6	30.1	29.7	...	...	...	...	...	...
61	34.6	33.9	33.3	32.6	32.0	31.4	30.8	30.2	29.7	29.2	28.7	...	...	...	...	...
62	34.4	33.7	33.0	32.3	31.7	31.0	30.4	29.9	29.3	28.8	28.3	27.8	...	...	...	...
63	34.2	33.5	32.7	32.0	31.4	30.7	30.1	29.5	28.9	28.4	27.8	27.3	26.9	...	...	...
64	34.0	33.2	32.5	31.8	31.1	30.4	29.8	29.2	28.6	28.0	27.4	26.9	26.4	25.9	...	...
65	33.8	33.0	32.3	31.6	30.9	30.2	29.5	28.9	28.2	27.6	27.1	26.5	26.0	25.5	25.0	...
66	33.6	32.9	32.1	31.4	30.6	29.9	29.2	28.6	27.9	27.3	26.7	26.1	25.6	25.1	24.6	24.1
67	33.5	32.7	31.9	31.2	30.4	29.7	29.0	28.3	27.6	27.0	26.4	25.8	25.2	24.7	24.2	23.7
68	33.4	32.5	31.8	31.0	30.2	29.5	28.8	28.1	27.4	26.7	26.1	25.5	24.9	24.3	23.8	23.3
69	33.2	32.4	31.6	30.8	30.1	29.3	28.6	27.8	27.1	26.5	25.8	25.2	24.6	24.0	23.4	22.9
70	33.1	32.3	31.5	30.7	29.9	29.1	28.4	27.6	26.9	26.2	25.6	24.9	24.3	23.7	23.1	22.5
71	33.0	32.2	31.4	30.5	29.7	29.0	28.2	27.5	26.7	26.0	25.3	24.7	24.0	23.4	22.8	22.2
72	32.9	32.1	31.2	30.4	29.6	28.8	28.1	27.3	26.5	25.8	25.1	24.4	23.8	23.1	22.5	21.9
73	32.8	32.0	31.1	30.3	29.5	28.7	27.9	27.1	26.4	25.6	24.9	24.2	23.5	22.9	22.2	21.6
74	32.8	31.9	31.1	30.2	29.4	28.6	27.8	27.0	26.2	25.5	24.7	24.0	23.3	22.7	22.0	21.4
75	32.7	31.8	31.0	30.1	29.3	28.5	27.7	26.9	26.1	25.3	24.6	23.8	23.1	22.4	21.8	21.1
76	32.6	31.8	30.9	30.1	29.2	28.4	27.6	26.8	26.0	25.2	24.4	23.7	23.0	22.3	21.6	20.9
77	32.6	31.7	30.8	30.0	29.1	28.3	27.5	26.7	25.9	25.1	24.3	23.6	22.8	22.1	21.4	20.7
78	32.5	31.7	30.8	29.9	29.1	28.2	27.4	26.6	25.8	25.0	24.2	23.4	22.7	21.9	21.2	20.5
79	32.5	31.6	30.7	29.9	29.0	28.2	27.3	26.5	25.7	24.9	24.1	23.3	22.6	21.8	21.1	20.4
80	32.5	31.6	30.7	29.8	29.0	28.1	27.3	26.4	25.6	24.8	24.0	23.2	22.4	21.7	21.0	20.2
81	32.4	31.5	30.7	29.8	28.9	28.1	27.2	26.4	25.5	24.7	23.9	23.1	22.3	21.6	20.8	20.1
82	32.4	31.5	30.6	29.7	28.9	28.0	27.2	26.3	25.5	24.6	23.8	23.0	22.3	21.5	20.7	20.0
83	32.4	31.5	30.6	29.7	28.8	28.0	27.1	26.3	25.4	24.6	23.8	23.0	22.2	21.4	20.6	19.9
84	32.3	31.4	30.6	29.7	28.8	27.9	27.1	26.2	25.4	24.5	23.7	22.9	22.1	21.3	20.5	19.8
85	32.3	31.4	30.5	29.6	28.8	27.9	27.0	26.2	25.3	24.5	23.7	22.8	22.0	21.3	20.5	19.7
86	32.3	31.4	30.5	29.6	28.7	27.9	27.0	26.1	25.3	24.5	23.6	22.8	22.0	21.2	20.4	19.6
87	32.3	31.4	30.5	29.6	28.7	27.8	27.0	26.1	25.3	24.4	23.6	22.8	21.9	21.1	20.4	19.6
88	32.3	31.4	30.5	29.6	28.7	27.8	27.0	26.1	25.2	24.4	23.5	22.7	21.9	21.1	20.3	19.5
89	32.3	31.4	30.5	29.6	28.7	27.8	26.9	26.1	25.2	24.4	23.5	22.7	21.9	21.1	20.3	19.5
90	32.3	31.3	30.5	29.5	28.7	27.8	26.9	26.1	25.2	24.3	23.5	22.7	21.8	21.0	20.2	19.4

Table VI — Ordinary Joint Life and Last Survivor Annuities — Two Lives — Expected Return Multiples

AGES	67	68	69	70	71	72	73	74	75	76	77	78	79	80	81	82
67	23.2	...	...	...	...	...	...	...	...	...	...	...	...	...	...	...
68	22.8	22.3	...	...	...	...	...	...	...	...	...	...	...	...	...	...
69	22.4	21.9	21.5	...	...	...	...	...	...	...	...	...	...	...	...	...
70	22.0	21.5	21.1	20.6	...	...	...	...	...	...	...	...	...	...	...	...
71	21.7	21.2	20.7	20.2	19.8	...	...	...	...	...	...	...	...	...	...	...
72	21.3	20.8	20.3	19.8	19.4	18.9	...	...	...	...	...	...	...	...	...	...
73	21.0	20.5	20.0	19.4	19.0	18.5	18.1	...	...	...	...	...	...	...	...	...
74	20.8	20.2	19.6	19.1	18.6	18.2	17.7	17.3	...	...	...	...	...	...	...	...
75	20.5	19.9	19.3	18.8	18.3	17.8	17.3	16.9	16.5	...	...	...	...	...	...	...
76	20.3	19.7	19.1	18.5	18.0	17.5	17.0	16.5	16.1	15.7	...	...	...	...	...	...
77	20.1	19.4	18.8	18.3	17.7	17.2	16.7	16.2	15.8	15.4	15.0	...	...	...	...	...
78	19.9	19.2	18.6	18.0	17.5	16.9	16.4	15.9	15.4	15.0	14.6	14.2	...	...	...	...
79	19.7	19.0	18.4	17.8	17.2	16.7	16.1	15.6	15.1	14.7	14.3	13.9	13.5	...	...	...
80	19.5	18.9	18.2	17.6	17.0	16.4	15.9	15.4	14.9	14.4	14.0	13.5	13.2	12.8	...	...
81	19.4	18.7	18.1	17.4	16.8	16.2	15.7	15.1	14.6	14.1	13.7	13.2	12.8	12.5	12.1	...
82	19.3	18.6	17.9	17.3	16.6	16.0	15.5	14.9	14.4	13.9	13.4	13.0	12.5	12.2	11.8	11.5
83	19.2	18.5	17.8	17.1	16.5	15.9	15.3	14.7	14.2	13.7	13.2	12.7	12.3	11.9	11.5	11.1
84	19.1	18.4	17.7	17.0	16.3	15.7	15.1	14.5	14.0	13.5	13.0	12.5	12.0	11.6	11.2	10.9
85	19.0	18.3	17.6	16.9	16.2	15.6	15.0	14.4	13.8	13.3	12.8	12.3	11.8	11.4	11.0	10.6
86	18.9	18.2	17.5	16.8	16.1	15.5	14.8	14.2	13.7	13.1	12.6	12.1	11.6	11.2	10.8	10.4
87	18.8	18.1	17.4	16.7	16.0	15.4	14.7	14.1	13.5	13.0	12.4	11.9	11.4	11.0	10.6	10.1
88	18.8	18.0	17.3	16.6	15.9	15.3	14.6	14.0	13.4	12.8	12.3	11.8	11.3	10.8	10.4	10.0
89	18.7	18.0	17.2	16.5	15.8	15.2	14.5	13.9	13.3	12.7	12.2	11.6	11.1	10.7	10.2	9.8
90	18.7	17.9	17.2	16.5	15.8	15.1	14.5	13.8	13.2	12.6	12.1	11.5	11.0	10.5	10.1	9.6

Table VI — Ordinary Joint Life and Last Survivor Annuities — Two Lives — Expected Return Multiples

AGES	83	84	85	86	87	88	89	90
83	10.8	...	...	...	...	...	...	...
84	10.5	10.2	...	...	...	...	...	...
85	10.2	9.9	9.6	...	...	...	...	...
86	10.0	9.7	9.3	9.1	...	...	...	...
87	9.8	9.4	9.1	8.8	8.5	...	...	...
88	9.6	9.2	8.9	8.6	8.3	8.0	...	...
89	9.4	9.0	8.7	8.3	8.1	7.8	7.5	...
90	9.2	8.8	8.5	8.2	7.9	7.6	7.3	7.1

Table VIA — Annuities for Joint Life Only — Two Lives — Expected Return Multiples

AGES	35	36	37	38	39	40	41	42	43	44	45	46	47	48	49	50
35	40.7	...	...	...	...	...	...	...	...	...	...	...	...	...	...	...
36	40.2	39.7	...	...	...	...	...	...	...	...	...	...	...	...	...	...
37	39.7	39.3	38.8	...	...	...	...	...	...	...	...	...	...	...	...	...
38	39.2	38.7	38.3	37.9	...	...	...	...	...	...	...	...	...	...	...	...
39	38.6	38.2	37.8	37.4	36.9	...	...	...	...	...	...	...	...	...	...	...
40	38.0	37.7	37.3	36.9	36.4	36.0	...	...	...	...	...	...	...	...	...	...
41	37.4	37.1	36.7	36.3	35.9	35.5	35.1	...	...	...	...	...	...	...	...	...
42	36.8	36.5	36.2	35.8	35.4	35.0	34.6	34.1	...	...	...	...	...	...	...	...
43	36.2	35.9	35.6	35.2	34.9	34.5	34.1	33.7	33.2	...	...	...	...	...	...	...
44	35.5	35.2	34.9	34.6	34.3	34.0	33.6	33.2	32.8	32.3	...	...	...	...	...	...
45	34.8	34.6	34.3	34.0	33.7	33.4	33.0	32.7	32.3	31.8	31.4	...	...	...	...	...
46	34.1	33.9	33.7	33.4	33.1	32.8	32.5	32.1	31.8	31.4	30.9	30.5	...	...	...	...
47	33.4	33.2	33.0	32.8	32.5	32.2	31.9	31.6	31.2	30.8	30.5	30.0	29.6	...	...	...
48	32.7	32.5	32.3	32.1	31.8	31.6	31.3	31.0	30.7	30.3	30.0	29.6	29.2	28.7	...	...
49	32.0	31.8	31.6	31.4	31.2	30.9	30.7	30.4	30.1	29.8	29.4	29.1	28.7	28.3	27.9	...
50	31.3	31.1	30.9	30.7	30.5	30.3	30.0	29.8	29.5	29.2	28.9	28.5	28.2	27.4	27.4	27.0
51	30.5	30.4	30.2	30.0	29.8	29.6	29.4	29.2	28.9	28.6	28.3	28.0	27.7	27.3	26.9	26.5
52	29.7	29.6	29.5	29.3	29.1	28.9	28.7	28.5	28.3	28.0	27.7	27.4	27.1	26.8	26.5	26.1
53	29.0	28.9	28.7	28.6	28.4	28.2	28.1	27.9	27.6	27.4	27.1	26.9	26.6	26.3	25.9	25.6
54	28.2	28.1	28.0	27.8	27.7	27.5	27.4	27.2	27.0	26.8	26.5	26.3	26.0	25.7	25.4	25.1
55	27.4	27.3	27.2	27.1	27.0	26.8	26.7	26.5	26.3	26.1	25.9	25.7	25.4	25.1	24.9	24.6
56	26.7	26.6	26.5	26.3	26.2	26.1	26.0	25.8	25.6	25.4	25.2	25.0	24.8	24.6	24.3	24.0
57	25.9	25.8	25.7	25.6	25.5	25.4	25.2	25.1	24.9	24.8	24.6	24.4	24.2	24.0	23.7	23.5
58	25.1	25.0	24.9	24.8	24.7	24.6	24.5	24.4	24.2	24.1	23.9	23.7	23.5	23.3	23.1	22.9
59	24.3	24.2	24.1	24.1	24.0	23.9	23.8	23.6	23.5	23.4	23.2	23.1	22.9	22.7	22.5	22.3
60	23.5	23.4	23.4	23.3	23.2	23.1	23.0	22.9	22.8	22.7	22.5	22.4	22.2	22.1	21.9	21.7
61	22.7	22.6	22.6	22.5	22.4	22.4	22.3	22.2	22.1	22.0	21.8	21.7	21.6	21.4	21.2	21.1
62	21.9	21.9	21.8	21.7	21.7	21.6	21.5	21.4	21.3	21.2	21.1	21.0	20.9	20.7	20.6	20.4
63	21.1	21.1	21.0	21.0	20.9	20.8	20.8	20.7	20.6	20.5	20.4	20.3	20.2	20.1	19.9	19.8
64	20.3	20.3	20.2	20.2	20.1	20.0	20.0	20.0	19.9	19.8	19.7	19.6	19.5	19.4	19.3	19.1
65	19.6	19.5	19.5	19.4	19.4	19.3	19.3	19.2	19.1	19.1	19.0	18.9	18.8	18.7	18.6	18.5
66	18.8	18.8	18.7	18.7	18.6	18.6	18.5	18.5	18.4	18.4	18.3	18.2	18.1	18.0	17.9	17.8
67	18.0	18.0	18.0	17.9	17.9	17.9	17.8	17.8	17.7	17.6	17.6	17.5	17.4	17.3	17.3	17.2
68	17.3	17.3	17.2	17.2	17.2	17.1	17.1	17.0	17.0	16.9	16.9	16.8	16.7	16.7	16.6	16.5
69	16.5	16.5	16.5	16.5	16.4	16.4	16.4	16.3	16.3	16.2	16.2	16.1	16.1	16.0	15.9	15.8
70	15.8	15.8	15.8	15.7	15.7	15.7	15.6	15.6	15.6	15.5	15.5	15.4	15.4	15.3	15.3	15.2
71	15.1	15.1	15.1	15.0	15.0	15.0	15.0	14.9	14.9	14.9	14.8	14.8	14.7	14.7	14.6	14.5
72	14.4	14.4	14.4	14.3	14.3	14.3	14.3	14.2	14.2	14.2	14.1	14.1	14.1	14.0	14.0	13.9
73	13.7	13.7	13.7	13.7	13.7	13.6	13.6	13.6	13.6	13.5	13.5	13.5	13.4	13.4	13.3	13.3
74	13.1	13.0	13.0	13.0	13.0	13.0	13.0	12.9	12.9	12.9	12.8	12.8	12.8	12.7	12.7	12.7
75	12.4	12.4	12.4	12.4	12.3	12.3	12.3	12.3	12.3	12.2	12.2	12.2	12.2	12.1	12.1	12.1
76	11.8	11.8	11.7	11.7	11.7	11.7	11.7	11.7	11.6	11.6	11.6	11.6	11.6	11.5	11.5	11.5
77	11.1	11.1	11.1	11.1	11.1	11.1	11.1	11.1	11.0	11.0	11.0	11.0	11.0	10.9	10.9	10.9
78	10.5	10.5	10.5	10.5	10.5	10.5	10.5	10.5	10.5	10.4	10.4	10.4	10.4	10.4	10.3	10.3
79	10.0	10.0	9.9	9.9	9.9	9.9	9.9	9.9	9.9	9.9	9.9	9.9	9.8	9.8	9.8	9.8
80	9.4	9.4	9.4	9.4	9.4	9.4	9.4	9.3	9.3	9.3	9.3	9.3	9.3	9.3	9.2	9.2
81	8.9	8.8	8.8	8.8	8.8	8.8	8.8	8.8	8.8	8.8	8.8	8.8	8.8	8.7	8.7	8.7
82	8.3	8.3	8.3	8.3	8.3	8.3	8.3	8.3	8.3	8.3	8.3	8.3	8.2	8.2	8.2	8.2
83	7.8	7.8	7.8	7.8	7.8	7.8	7.8	7.8	7.8	7.8	7.8	7.8	7.8	7.7	7.7	7.7
84	7.3	7.3	7.3	7.3	7.3	7.3	7.3	7.3	7.3	7.3	7.3	7.3	7.3	7.3	7.3	7.2
85	6.9	6.9	6.9	6.9	6.9	6.9	6.9	6.9	6.9	6.9	6.9	6.8	6.8	6.8	6.8	6.8
86	6.5	6.5	6.5	6.5	6.4	6.4	6.4	6.4	6.4	6.4	6.4	6.4	6.4	6.4	6.4	6.4
87	6.1	6.0	6.0	6.0	6.0	6.0	6.0	6.0	6.0	6.0	6.0	6.0	6.0	6.0	6.0	6.0
88	5.7	5.7	5.7	5.7	5.7	5.7	5.7	5.6	5.6	5.6	5.6	5.6	5.6	5.6	5.6	5.6
89	5.3	5.3	5.3	5.3	5.3	5.3	5.3	5.3	5.3	5.3	5.3	5.3	5.3	5.3	5.3	5.3
90	5.0	5.0	5.0	5.0	5.0	5.0	5.0	5.0	5.0	5.0	5.0	4.9	4.9	4.9	4.9	4.9

(Table VIA continues on the following page.)

Table VIA — Annuities for Joint Life Only — Two Lives — Expected Return Multiples

AGES	51	52	53	54	55	56	57	58	59	60	61	62	63	64	65	66
51	26.1															
52	25.7	25.3														
53	25.2	24.8	24.4													
54	24.7	24.4	24.0	23.6												
55	24.2	23.9	23.5	23.2	22.7											
56	23.7	23.4	23.1	22.7	22.3	21.9										
57	23.2	22.9	22.6	22.2	21.9	21.5	21.1									
58	22.6	22.4	22.1	21.7	21.4	21.1	20.7	20.3								
59	22.1	21.8	21.5	21.2	20.9	20.6	20.3	19.9	19.5							
60	21.5	21.2	21.0	20.7	20.4	20.1	19.8	19.5	19.1	18.7						
61	20.9	20.6	20.4	20.2	19.9	19.6	19.3	19.0	18.7	18.3	17.9					
62	20.2	20.0	19.8	19.6	19.4	19.1	18.8	18.5	18.2	17.9	17.5	17.1				
63	19.6	19.4	19.2	19.0	18.8	18.6	18.3	18.0	17.7	17.4	17.1	16.8	16.4			
64	19.0	18.8	18.6	18.5	18.3	18.0	17.8	17.5	17.3	17.0	16.7	16.3	16.0	15.6		
65	18.3	18.2	18.0	17.9	17.7	17.5	17.3	17.0	16.8	16.5	16.2	15.9	15.6	15.3	14.9	
66	17.7	17.6	17.4	17.3	17.1	16.9	16.7	16.5	16.3	16.0	15.8	15.5	15.2	14.9	14.5	14.2
67	17.1	16.9	16.8	16.7	16.5	16.3	16.2	16.0	15.8	15.5	15.3	15.0	14.7	14.5	14.1	13.8
68	16.4	16.3	16.2	16.1	15.9	15.8	15.6	15.4	15.2	15.0	14.8	14.6	14.3	14.0	13.7	13.4
69	15.8	15.7	15.6	15.4	15.3	15.2	15.0	14.9	14.7	14.5	14.3	14.1	13.9	13.6	13.3	13.1
70	15.1	15.0	14.9	14.8	14.7	14.6	14.5	14.3	14.2	14.0	13.8	13.6	13.4	13.2	12.9	12.6
71	14.5	14.4	14.3	14.2	14.1	14.0	13.9	13.8	13.6	13.5	13.3	13.1	12.9	12.7	12.5	12.2
72	13.8	13.8	13.7	13.6	13.5	13.4	13.3	13.2	13.1	12.9	12.8	12.6	12.4	12.3	12.0	11.8
73	13.2	13.2	13.1	13.0	13.0	12.9	12.8	12.7	12.5	12.4	12.3	12.1	12.0	11.8	11.6	11.4
74	12.6	12.6	12.5	12.5	12.4	12.3	12.2	12.1	12.0	11.9	11.8	11.6	11.5	11.3	11.2	11.0
75	12.0	12.0	11.9	11.9	11.8	11.7	11.7	11.6	11.5	11.4	11.3	11.1	11.0	10.9	10.7	10.5
76	11.4	11.4	11.3	11.3	11.2	11.2	11.1	11.0	10.9	10.8	10.8	10.6	10.5	10.4	10.3	10.1
77	10.8	10.8	10.8	10.7	10.7	10.6	10.6	10.5	10.4	10.3	10.3	10.2	10.0	10.0	9.8	9.7
78	10.3	10.2	10.2	10.2	10.1	10.1	10.0	10.0	9.9	9.8	9.8	9.7	9.6	9.5	9.4	9.2
79	9.7	9.7	9.7	9.6	9.6	9.6	9.5	9.5	9.4	9.3	9.3	9.2	9.1	9.0	8.9	8.8
80	9.2	9.2	9.1	9.1	9.1	9.0	9.0	9.0	8.9	8.9	8.8	8.7	8.7	8.6	8.5	8.4
81	8.7	8.7	8.6	8.6	8.6	8.5	8.5	8.5	8.4	8.4	8.3	8.3	8.2	8.1	8.0	8.0
82	8.2	8.2	8.1	8.1	8.1	8.1	8.0	8.0	8.0	7.9	7.9	7.8	7.8	7.7	7.6	7.5
83	7.7	7.7	7.7	7.6	7.6	7.6	7.6	7.5	7.5	7.5	7.4	7.4	7.3	7.3	7.2	7.1
84	7.2	7.2	7.2	7.2	7.2	7.1	7.1	7.1	7.1	7.0	7.0	7.0	6.9	6.9	6.8	6.7
85	6.8	6.8	6.8	6.7	6.7	6.7	6.7	6.7	6.6	6.6	6.6	6.5	6.5	6.5	6.4	6.4
86	6.4	6.4	6.3	6.3	6.3	6.3	6.3	6.3	6.2	6.2	6.2	6.2	6.1	6.1	6.0	6.0
87	6.0	6.0	6.0	5.9	5.9	5.9	5.9	5.9	5.9	5.8	5.8	5.8	5.8	5.7	5.7	5.6
88	5.6	5.6	5.6	5.6	5.6	5.5	5.5	5.5	5.5	5.5	5.5	5.4	5.4	5.4	5.3	5.3
89	5.2	5.2	5.2	5.2	5.2	5.2	5.2	5.2	5.2	5.1	5.1	5.1	5.1	5.1	5.0	5.0
90	4.9	4.9	4.9	4.9	4.9	4.9	4.9	4.9	4.9	4.8	4.8	4.8	4.8	4.8	4.7	4.7

Table VIA — Annuities for Joint Life Only — Two Lives — Expected Return Multiples

AGES	67	68	69	70	71	72	73	74	75	76	77	78	79	80	81	82
67	13.5															
68	13.1	12.8														
69	12.8	12.5	12.1													
70	12.4	12.1	11.8	11.5												
71	12.0	11.7	11.4	11.2	10.9											
72	11.6	11.4	11.1	10.8	10.5	10.2										
73	11.2	11.0	10.7	10.5	10.2	9.9	9.7									
74	10.8	10.6	10.4	10.1	9.9	9.6	9.4	9.1								
75	10.4	10.2	10.0	9.8	9.5	9.3	9.1	8.8	8.6							
76	9.9	9.8	9.6	9.4	9.2	9.0	8.8	8.5	8.3	8.0						
77	9.5	9.4	9.2	9.0	8.8	8.6	8.4	8.2	8.0	7.8	7.5					
78	9.1	9.0	8.8	8.7	8.5	8.3	8.1	7.9	7.7	7.5	7.3	7.0				
79	8.7	8.6	8.4	8.3	8.1	8.0	7.8	7.6	7.4	7.2	7.0	6.8	6.6			
80	8.3	8.2	8.0	7.9	7.8	7.6	7.5	7.3	7.1	6.9	6.8	6.6	6.3	6.1		
81	7.9	7.9	7.7	7.5	7.4	7.3	7.1	7.0	6.8	6.7	6.5	6.3	6.1	5.9	5.7	
82	7.5	7.4	7.3	7.2	7.1	6.9	6.8	6.7	6.5	6.4	6.2	6.0	5.9	5.7	5.5	5.3
83	7.1	7.0	6.9	6.8	6.7	6.6	6.5	6.4	6.2	6.1	5.9	5.8	5.6	5.5	5.3	5.1
84	6.7	6.6	6.5	6.4	6.4	6.3	6.2	6.0	5.9	5.8	5.7	5.5	5.4	5.3	5.2	4.9
85	6.3	6.2	6.2	6.1	6.0	5.9	5.8	5.7	5.6	5.5	5.4	5.3	5.1	5.0	4.9	4.7
86	5.9	5.9	5.8	5.8	5.7	5.6	5.5	5.4	5.4	5.3	5.1	5.0	4.9	4.8	4.7	4.5
87	5.6	5.6	5.5	5.4	5.4	5.3	5.2	5.2	5.1	5.0	4.9	4.8	4.7	4.6	4.4	4.3
88	5.3	5.2	5.2	5.1	5.1	5.0	5.0	4.9	4.8	4.7	4.6	4.5	4.4	4.3	4.2	4.1
89	5.0	4.9	4.9	4.8	4.8	4.7	4.7	4.6	4.5	4.5	4.4	4.3	4.2	4.1	4.0	3.9
90	4.7	4.6	4.6	4.6	4.5	4.5	4.4	4.4	4.3	4.2	4.2	4.1	4.0	3.9	3.8	3.8

AGES	83	84	85	86	87	88	89	90
83	4.9							
84	4.7	4.6						
85	4.6	4.4	4.2					
86	4.4	4.2	4.1	3.9				
87	4.2	4.1	3.9	3.8	3.6			
88	4.0	3.9	3.8	3.6	3.5	3.4		
89	3.8	3.7	3.6	3.5	3.4	3.2	3.1	
90	3.7	3.5	3.4	3.3	3.2	3.1	3.0	2.9

Table VII — Percent Value of Refund Feature
Duration of Guaranteed Amount

Age	1 Yr.	2 Yrs.	3 Yrs.	4 Yrs.	5 Yrs.	6 Yrs.	7 Yrs.	8 Yrs.	9 Yrs.	10 Yrs.	11 Yrs.	12 Yrs.	13 Yrs.	14 Yrs.	15 Yrs.	16 Yrs.	17 Yrs.	18 Yrs.	19 Yrs.	20 Yrs.
19	...	...	...	...	...	...	...	...	...	...	...	...	...	...	...	...	...	...	...	...
20	...	...	...	...	...	...	...	...	...	...	...	...	...	...	...	...	...	...	...	1
21	...	...	...	...	...	...	...	...	...	...	...	...	...	...	...	...	...	...	...	1
22	...	...	...	...	...	...	...	...	...	...	...	...	...	...	...	...	...	...	...	1
23	...	...	...	...	...	...	...	...	...	...	...	...	...	...	...	...	...	...	1	1
24	...	...	...	...	...	...	...	...	...	...	...	...	...	...	...	...	...	1	1	1
25	...	...	...	...	...	...	...	...	...	...	...	...	...	...	...	...	1	1	1	1
26	...	...	...	...	...	...	...	...	...	...	...	...	...	...	...	...	1	1	1	1
27	...	...	...	...	...	...	...	...	...	...	...	...	...	...	...	1	1	1	1	1
28	...	...	...	...	...	...	...	...	...	...	...	...	...	...	1	1	1	1	1	1
29	...	...	...	...	...	...	...	...	...	...	...	...	...	...	1	1	1	1	1	1
30	...	...	...	...	...	...	...	...	...	...	...	...	...	1	1	1	1	1	1	1
31	...	...	...	...	...	...	...	...	...	...	...	...	...	1	1	1	1	1	1	1
32	...	...	...	...	...	...	...	...	...	...	...	...	...	1	1	1	1	1	1	1
33	...	...	...	...	...	...	...	...	...	...	...	...	1	1	1	1	1	1	1	1
34	...	...	...	...	...	...	...	...	...	...	...	1	1	1	1	1	1	1	1	1
35	...	...	...	...	...	...	...	...	...	...	...	1	1	1	1	1	1	1	1	1
36	...	...	...	...	...	...	...	...	...	...	1	1	1	1	1	1	1	1	1	1
37	...	...	...	...	...	...	...	...	...	1	1	1	1	1	1	1	1	1	1	1
38	...	...	...	...	...	...	...	...	1	1	1	1	1	1	1	1	1	1	1	2
39	...	...	...	...	...	...	...	...	1	1	1	1	1	1	1	1	1	1	2	2
40	...	...	...	...	...	...	...	1	1	1	1	1	1	1	1	1	1	2	2	2
41	...	...	...	...	...	...	...	1	1	1	1	1	1	1	1	1	2	2	2	2
42	...	...	...	...	...	...	1	1	1	1	1	1	1	1	1	2	2	2	2	2
43	...	...	...	...	...	...	1	1	1	1	1	1	1	1	2	2	2	2	2	3
44	...	...	...	...	...	1	1	1	1	1	1	1	1	2	2	2	2	2	3	3
45	...	...	...	...	...	1	1	1	1	1	1	1	1	2	2	2	2	3	3	3
46	...	...	...	...	1	1	1	1	1	1	1	1	1	2	2	2	2	3	3	3
47	...	...	...	...	1	1	1	1	1	1	1	1	2	2	2	2	2	3	3	4
48	...	...	...	...	1	1	1	1	1	1	1	2	2	2	2	2	3	3	3	4
49	...	...	...	1	1	1	1	1	1	1	1	2	2	2	2	2	3	3	3	4
50	...	...	...	1	1	1	1	1	1	1	1	2	2	2	2	3	3	3	4	5
51	...	...	...	1	1	1	1	1	1	1	2	2	2	2	2	3	3	3	4	5
52	...	...	...	1	1	1	1	1	1	2	2	2	2	2	3	3	3	4	4	5
53	...	...	1	1	1	1	1	1	2	2	2	2	2	3	3	3	4	4	5	6
54	...	...	1	1	1	1	1	2	2	2	2	2	3	3	3	4	4	5	6	7
55	...	...	1	1	1	1	1	2	2	2	2	3	3	3	4	4	5	6	7	7
56	...	...	1	1	1	1	2	2	2	2	2	3	3	3	4	4	5	6	7	8
57	...	...	1	1	1	1	2	2	2	2	3	3	3	4	4	5	6	7	8	9
58	...	1	1	1	1	2	2	2	2	3	3	3	4	4	5	6	7	8	9	9
59	...	1	1	1	2	2	2	2	3	3	3	4	4	5	5	6	7	8	9	10
60	...	1	1	1	2	2	2	3	3	3	4	4	5	6	7	8	9	9	10	11
61	...	1	1	1	2	2	3	3	3	4	4	5	6	7	8	9	10	11	12	13
62	...	1	1	2	2	2	3	3	4	4	5	6	7	8	9	10	11	12	13	14
63	...	1	1	2	2	3	3	4	4	5	6	7	8	9	10	11	12	13	14	15
64	...	1	1	2	2	3	4	5	6	7	8	9	10	11	12	13	14	15	16	17
65	...	1	2	2	3	4	4	5	6	7	8	9	10	11	12	13	14	15	17	18
66	1	1	2	2	3	4	5	5	6	7	8	9	10	12	13	14	15	17	18	20
67	1	1	2	3	3	4	5	6	7	8	9	10	11	13	14	15	17	18	20	22
68	1	1	2	3	4	5	6	7	8	9	10	11	13	14	15	17	19	20	22	24
69	1	1	2	3	4	5	6	7	8	10	11	12	14	15	17	19	20	22	24	26
70	1	2	3	4	5	6	7	8	9	11	12	14	15	17	19	20	22	24	26	28
71	1	2	3	4	5	6	8	9	10	12	13	15	17	18	20	22	24	26	28	30
72	1	2	3	4	6	7	8	10	11	13	15	17	18	20	22	24	26	28	30	32
73	1	2	4	5	6	8	9	11	13	14	16	18	20	22	24	26	28	31	33	35
74	1	3	4	5	7	9	10	12	14	16	18	20	22	24	26	28	31	33	35	37
75	1	3	4	6	8	9	11	13	15	17	19	22	24	26	28	31	33	35	38	40
76	2	3	5	7	9	10	12	15	17	19	21	24	26	28	31	33	36	38	40	43
77	2	4	5	7	9	12	14	16	18	21	23	26	28	31	33	36	38	41	43	45
78	2	4	6	8	10	13	15	18	20	23	25	28	31	33	36	38	41	43	46	48
79	2	4	7	9	11	14	17	19	22	25	28	30	33	36	38	41	44	46	48	51
80	2	5	7	10	13	15	18	21	24	27	30	33	36	38	41	44	46	49	51	53
81	3	5	8	11	14	17	20	23	26	29	32	35	38	41	44	47	48	51	54	56
82	3	6	9	12	15	19	22	25	28	32	35	38	41	44	47	49	52	54	56	58
83	3	7	10	13	17	20	24	27	31	34	38	41	44	47	49	52	54	57	59	61
84	4	7	11	15	19	22	26	30	33	37	40	44	47	49	52	55	57	59	61	63
85	4	8	12	16	20	24	28	32	36	40	43	46	49	52	55	57	59	62	63	65
86	4	9	13	18	22	27	31	35	39	42	46	49	52	55	57	60	62	64	66	67
87	5	10	15	20	24	29	33	37	41	45	48	52	55	57	60	62	64	66	68	69
88	5	11	16	21	26	31	36	40	44	48	51	54	57	60	62	64	66	68	70	71
89	6	12	17	23	28	33	38	43	47	50	54	57	60	62	65	67	68	70	72	73
90	7	13	19	25	31	36	41	45	49	53	56	59	62	64	67	69	70	72	74	75

Table VII — Percent Value of Refund Feature
Duration of Guaranteed Amount

Age	21 Yrs.	22 Yrs.	23 Yrs.	24 Yrs.	25 Yrs.	26 Yrs.	27 Yrs.	28 Yrs.	29 Yrs.	30 Yrs.	31 Yrs.	32 Yrs.	33 Yrs.	34 Yrs.	35 Yrs.	36 Yrs.	37 Yrs.	38 Yrs.	39 Yrs.	40 Yrs.
5	...	...	...	...	...	...	...	...	...	...	...	1	1	1	1	1	1	1	1	1
6	...	...	...	...	...	...	...	...	...	...	1	1	1	1	1	1	1	1	1	1
7	...	...	...	...	...	...	...	...	...	...	1	1	1	1	1	1	1	1	1	1
8	...	...	...	...	...	...	...	...	...	1	1	1	1	1	1	1	1	1	1	1
9	...	...	...	...	...	...	...	...	...	1	1	1	1	1	1	1	1	1	1	1
10	...	...	...	...	...	...	...	1	1	1	1	1	1	1	1	1	1	1	1	1
11	...	...	...	...	...	...	1	1	1	1	1	1	1	1	1	1	1	1	1	1
12	...	...	...	...	...	...	1	1	1	1	1	1	1	1	1	1	1	1	1	1
13	...	...	...	...	...	1	1	1	1	1	1	1	1	1	1	1	1	1	1	1
14	...	...	...	1	1	1	1	1	1	1	1	1	1	1	1	1	1	1	1	1
15	...	...	...	1	1	1	1	1	1	1	1	1	1	1	1	1	1	1	1	1
16	...	...	1	1	1	1	1	1	1	1	1	1	1	1	1	1	1	1	1	1
17	...	...	1	1	1	1	1	1	1	1	1	1	1	1	1	1	1	1	1	1
18	...	1	1	1	1	1	1	1	1	1	1	1	1	1	1	1	1	1	1	2
19	1	1	1	1	1	1	1	1	1	1	1	1	1	1	1	1	1	1	2	2
20	1	1	1	1	1	1	1	1	1	1	1	1	1	1	1	1	1	2	2	2
21	1	1	1	1	1	1	1	1	1	1	1	1	1	1	1	1	2	2	2	2
22	1	1	1	1	1	1	1	1	1	1	1	1	1	1	1	2	2	2	2	2
23	1	1	1	1	1	1	1	1	1	1	1	1	1	1	2	2	2	2	2	2
24	1	1	1	1	1	1	1	1	1	1	1	1	2	2	2	2	2	2	2	3
25	1	1	1	1	1	1	1	1	1	1	1	2	2	2	2	2	2	2	3	3
26	1	1	1	1	1	1	1	1	1	1	2	2	2	2	2	2	2	3	3	3
27	1	1	1	1	1	1	1	1	1	2	2	2	2	2	2	2	3	3	3	3
28	1	1	1	1	1	1	1	1	2	2	2	2	2	2	2	3	3	3	3	4
29	1	1	1	1	1	1	1	2	2	2	2	2	2	2	3	3	3	3	4	4
30	1	1	1	1	1	1	2	2	2	2	2	2	2	3	3	3	3	4	4	4
31	1	1	1	1	1	2	2	2	2	2	2	2	3	3	3	3	4	4	4	4
32	1	1	1	1	2	2	2	2	2	2	2	3	3	3	3	4	4	4	4	5
33	1	1	1	1	2	2	2	2	2	2	3	3	3	3	4	4	4	4	5	5
34	1	1	2	2	2	2	2	2	3	3	3	3	4	4	4	4	5	5	5	5
35	1	2	2	2	2	2	2	3	3	3	3	4	4	4	4	5	5	5	5	6
36	2	2	2	2	2	2	3	3	3	3	4	4	4	4	5	5	5	5	6	6
37	2	2	2	2	2	3	3	3	3	4	4	4	4	5	5	5	5	6	6	7
38	2	2	2	2	3	3	3	3	4	4	4	4	5	5	5	5	6	6	7	8
39	2	2	2	3	3	3	3	4	4	4	5	5	5	6	6	6	7	7	8	8
40	2	2	2	3	3	3	3	4	4	4	5	5	5	6	6	7	7	8	8	9
41	2	3	3	3	3	4	4	4	5	5	5	6	6	7	7	8	8	9	9	10
42	3	3	3	3	3	4	4	4	5	5	6	6	7	7	8	8	9	9	10	11
43	3	3	3	4	4	4	4	5	5	6	6	7	7	8	8	9	10	10	11	12
44	3	3	4	4	4	4	5	5	6	6	7	7	8	8	9	10	10	11	12	13
45	3	4	4	4	5	5	5	6	6	7	7	8	8	9	10	11	11	12	13	14
46	4	4	4	5	5	5	6	6	7	7	8	8	9	10	11	11	12	13	14	15
47	4	4	5	5	5	6	6	7	7	8	9	9	10	11	12	13	13	14	15	16
48	4	5	5	5	6	6	6	7	8	8	9	10	11	12	13	14	14	15	16	18
49	5	5	5	6	6	7	7	8	8	9	10	11	12	13	14	15	16	16	17	19
50	5	5	6	6	7	7	8	8	9	10	10	11	12	13	14	15	16	17	18	20
51	5	6	6	7	8	8	9	10	11	11	12	13	14	15	16	17	18	19	20	22
52	6	7	7	8	8	9	10	11	12	13	14	15	15	16	17	18	20	21	23	24
53	7	7	8	8	9	10	11	12	13	14	15	16	17	18	19	20	22	23	24	26
54	7	8	8	9	10	11	12	13	14	15	16	17	18	19	21	22	23	25	26	28
55	8	9	9	10	11	12	13	14	15	16	17	18	20	21	22	24	25	27	28	30
56	9	9	10	11	12	13	14	15	16	18	19	20	21	23	24	26	27	29	30	32
57	9	10	11	12	13	14	15	17	18	19	20	22	23	25	26	28	29	31	32	34
58	10	11	12	13	14	16	17	18	19	21	22	24	25	27	28	30	31	33	34	36
59	11	12	13	15	16	17	18	20	21	22	24	25	27	28	30	32	33	35	36	38
60	12	14	15	16	17	19	20	21	23	24	26	27	29	31	32	34	35	37	38	40
61	14	15	16	17	19	20	22	23	25	26	28	29	31	33	34	36	37	39	40	42
62	15	16	18	19	20	22	23	25	27	28	30	32	33	35	36	38	40	41	42	44
63	16	18	19	21	22	24	25	27	29	30	32	34	35	37	39	40	42	43	45	46
64	18	19	21	23	24	26	28	29	31	33	34	36	38	39	41	42	44	45	47	48
65	20	21	23	25	26	28	30	31	33	35	37	38	40	42	43	45	46	47	49	50
66	21	23	25	27	28	30	32	34	35	37	39	41	42	44	45	47	48	50	51	52
67	23	25	27	29	31	32	34	36	38	40	41	43	45	46	48	49	50	51	53	54
68	25	27	29	31	33	35	37	38	40	42	44	45	47	48	50	51	52	54	55	56
69	28	29	31	33	35	37	39	41	43	44	46	48	49	51	52	53	54	55	56	58
70	30	32	34	36	38	40	42	43	45	47	48	50	51	53	54	55	56	57	59	60
71	32	34	36	38	40	42	44	46	47	49	51	52	54	55	56	57	58	59	61	62
72	35	37	39	41	43	45	46	48	50	51	53	54	56	57	58	59	60	61	62	63
73	37	39	41	43	45	47	49	51	52	54	55	57	58	59	60	61	62	63	64	65
74	40	42	44	46	48	50	51	53	54	56	57	59	60	61	62	63	64	65	66	67
75	42	44	46	48	50	52	54	55	57	58	60	61	62	63	64	65	66	67	68	69
76	45	47	49	51	53	54	56	58	59	60	62	63	64	65	66	67	68	69	69	70
77	47	50	51	53	55	57	58	60	61	62	64	65	66	67	68	69	70	70	71	72
78	50	52	54	56	57	59	61	62	63	64	66	67	68	69	70	70	71	72	73	73
79	53	55	56	58	60	61	63	64	65	66	68	69	70	71	72	72	73	73	74	75
80	55	57	59	60	62	63	65	66	67	68	69	70	71	72	73	73	74	74	75	76
81	58	59	61	63	64	66	67	68	69	70	71	72	73	74	74	75	76	76	77	78
82	60	62	63	65	66	68	69	70	71	72	73	74	74	75	76	76	77	77	78	79
83	62	64	66	67	68	70	71	72	73	74	74	75	76	77	77	78	79	79	80	80
84	65	66	68	69	70	71	72	73	74	75	76	77	77	78	79	79	80	80	81	81
85	67	68	70	71	72	73	74	75	76	77	77	78	79	79	80	81	81	82	82	83
86	69	70	72	73	74	75	76	77	77	78	79	80	80	81	81	82	82	83	83	84
87	71	72	73	75	76	76	77	78	79	80	80	81	81	82	83	83	84	84	84	85
88	73	74	75	76	77	78	79	79	80	80	81	82	82	83	83	84	84	85	85	86
89	74	76	77	78	79	79	80	81	81	82	83	83	84	84	85	85	85	86	86	87
90	76	77	78	79	80	81	81	82	83	83	84	84	85	85	86	86	86	87	87	87

Appendix B

Examples of Exclusion Ratio Calculations

Single Life Annuity

Example 1. On October 1, 2005, Mr. Smith purchased an immediate nonrefund annuity which will pay him $125 a month ($1,500 a year) for life, beginning November 1, 2005. He paid $16,000 for the contract. Mr. Smith's age on his birthday nearest the annuity starting date (October 1st) was 68. According to Table V (which he uses because his investment in the contract is post-June 1986), his life expectancy is 17.6 years. Consequently, the expected return under the contract is $26,400 (12 x $125 x 17.6). And the exclusion percentage for the annuity payments is 60.6% ($16,000 ÷ $26,400). Since Mr. Smith received 2 monthly payments in 2005 (a total of $250), he will exclude $151.50 (60.6% of $250) from his gross income for 2005, and he must include $98.50 ($250 – $151.50). Mr. Smith will exclude the amounts so determined for 17.6 years. In 2005, he could exclude $151.50; each year thereafter through 2022, he could exclude $909, for a total exclusion of $15,604.50 ($151.50 excluded in 2005 and $15,453 excluded over the next 17 years). In 2023, he could exclude only $395.50 ($16,000 – $15,604.50). In 2023, he would include in his income $1,104.50 ($1,500 – $395.50) and $1,500 in 2024 and in each year thereafter.

Example 2. If Mr. Smith purchased the contract illustrated above on October 1, 1986 (so that it had an annuity starting date before January 1, 1987), he would exclude $151.50 (60.6% of $250) from his 1986 gross income and would include $98.50 ($250 – $151.50). For each succeeding tax year in which he receives 12 monthly payments (even if he outlives his life expectancy of 17.6 years), he will exclude $909 (60.6% of $1,500), and he will include $591 ($1,500 – $909).

Refund or Period Certain Guarantee

Example 1. On January 1, 2005, a husband, age 65, purchased for $21,053 an immediate installment refund annuity which pays $100 a month for life. The contract provides that in the event the husband does not live long enough to recover the full purchase price, payments will be made to his wife until the total payments under the contract equal the purchase price. The investment in the contract is adjusted for the purpose of determining the exclusion ratio as follows:

```
Unadjusted investment in the contract .........................................$ 21,053
Amount to be received annually.....................................................$ 1,200
Duration of guaranteed amount ($21,053 ÷ $1,200).....................17.5 yrs.
Rounded to nearest whole number of years ...............................18
Percentage value of guaranteed refund
(Table VII for age 65 and 18 years)........................................15%
Value of refund feature rounded to nearest dollar (15% of $21,053)$ 3,158
Adjusted investment in the contract ($21,053 - $3,158)................$ 17,895
```

Example 2. Assume the contract in Example 1 was purchased as a deferred annuity and the pre-July 1986 investment in the contract is $10,000 and the post-June 1986 investment in the contract is $11,053. If the annuitant elects, as explained earlier, to compute a separate exclusion percentage for the pre-July 1986 and the post-June 1986 amounts, separate computations must be performed to determine the adjusted investment in the contract. The pre-July 1986 investment in the contract and the post-June 1986 investment in the contract are adjusted for the purpose of determining the exclusion ratios in the following manner:

```
Pre-July 1986 adjustment:
Unadjusted investment in the contract.........................................$ 10,000
Allocable part of amount to be received annually
(($10,000 ÷ $21,053) x $1,200)......................................................$ 570
Duration of guaranteed amount ($10,000 ÷ $570) ............................17.5
Rounded to nearest whole number of years..............................18
Percentage in Table III for age 65 and 18 years................................30%
Present value of refund feature rounded to nearest dollar
(30% of $10,000).......................................................................$ 3,000
Adjusted pre-July 1986 investment in the contract
($10,000 - $3,000)....................................................................$ 7,000
```

Post-June 1986 adjustment:
Unadjusted investment in the contract...$ 11,053
Allocable part of amount to be received annually
  (($11,053 ÷ $21,053) x $1,200..$ 630
Duration of guaranteed amount ($11,053 ÷ $630)............................17.54
Rounded to nearest whole number of years..18
Percentage in Table VII for age 65 and 18 years 15%
Present value of refund feature rounded to nearest dollar
  (15% of $11,054)...$ 1,658
Adjusted post-June 1986 investment in the contract
  ($11,053 - $1,658)...$ 9,395

Once the investment in the contract has been adjusted by subtracting the value of the refund or period certain guarantee, an exclusion ratio is determined in the same way as for a straight life annuity. Expected return is computed; then the *adjusted* investment in the contract is divided by expected return. Taking the two examples above, the exclusion ratio for each contract is determined as follows.

Example (1) above.

Investment in the contract (adjusted for refund guarantee) ....$ 17,895
One year's guaranteed annuity payments (12 x $100)......................$ 1,200
Life expectancy for Table V, age 65 ....20 yrs.
Expected return (20 x $1,200)..$ 24,000
Exclusion ratio ($17,895 ÷ $24,000)...74.6%
Amount excludable from gross income each year in which 12
  payments are received (74.6% of $1,200)*....................................$ 895.20
Amount includable in gross income ($1,200 - $895.20)*..............$ 304.80

* Since the annuity starting date is after December 31, 1986, the total amount excludable is limited to the investment in the contract; after that has been recovered, the remaining amounts received are includable in income. However, the Small Business Job Protection Act of 1996 (P.L. 104-188) changed the manner in which the "unrecovered investment" in the contract is calculated when the annuity has a refund or guarantee feature. Generally, the portion of any amount received as an annuity that can be excluded using the exclusion ratio is not to exceed the unrecovered investment in the contract. In calculating this figure, the value of the refund or guarantee feature was subtracted prior to the 1996 Act. After the 1996 Act, for this purpose, the value of the refund or guarantee feature is not subtracted. Although this change was made in 1996 legislation, it is effective for individuals with annuity starting dates after December 31, 1986. IRC Sec. 72(b)(4). Please note, this change does not affect the calculation of the refund or guarantee feature for purposes of calculating the exclusion ratio; it only affects the unrecovered investment in the contract and, thus, the date on which the investment in the contract is recovered.

Example (2) above.

Pre-July 1986 investment in the contract
   (adjusted for period certain guarantee) ....$ 7,000
One year's guaranteed annuity payments (12 x $100).....................$ 1,200
Life expectancy from Table I, male age 65 ....15 yrs.
Expected return (15 x $1,200)...$ 18,000
Exclusion ratio ($7,000 ÷ $18,000)..38.9%

Post-June 1986 investment in the contract
   (adjusted for period certain guarantee) ....$ 9,395
One year's guaranteed annuity payments (12 x $100).....................$ 1,200
Life expectancy from Table V, age 65..20 yrs.
Expected return (20 x $1,200)...$ 24,000
Exclusion ratio ($9,395 ÷ $24,000)..39.1%
Sum of pre-July and post-June 1986 ratios.....................................78%
Amount excludable from gross income each year in which
   twelve payments are received (78% of $1,200)*.......................$ 936.00
Amount includable in gross income ($1,200 - 936.00)*................$ 264.00

* Since the annuity starting date is after December 31, 1986, the total amount excludable is limited to the investment in the contract; after that has been recovered, the remaining amounts received are includable in income. (Note that 1996 legislation changed the manner in which the unrecovered investment in the contract is calculated for this purpose as explained above in Example 1.)

Joint and Survivor Annuity (Same Income to Survivor as to Both Annuitants Before Any Death)

Example 1. After June 30, 1986, Mr. and Mrs. Jones purchase an immediate joint and survivor annuity. The annuity will provide payments of $100 a month while both are alive and until the death of the survivor. Mr. Jones' age on his birthday nearest the annuity starting date is 65; Mrs. Jones', 63. The single premium is $22,000.

Investment in the contract..$ 22,000
One year's annuity payments (12 x $100)..1,200
Joint and survivor multiple from Table VI
   (age 65, 63)..26
Expected return (26 x $1,200)...$ 31,200
Exclusion ratio ($22,000 ÷ $31,200)..70.5%
Amount excludable from gross income each year in which 12
   payments are received (70.5% of $1,200)* ....$ 846.00
Amount includable in gross income
   ($1,200 - $846.00)*...354.00

* If the annuity starting date is after December 31, 1986, the total amount excludable is limited to the investment in the contract; after that has been recovered, the remaining amounts received are includable in income.

Joint and Survivor Annuity (Income To Survivor Differs From Income Before First Death)

Example 1. After July 30, 1986, Mr. and Mrs. Smith buy an immediate joint and survivor annuity which will provide monthly payments of $117 ($1,404 a year) for as long as both live, and monthly payments of $78 ($936 a year) to the survivor. As of the annuity starting date he is 65 years old; she is 63. The expected return is computed as follows.

Joint and survivor multiple from Table VI (ages 65, 63).....................................26
Portion of expected return (26 x $936)..$24,366.00
Joint life multiple from Table VIA (ages 65, 63)..15.6
Difference between annual annuity payment before the first death
   and annual annuity payment to the survivor ($1,404 - $936)..................$468
Portion of expected return (15.6 x $468)...$ 7,300.80
Expected return...$31,636.80

Assuming that Mr. Smith paid $22,000 for the contract, the exclusion ratio is 69.5% ($22,000 ÷ $31,636.80). During their joint lives the portion of each monthly payment to be excluded from gross income is $81.31 (69.5% of $117), or $975.72 a year. The portion to be included is $35.69 ($117 − $81.31), or $428.28 a year. After the first death, the portion of each monthly payment to be excluded from gross income will be $54.21 (69.5% of $78), or $650.52 a year. And $23.79 of each payment ($78 − $54.21), or $285.48 a year, will be included. If the annuity starting date is after December 31, 1986, the total amount excludable is limited to the investment in the contract. Thus, if Mr. Smith lives for 23 years, he may exclude $81.31 from each payment for 22 years ((12 x 22) x $81.31 = $21,465.84). In the 23rd year he may exclude $534.16 ($22,000 − $21,465.84) or $81.31 from each of the first six payments, but only $46.30 from the seventh. The balance is entirely includable in his income, and on his death, his widow must include the full amount of each payment in income.

Example 2. Assume that in the example above, there is a pre-July 1986 investment in the contract of $12,000 and a post-June 1986 investment in the contract of $10,000. Mr. Smith elects to calculate the exclusion percentage for each portion. The pre-July exclusion ratio would be 44.6% ($12,000 ÷ $26,910–the expected return on the contract determined by using Tables II and IIA and the age and sex of both annuitants). The post-June 1986 exclusion ratio is $10,000 ÷ $31,636.80 or 31.6%. The amount excludable from each monthly payment while both are alive would be $89.15 (44.6% of $117 plus 31.6% of $117) and the remaining $27.85 would be included in gross income. If the annuity starting date is after December 31, 1986, the total amount excludable is limited to the investment in the contract.

Appendix C

Internal Revenue Code Sections

Internal Revenue Code Section 72

72. ANNUITIES; CERTAIN PROCEEDS OF ENDOWMENT AND LIFE INSURANCE CONTRACTS

(a) GENERAL RULE FOR ANNUITIES

Except as otherwise provided in this chapter, gross income includes any amount received as an annuity (whether for a period certain or during one or more lives) under an annuity, endowment, or life insurance contract.

(b) EXCLUSION RATIO

(1) IN GENERAL

Gross income does not include that part of any amount received as an annuity under an annuity, endowment, or life insurance contract which bears the same ratio to such amount as the investment in the contract (as of the annuity starting date) bears to the expected return under the contract (as of such date).

(2) EXCLUSION LIMITED TO INVESTMENT

The portion of any amount received as an annuity which is excluded from gross income under paragraph (1) shall not exceed the unrecovered investment in the contract immediately before the receipt of such amount.

(3) DEDUCTION WHERE ANNUITY PAYMENTS CEASE BEFORE ENTIRE INVESTMENT RECOVERED

(A) IN GENERAL

If–

(i) after the annuity starting date, payments as an annuity under the contract cease by reason of the death of an annuitant, and

(ii) as of the date of such cessation, there is unrecovered investment in the contract, the amount of such unrecovered investment (in excess of any amount specified in subsection (e)(5) which was not included in gross income) shall be allowed as a deduction to the annuitant for his last taxable year.

(B) PAYMENTS TO OTHER PERSONS

In the case of any contract which provides for payments meeting the requirements of subparagraphs (B) and (C) of subsection (c)(2), the deduction under subparagraph (A) shall be allowed to the person entitled to such payments for the taxable year in which such payments are received.

(C) NET OPERATING LOSS DEDUCTIONS PROVIDED

For purposes of section 172, a deduction allowed under this paragraph shall be treated as if it were attributable to a trade or business of the taxpayer.

(4) UNRECOVERED INVESTMENT

For purposes of this subsection, the unrecovered investment in the contract as of any date is–

(A) the investment in the contract (determined without regard to subsection (c)(2)) as of the annuity starting date, reduced by

(B) the aggregate amount received under the contract on or after such annuity starting date and before the date as of which the determination is being made, to the extent such amount was excludable from gross income under this subtitle.

(c) DEFINITIONS

(1) INVESTMENT IN THE CONTRACT

For purposes of subsection (b), the investment in the contract as of the annuity starting date is–

(A) the aggregate amount of premiums or other consideration paid for the contract, minus

(B) the aggregate amount received under the contract before such date, to the extent that such amount was excludable from gross income under this subtitle or prior income tax laws.

(2) ADJUSTMENT IN INVESTMENT WHERE THERE IS REFUND FEATURE

If–

(A) the expected return under the contract depends in whole or in part on the life expectancy of one or more individuals;

(B) the contract provides for payments to be made to a beneficiary (or to the estate of an annuitant) on or after the death of the annuitant or annuitants; and

(C) such payments are in the nature of a refund of the consideration paid, then the value (computed without discount for interest) of such payments on the annuity starting date shall be subtracted from the amount determined under paragraph (1). Such value shall be computed in accordance with actuarial tables prescribed by the Secretary. For purposes of this paragraph and of subsection (e)(2)(A), the term "refund of the consideration paid" includes amounts payable after the death of an annuitant by reason of a provision in the contract for a life annuity with minimum period of payments certain, but (if part of the consideration was contributed by an employer) does not include that part of any payment to a beneficiary (or to the estate of the annuitant) which is not attributable to the consideration paid by the employee for the contract as determined under paragraph (1)(A).

(3) EXPECTED RETURN

For purposes of subsection (b), the expected return under the contract shall be determined as follows:

(A) LIFE EXPECTANCY

If the expected return under the contract, for the period on and after the annuity starting date, depends in whole or in part on the life expectancy of one or more individuals, the expected return shall be computed with reference to actuarial tables prescribed by the Secretary.

(B) INSTALLMENT PAYMENTS

If subparagraph (A) does not apply, the expected return is the aggregate of the amounts receivable under the contract as an annuity.

(4) ANNUITY STARTING DATE

For purposes of this section, the annuity starting date in the case of any contract is the first day of the first period for which an amount is received as an annuity under the contract; except that if such date was before January 1, 1954, then the annuity starting date is January 1, 1954.

*   *   *

(e) AMOUNTS NOT RECEIVED AS ANNUITIES

(1) APPLICATION OF SUBSECTION

(A) IN GENERAL

This subsection shall apply to any amount which–

(i) is received under an annuity, endowment, or life insurance contract, and

(ii) is not received as an annuity, if no provision of this subtitle (other than this subsection) applies with respect to such amount.

(B) DIVIDENDS

For purposes of this section, any amount received which is in the nature of a dividend or similar distribution shall be treated as an amount not received as an annuity.

(2) GENERAL RULE

Any amount to which this subsection applies–

(A) if received on or after the annuity starting date, shall be included in gross income, or

(B) if received before the annuity starting date–

(i) shall be included in gross income to the extent allocable to income on the contract, and

(ii) shall not be included in gross income to the extent allocable to the investment in the contract.

(3) ALLOCATION OF AMOUNTS TO INCOME AND INVESTMENT

For purposes of paragraph (2)(B)–

(A) ALLOCATION TO INCOME

Any amount to which this subsection applies shall be treated as allocable to income on the contract to the extent that such amount does not exceed the excess (if any) of–

(i) the cash value of the contract (determined without regard to any surrender charge) immediately before the amount is received, over

(ii) the investment in the contract at such time.

(B) ALLOCATION TO INVESTMENT

Any amount to which this subsection applies shall be treated as allocable to investment in the contract to the extent that such amount is not allocated to income under subparagraph (A).

(4) SPECIAL RULES FOR APPLICATION OF PARAGRAPH (2)(B)

For purposes of paragraph (2)(B)–

(A) LOANS TREATED AS DISTRIBUTIONS

If, during any taxable year, an individual–

(i) receives (directly or indirectly) any amount as a loan under any contract to which this subsection applies, or

(ii) assigns or pledges (or agrees to assign or pledge) any portion of the value of any such contract, such amount or portion shall be treated as received under the contract as an amount not received as an annuity. The preceding sentence shall not apply for purposes of determining investment in the contract, except that the investment in the contract shall be increased by any amount included in gross income by reason of the amount treated as received under the preceding sentence.

(B) TREATMENT OF POLICYHOLDER DIVIDENDS

Any amount described in paragraph (1)(B) shall not be included in gross income under paragraph (2)(B)(i) to the extent such amount is retained by the insurer as a premium or other consideration paid for the contract.

(C) TREATMENT OF TRANSFERS WITHOUT ADEQUATE CONSIDERATION

(i) IN GENERAL

If an individual who holds an annuity contract transfers it without full and adequate consideration, such individual shall be treated as receiving an amount equal to the excess of–

(I) the cash surrender value of such contract at the time of transfer, over

(II) the investment in such contract at such time, under the contract as an amount not received as an annuity.

(ii) EXCEPTION FOR CERTAIN TRANSFERS BETWEEN SPOUSES OR FORMER SPOUSES

Clause (i) shall not apply to any transfer to which section 1041(a) (relating to transfers of property between spouses or incident to divorce) applies.

(iii) ADJUSTMENT TO INVESTMENT IN CONTRACT OF TRANSFEREE

If under clause (i) an amount is included in the gross income of the transferor of an annuity contract, the investment in the contract of the transferee in such contract shall be increased by the amount so included.

(5) RETENTION OF EXISTING RULES IN CERTAIN CASES

(A) IN GENERAL

In any case to which this paragraph applies–

(i) paragraphs (2)(B) and (4)(A) shall not apply, and

(ii) if paragraph (2)(A) does not apply, the amount shall be included in gross income, but only to the extent it exceeds the investment in the contract.

(B) EXISTING CONTRACTS

This paragraph shall apply to contracts entered into before August 14, 1982. Any amount allocable to investment in the contract after August 13, 1982, shall be treated as from a contract entered into after such date.

(C) CERTAIN LIFE INSURANCE AND ENDOWMENT CONTRACTS

Except as provided in paragraph (10) and except to the extent prescribed by the Secretary by regulations, this paragraph shall apply to any amount not received as an annuity which is received under a life insurance or endowment contract.

(D) CONTRACTS UNDER QUALIFIED PLANS

Except as provided in paragraph (8), this paragraph shall apply to any amount received–

(i) from a trust described in section 401(a) which is exempt from tax under section 501(a),

(ii) from a contract–

(I) purchased by a trust described in clause (i),

(II) purchased as part of a plan described in section 403(a),

(III) described in section 403(b), or

(IV) provided for employees of a life insurance company under a plan described in section 818(a)(3), or

(iii) from an individual retirement account or an individual retirement annuity. Any dividend described in section 404(k) which is received by a participant or beneficiary shall, for purposes of this subparagraph, be treated as paid under a separate contract to which clause (ii)(I) applies.

(E) FULL REFUNDS, SURRENDERS, REDEMPTIONS, AND MATURITIES

This paragraph shall apply to–

(i) any amount received, whether in a single sum or otherwise, under a contract in full discharge of the obligation under the contract which is in the nature of a refund of the consideration paid for the contract, and

(ii) any amount received under a contract on its complete surrender, redemption, or maturity. In the case of any amount to which the preceding sentence applies, the rule of paragraph (2)(A) shall not apply.

(6) INVESTMENT IN THE CONTRACT

For purposes of this subsection, the investment in the contract as of any date is–

(A) the aggregate amount of premiums or other consideration paid for the contract before such date, minus

(B) the aggregate amount received under the contract before such date, to the extent that such amount was excludable from gross income under this subtitle or prior income tax laws.

(7) [Repealed. Pub. L. 100-647, title I, 1011A(b)(9)(A), Nov. 10, 1988, 102 Stat. 3474]

(8) EXTENSION OF PARAGRAPH (2)(B) TO QUALIFIED PLANS

(A) IN GENERAL

Notwithstanding any other provision of this subsection, in the case of any amount received before the annuity starting date from a trust or contract described in paragraph (5)(D), paragraph (2)(B) shall apply to such amounts.

(B) ALLOCATION OF AMOUNT RECEIVED

For purposes of paragraph (2)(B), the amount allocated to the investment in the contract shall be the portion of the amount described in subparagraph (A) which bears the same ratio to such amount as the investment in the contract bears to the account balance. The determination under the preceding sentence shall be made as of the time of the distribution or at such other time as the Secretary may prescribe.

(C) TREATMENT OF FORFEITABLE RIGHTS

If an employee does not have a nonforfeitable right to any amount under any trust or contract to which subparagraph (A) applies, such amount shall not be treated as part of the account balance.

(D) INVESTMENT IN THE CONTRACT BEFORE 1987

In the case of a plan which on May 5, 1986, permitted withdrawal of any employee contributions before separation from service, subparagraph (A) shall apply only to the extent that amounts received before the annuity starting date (when increased by amounts previously received under the contract after December 31, 1986) exceed the investment in the contract as of December 31, 1986.

(9) EXTENSION OF PARAGRAPH (2)(B) TO QUALIFIED STATE TUITION PROGRAMS AND EDUCATION INDIVIDUAL RETIREMENT ACCOUNTS

Notwithstanding any other provision of this subsection, paragraph (2)(B) shall apply to amounts received under a qualified tuition program (as defined in section 529(b)) or under a Coverdell education savings account (as defined in section 530(b)). The rule of paragraph (8)(B) shall apply for purposes of this paragraph.

(10) TREATMENT OF MODIFIED ENDOWMENT CONTRACTS

(A) IN GENERAL

Notwithstanding paragraph (5)(C), in the case of any modified endowment contract (as defined in section 7702A)–

(i) paragraphs (2)(B) and (4)(A) shall apply, and

(ii) in applying paragraph (4)(A), "any person" shall be substituted for "an individual".

(B) TREATMENT OF CERTAIN BURIAL CONTRACTS

Notwithstanding subparagraph (A), paragraph (4)(A) shall not apply to any assignment (or pledge) of a modified endowment contract if such assignment (or pledge) is solely to cover the payment of expenses referred to in section 7702(e)(2)(C)(iii) and if the maximum death benefit under such contract does not exceed $25,000.

(11) ANTI-ABUSE RULES

(A) IN GENERAL

For purposes of determining the amount includible in gross income under this subsection–

(i) all modified endowment contracts issued by the same company to the same policyholder during any calendar year shall be treated as 1 modified endowment contract, and

(ii) all annuity contracts issued by the same company to the same policyholder during any calendar year shall be treated as 1 annuity contract. The preceding sentence shall not apply to any contract described in paragraph (5)(D).

(B) REGULATORY AUTHORITY

The Secretary may by regulations prescribe such additional rules as may be necessary or appropriate to prevent avoidance of the purposes of this subsection through serial purchases of contracts or otherwise.

* * *

(g) RULES FOR TRANSFEREE WHERE TRANSFER WAS FOR VALUE

Where any contract (or any interest therein) is transferred (by assignment or otherwise) for a valuable consideration, to the extent that the contract (or interest therein) does not, in the hands of the transferee, have a basis which is determined by reference to the basis in the hands of the transferor, then–

(1) for purposes of this section, only the actual value of such consideration, plus the amount of the premiums and other consideration paid by the transferee after the transfer, shall be taken into account in computing the aggregate amount of the premiums or other consideration paid for the contract;

(2) for purposes of subsection (c)(1)(B), there shall be taken into account only the aggregate amount received under the contract by the transferee before the annuity starting date, to the extent that such amount was excludable from gross income under this subtitle or prior income tax laws; and

(3) the annuity starting date is January 1, 1954, or the first day of the first period for which the transferee received an amount under the contract as an annuity, whichever is the later. For purposes of this subsection, the term "transferee" includes a beneficiary of, or the estate of, the transferee.

(h) OPTION TO RECEIVE ANNUITY IN LIEU OF LUMP SUM

If–

(1) a contract provides for payment of a lump sum in full discharge of an obligation under the contract, subject to an option to receive an annuity in lieu of such lump sum;

(2) the option is exercised within 60 days after the day on which such lump sum first became payable; and

(3) part or all of such lump sum would (but for this subsection) be includible in gross income by reason of subsection (e)(1), then, for purposes of this subtitle, no part of such lump sum shall be considered as includible in gross income at the time such lump sum first became payable.

* * *

(j) INTEREST

Notwithstanding any other provision of this section, if any amount is held under an agreement to pay interest thereon, the interest payments shall be included in gross income.

* * *

(n) ANNUITIES UNDER RETIRED SERVICEMAN'S FAMILY PROTECTION PLAN OR SURVIVOR BENEFIT PLAN

Subsection (b) shall not apply in the case of amounts received after December 31, 1965, as an annuity under chapter 73 of title 10 of the United

States Code, but all such amounts shall be excluded from gross income until there has been so excluded (under section 122(b)(1) or this section, including amounts excluded before January 1, 1966) an amount equal to the consideration for the contract (as defined by section 122(b)(2)), plus any amount treated pursuant to section 101(b)(2)(D) (as in effect on the day before the enactment of the Small Business Job Protection Act of 1996) as additional consideration paid by the employee. Thereafter all amounts so received shall be included in gross income.

* * *

(q) 10-PERCENT PENALTY FOR PREMATURE DISTRIBUTIONS FROM ANNUITY CONTRACTS

(1) IMPOSITION OF PENALTY

If any taxpayer receives any amount under an annuity contract, the taxpayer's tax under this chapter for the taxable year in which such amount is received shall be increased by an amount equal to 10 percent of the portion of such amount which is includible in gross income.

(2) SUBSECTION NOT TO APPLY TO CERTAIN DISTRIBUTIONS

Paragraph 1 shall not apply to any distribution–

(A) made on or after the date on which the taxpayer attains age 59½,

(B) made on or after the death of the holder (or, where the holder is not an individual, the death of the primary annuitant (as defined in subsection (s)(6)(B))),

(C) attributable to the taxpayer's becoming disabled within the meaning of subsection (m)(7),

(D) which is a part of a series of substantially equal periodic payments (not less frequently than annually) made for the life (or life expectancy) of the taxpayer or the joint lives (or joint life expectancies) of such taxpayer and his designated beneficiary,

(E) from a plan, contract, account, trust, or annuity described in subsection (e)(5)(D),

(F) allocable to investment in the contract before August 14, 1982, or

(G) under a qualified funding asset (within the meaning of section 130(d), but without regard to whether there is a qualified assignment),

(H) to which subsection (t) applies (without regard to paragraph (2) thereof),

(I) under an immediate annuity contract (within the meaning of section 72(u)(4)), or

(J) which is purchased by an employer upon the termination of a plan described in section 401(a) or 403(a) and which is held by the employer until such time as the employee separates from service.

(3) CHANGE IN SUBSTANTIALLY EQUAL PAYMENTS

If–

(A) paragraph (1) does not apply to a distribution by reason of paragraph (2)(D), and

(B) the series of payments under such paragraph are subsequently modified (other than by reason of death or disability)–

(i) before the close of the 5-year period beginning on the date of the first payment and after the taxpayer attains age 59½, or

(ii) before the taxpayer attains age 59½, the taxpayer's tax for the 1st taxable year in which such modification occurs shall be increased by an amount, determined under regulations, equal to the tax which (but for paragraph (2)(D)) would have been imposed, plus interest for the deferral period (within the meaning of subsection (t)(4)(B)).

* * *

(s) REQUIRED DISTRIBUTIONS WHERE HOLDER DIES BEFORE ENTIRE INTEREST IS DISTRIBUTED

(1) IN GENERAL

A contract shall not be treated as an annuity contract for purposes of this title unless it provides that–

(A) if any holder of such contract dies on or after the annuity starting date and before the entire interest in such contract has been distributed, the remaining portion of such interest will be distributed at least as rapidly as under the method of distributions being used as of the date of his death, and

(B) if any holder of such contract dies before the annuity starting date, the entire interest in such contract will be distributed within 5 years after the death of such holder.

(2) EXCEPTION FOR CERTAIN AMOUNTS PAYABLE OVER LIFE OF BENEFICIARY

If–

(A) any portion of the holder's interest is payable to (or for the benefit of) a designated beneficiary,

(B) such portion will be distributed (in accordance with regulations) over the life of such designated beneficiary(or over a period not extending beyond the life expectancy of such beneficiary), and

(C) such distributions begin not later than 1 year after the date of the holder's death or such later date as the Secretary may by regulations prescribe, then for purposes of paragraph (1), the portion referred to in subparagraph (A) shall be treated as distributed on the day on which such distributions begin.

(3) SPECIAL RULE WHERE SURVIVING SPOUSE BENEFICIARY

If the designated beneficiary referred to in paragraph (2)(A) is the surviving spouse of the holder of the contract, paragraphs (1) and (2) shall be applied by treating such spouse as the holder of such contract.

(4) DESIGNATED BENEFICIARY

For purposes of this subsection, the term "designated beneficiary" means any individual designated a beneficiary by the holder of the contract.

(5) EXCEPTION FOR CERTAIN ANNUITY CONTRACTS

This subsection shall not apply to any annuity contract–

(A) which is provided–

(i) under a plan described in section 401(a) which includes a trust exempt from tax under section 501, or

(ii) under a plan described in section 403(a),

(B) which is described in section 403(b),

(C) which is an individual retirement annuity or provided under an individual retirement account or annuity, or

(D) which is a qualified funding asset (as defined in section 130(d), but without regard to whether there is a qualified assignment).

(6) SPECIAL RULE WHERE HOLDER IS CORPORATION OR OTHER NON-INDIVIDUAL

(A) IN GENERAL

For purposes of this subsection, if the holder of the contract is not an individual, the primary annuitant shall be treated as the holder of the contract.

(B) PRIMARY ANNUITANT

For purposes of subparagraph (A), the term "primary annuitant" means the individual, the events in the life of whom are of primary importance in affecting the timing or amount of the payout under the contract.

(7) TREATMENT OF CHANGES IN PRIMARY ANNUITANT WHERE HOLDER OF CONTRACT IS NOT AN INDIVIDUAL

For purposes of this subsection, in the case of a holder of an annuity contract which is not an individual, if there is a change in a primary annuitant (as defined in paragraph (6)(B)), such change shall be treated as the death of the holder.

* * *

(u) TREATMENT OF ANNUITY CONTRACTS NOT HELD BY NATURAL PERSONS

(1) IN GENERAL

If any annuity contract is held by a person who is not a natural person—

(A) such contract shall not be treated as an annuity contract for purposes of this subtitle (other than subchapter L), and

(B) the income on the contract for any taxable year of the policyholder shall be treated as ordinary income received or accrued by the owner during such taxable year. For purposes of this paragraph, holding by a trust or other entity as an agent for a natural person shall not be taken into account.

(2) INCOME ON THE CONTRACT

(A) IN GENERAL

For purposes of paragraph (1), the term "income on the contract" means, with respect to any taxable year of the policyholder, the excess of—

(i) the sum of the net surrender value of the contract as of the close of the taxable year plus all distributions under the contract received during the taxable year or any prior taxable year, reduced by

(ii) the sum of the amount of net premiums under the contract for the taxable year and prior taxable years and amounts includible in gross income for prior taxable years with respect to such contract under this subsection. Where necessary to prevent the avoidance of this subsection, the Secretary may substitute "fair market value of the contract" for "net surrender value of the contract" each place it appears in the preceding sentence.

(B) NET PREMIUMS

For purposes of this paragraph, the term "net premiums" means the amount of premiums paid under the contract reduced by any policyholder dividends.

(3) EXCEPTIONS

This subsection shall not apply to any annuity contract which–

(A) is acquired by the estate of a decedent by reason of the death of the decedent,

(B) is held under a plan described in section 401(a) or 403(a), under a program described in section 403(b), or under an individual retirement plan,

(C) is a qualified funding asset (as defined in section 130(d), but without regard to whether there is a qualified assignment),

(D) is purchased by an employer upon the termination of a plan described in section 401(a) or 403(a) and is held by the employer until all amounts under such contract are distributed to the employee for whom such contract was purchased or the employee's beneficiary, or

(E) is an immediate annuity.

(4) IMMEDIATE ANNUITY

For purposes of this subsection, the term "immediate annuity" means an annuity–

(A) which is purchased with a single premium or annuity consideration,

(B) the annuity starting date (as defined in subsection (c)(4)) of which commences no later than 1 year from the date of the purchase of the annuity, and

(C) which provides for a series of substantially equal periodic payments (to be made not less frequently than annually) during the annuity period.

* * *

(x) CROSS REFERENCE

For limitation on adjustments to basis of annuity contracts sold, see section 1021.

Internal Revenue Code Section 1035

1035. CERTAIN EXCHANGES OF INSURANCE POLICIES.

(a) GENERAL RULES

No gain or loss shall be recognized on the exchange of–

(1) a contract of life insurance for another contract of life insurance or for an endowment or annuity contract; or

(2) a contract of endowment insurance (A) for another contract of endowment insurance which provides for regular payments beginning at a date not later than the date payments would have begun under the contract exchanged, or (B) for an annuity contract; or

(3) an annuity contract for an annuity contract.

(b) DEFINITIONS

For the purpose of this section–

(1) ENDOWMENT CONTRACT

A contract of endowment insurance is a contract with an insurance company which depends in part on the life expectancy of the insured, but which may be payable in full in a single payment during his life.

(2) ANNUITY CONTRACT

An annuity contract is a contract to which paragraph (1) applies but which may be payable during the life of the annuitant only in installments.

(3) LIFE INSURANCE CONTRACT

A contract of life insurance is a contract to which paragraph (1) applies but which is not ordinarily payable in full during the life of the insured.

(c) EXCHANGES INVOLVING FOREIGN PERSONS

To the extent provided in regulations, subsection (a) shall not apply to any exchange having the effect of transferring property to any person other than a United States person.

(d) CROSS REFERENCES

(1) For rules relating to recognition of gain or loss where an exchange is not solely in kind, see subsections (b) and (c) of section 1031.

(2) For rules relating to the basis of property acquired in an exchange described in subsection (a), see subsection (d) of section 1031.

Internal Revenue Code Section 2033

2033. PROPERTY IN WHICH THE DECEDENT HAD AN INTEREST.

The value of the gross estate shall include the value of all property to the extent of the interest therein of the decedent at the time of his death.

Internal Revenue Code Section 2039

2039. ANNUITIES.

(a) GENERAL

The gross estate shall include the value of an annuity or other payment receivable by any beneficiary by reason of surviving the decedent under any form of contract or agreement entered into after March 3, 1931 (other than as insurance under policies on the life of the decedent), if, under such contract or agreement, an annuity or other payment was payable to the decedent, or the decedent possessed the right to receive such annuity or payment, either alone or in conjunction with another for his life or for any period not ascertainable without reference to his death or for any period which does not in fact end before his death.

(b) AMOUNT INCLUDIBLE

Subsection (a) shall apply to only such part of the value of the annuity or other payment receivable under such contract or agreement as is proportionate to that part of the purchase price therefor contributed by the decedent. For purposes of this section, any contribution by the decedent's employer or former employer to the purchase price of such contract or agreement (whether or not to an employee's trust or fund forming part of a pension, annuity, retirement, bonus or profit sharing plan) shall be considered to be contributed by the decedent if made by reason of his employment.

Index